**To the memory of my grandmother,
Mary Rebecca Loveland McCann (1882–1967)**

Contents

Acknowledgments

Portions of Chapters 1 and 7 were originally presented at the 26th annual meeting of the History of Economics Society, held at the University of North Carolina, Greensboro, 25–28 June 1999; the Seminar in Critical Realism at King's College, Cambridge University, 8 November 1999; and the J. M. Kaplan Seminar in Political Economy at George Mason University, 25 February 2000. In addition, portions of Chapters 1, 6, and 7 appeared as "F. A. Hayek: The Liberal as Communitarian," published in *The Review of Austrian Economics* (March 2002).

I wish to thank Stephan Boehm, Peter Boettke, Robert Dimand, Susumu Egashira, Tony Lawson, Mark Perlman, Mario Rizzo, Jochen Runde, Karen Vaughn, and participants in these groups for their comments on early drafts, as well as several anonymous readers.

This book would not have been possible without a generous grant from the Earhart Foundation, Ann Arbor, Michigan, for which I am truly grateful.

Introduction

What follows is an extended essay on the social nature of man as represented in the philosophy of liberalism, in the classical sense of the term. This is not a presentation of the historical development of liberalism as a political philosophy. The purpose of this book is not to make some grand statement of the nature of liberalism, nor is it to identify the fundamental principles of that philosophy. The aim here is much more limited: to challenge the familiar characterization of liberalism (especially by those opposed to what they perceive as its central tenets) by addressing within the liberal tradition the place of community and obligation. This is in essence an essay in intellectual history, attempting to explicate through textual exegesis of some prominent exponents of liberalism the principles underlying political society.

It may not be much of an exaggeration to suggest that liberalism is one of the most misunderstood, mischaracterized, and maligned of political philosophies. It has been variously identified by its opponents – including in the list anarchists, conservatives, communitarians, institutionalists, Marxists, and others one may care to identify – as a philosophy of detachment, egoism, greed, individualism, isolation, *laissez-faire*, self-interest, and selfishness (the latter two to be seen as distinct), as it is denigrated as providing the intellectual foundation of capitalism, fostering a free market mentality within a competitive order and, *ipso facto*, engendering commodification and exploitation. Liberalism is said to ignore questions of the good in favor of promoting the right, to favor the personal over the social, to favor process over result, as though these were contrasting and competitive virtues and not complementary ones. More often than not, liberalism has been presented as an illustration in caricature, devoid of meaning, the denigration typically gratuitous and in the defense of alternative social philosophies.

The question is whether the perceptions of liberalism are valid and sustainable, and the answer must be ascertained through reference to the works of those who have identified themselves as within the liberal tradition. In the writings of some of its most ardent advocates – John Locke, David Hume, Adam Ferguson, Adam Smith, to name but a few of the more prominent – the caricature of liberal thought simply cannot be found, at least in the simplistic form in which it is often presented. Consider first, however, the characterizations of human nature as promulgated by Thomas Hobbes and Jean-Jacques Rousseau, two proto-liberal philosophers whose positions are typically viewed as diametric opposites. Hobbes, despite the fact that his great work, *Leviathan*, presents man in the state of nature as in a state of war, and provides in the end a justification for an absolutist monarchy, none the less begins his inquiry into the nature and form of a commonwealth with the premises of individual equality and a community purpose – this being the formation of a compact through which is facilitated escape from the misery of the base state. This common desire for security in community, not any natural sociality or comity, provides legitimacy (creates conditions favorable) to the apparatus of the social contract. Certainly, self-interest (as self-preservation) is a significant factor in the move to social union, and Hobbes may be held to account for the depiction of the individual as consti-tuted of the more base qualities of human nature, a depiction that in some sense is debilitating to the liberal theory even today. Yet self-interest *alone* is insufficient as an explanation of the form of the contract, and cannot explain cohesiveness of community and society in their more complex arrangements.

Rousseau, in *The Social Contract* and *Discourse Upon the Origin and Foundation of Inequality Among Mankind*, presents man as the gentle and selfless primitive with the simplest of desires, existing in harmony and conformity with nature, the natural bounty sufficient to inhibit conflict in the search for sustenance. It is when he is brought into competition with others and so coerced into social inter-course that difficulties arise. Rousseau's primitive, then, is in his base state not a gregarious but a solitary figure, lacking in sentiments of sociality, benevolence, and fellow-feeling, who must ultimately resist his natural inclinations as he subor-dinates his personal desires to the demands of social purpose through the device of the social contract. In both Hobbes and Rousseau we see the natural state of man as solitary, not social; the move into society is artificial, the result of felt needs, and a source of conflict unless constrained by force (Hobbes) or circum-scribed by the general will (Rousseau).

With Locke, we see a fundamental redefinition and reorientation of the nature of man. Locke's form of the social contract, in contrast to that of Hobbes and Rousseau, requires of individuals a social attachment, a feeling of community. Here, the desire to form social bonds is not so much for self-preservation as it is instinctual (this despite the fact that, for Locke, the mind is a "white paper," and so our ideas of social organization are socially constructed): man seeks society because he is endowed with the conviction that this is the most natural arrangement:

> God having made Man such a Creature, that, in his own Judgment, it was not good for him to be alone, put him under strong Obligations of Necessity, Convenience, and Inclination to drive him into *Society*, as well as fitted him with Understanding and Language to continue and enjoy it.
> (Locke 1698, Second Treatise, Ch.VII, §77; emphasis in original)

Thus does Locke provide in a single sentence one of the principal tenets of the liberal philosophy, and yet one that, over the three centuries since its offering, has been ignored by many antagonistic to its message, this tenet being the place of natural obligation in the formation of society. It is this understanding of obligation as an integral part of the human outfit, and not the emphasis on the individual as shaped by the forces of his environment, that results in social cohesion and social continuity.

While Locke is a significant figure in the promulgation of liberalism, the philosophers of the Scottish Enlightenment are even more so, as they may be seen to have been even more explicit in their considerations of the inherently social nature of man and so more emphatic in their rejection of the egoistic individual. Hume, Ferguson, and Smith, while advancing political and social theories of justice and right predicated on the primacy of the individual, all require as a first condition a social apprehension of the good – the moral sentiment is not by any stretch of the imagination even conceivable in the absence of an appreciation of the *social* nature of being. Consider first Hume's *An Enquiry Concerning the Principles of Morals* (1751; posthumous edition 1777). For Hume, the original state of man was the social, as the very nature of the individual derives from his association with others. Man did not, *contra* Hobbes, originate in a savage state, isolated, selfish, distrustful, ignorant, in a contest for survival against others for whom the concepts of justice, comity, equity, community, and reciprocity had no meaning. This depiction of the origins of mankind is little more than a philosophical fiction. In reality, notes Hume, individuals "are necessarily born in a family-society," conditioned to behave in accordance with the dictates of that society (Hume 1777, pp. 189–90). It is not self-love which motivates the moral sentiments, but a coincident social nature; personal interest "is, in general, so closely connected with that of the community, that those philosophers were excusable, who fancied that all our concern for the public might be resolved into a concern for our own happiness and preservation" (p. 218). Philosophers must be aware of this basic fact, *viz.*, "that the interests of society are not, even on their own account, entirely indifferent to us," and so "must renounce the theory, which accounts for every moral sentiment by the principle of self-love" (p. 219).

The society of Hobbes, according to Hume, and in contrast to his own theory of the formation of human society, allows no place for social intercourse or for notions of justice and right, notions that are predicated on understandings of morality; morality in turn arises from mutual regard and sympathy. Hume explicitly rejects those social and political philosophies predicated on egoism as being "contrary to common feeling and our most unprejudiced notions" (Hume 1777, p. 298). Indeed, "no qualities are more intitled to the general good-will and approbation of mankind than beneficence and humanity, friendship and gratitude, natural affection and public spirit, or whatever proceeds from a tender sympathy with others, and a generous concern for our kind and species" (p. 178). In the end, he goes even further: "I hate or despise him, who has no regard to any thing beyond his own gratifications and enjoyments" (p. 297).

Now consider Adam Ferguson. Ferguson, at the beginning of his *Essay on the History of Civil Society* (1767), is explicit in his characterization of the social nature of man. "The history of the individual is but a detail of the sentiments and thoughts he has entertained in the view of his species: and every experiment relative to this subject should be made with entire societies, not with single men" (Ferguson 1767, p. 10). This sentiment to sociality is inherent in the nature of man, and neither a historical artifact (valid for a particular time and circumstance), nor a philosophical abstraction offered as a means to initiate inquiry (as one might regard the original state of nature or the veil of ignorance). Man achieves happiness to the extent that he identifies himself as a "member of a community, for whose general good his heart may glow with an ardent zeal, to the suppression of those personal cares which are the foundation of painful anxieties, fear, jealousy, and envy" (p. 56). The social concern and the individual concern cannot be separated. This predilection to community is so obvious and evident that Ferguson proposes that should "a colony of children [be] transplanted from the nursery, and left to form a society apart, untaught and undisciplined, we should only have the same things repeated ..." (p. 10).

Ultimately, it is to Adam Smith we must turn for the fullest statement of the relationship of the individual to the whole. It is in Smith and not in Hobbes that we find the true nature of man in the liberal philosophy. For Smith, sympathy and benevolence are sufficient to allow that, once all restraint is removed and the "system of natural liberty" is re-established, the individual pursuit of self-interest will comport with the fulfillment of the social good. In the opening sentence of *Theory of Moral Sentiments* (1759; 6th edition 1790), Smith, whose reputation as the father of modern economics is enough for some *soi disant* Smithians to attribute to him positions on the nature of man as *homo economicus* that simply cannot be sustained, offers the following assessment:

> How selfish soever man may be supposed, there are evidently some principles in his nature, which interest him in the fortune of others, and render their happiness necessary to him, though he derives nothing from it except the pleasure of seeing it.
>
> (A. Smith 1790, Part I, Sec. I, Ch. I, p. 9)

As with Hume and Ferguson, Smith is quite emphatic in his declaration of the social aspects of man. Consider only the following passages in support of this contention:

> that to feel much for others and little for ourselves, that to restrain our selfish, and to indulge our benevolent affections, constitutes the perfection of human nature; and can alone produce among mankind that harmony of sentiments and passions in which consists their whole grace and propriety.
>
> (Ch. V, p. 25)

> It is thus that man, who can subsist only in society, was fitted by nature to that situation for which he was made. All the members of human society stand in need of each others assistance ... All the different members of it [society] are bound together by the agreeable bands of love and affection, and are, as it were, drawn to one common centre of mutual good offices.
>
> (Part II, Sec. II, Ch. III, p. 85)

The man of the most perfect virtue, the man whom we naturally love and revere the most, is he who joins, to the most perfect command of his own original and selfish feelings, the most exquisite sensibility both to the original and sympathetic feelings of others.

(Part III, Ch. III, p. 152)

The wise and virtuous man is at all times willing that his own private interest should be sacrificed to the public interest of his own particular order or society.

(Part VI, Sec. II, Ch. III, p. 235)

Smith's notion of self-interest cannot therefore be regarded as tantamount to selfishness or egoism, but must be seen as consistent with a view of man best summed up in Seneca's phrase, *homo est sociale animal*.

As one proceeds through the philosophies of the writers presented herein, the themes of society and connectedness will become clear. Each of our characters accepts this as a matter of course, as each rejects the idea of man as isolated individual and self-absorbed narcissist. This is not to suggest that they agree on every tenet of liberalism, even were it possible to define such, as each has his own understanding of the liberal philosophy. This leads to our second generality: one cannot generalize a modal liberalism, as its form differs among its advocates. Utilitarian and anti-utilitarian, formalist and pragmatist, rationalist and anti-rationalist philosophies are all present. It is this divergence of outlook perhaps more than anything which makes the liberal philosophy so compelling.

1 Forms of community

The theme of "community" is one that pervades much that passes for political philosophy and social (and even legal) theory. That this is so is of course abundantly clear with respect to the philosophies of conservatism and communitarianism. Conservatism as a philosophy (as distinct from a political movement) is predicated on the existence of a *social* morality, a set of imperatives the form and substance of which transcend the moral concerns of those comprising the community; communitarianism as a political philosophy (again, distinct from any political movement that may seek to capitalize on the term), while in some senses antithetical to conservatism, none the less also accepts the predicate of the *socially constituted* – non-individuated – person. Each maintains a social ontology, i.e., each holds (to some extent) that society has an existence beyond that of the individuals comprising it, that the community is an organic whole that subsumes its constituent elements, and that the social, not the individual, is the unit of account.

The place of community, of the social, is somewhat less distinctly defined when one comes to examine liberalism. Communitarianism and conservatism, as we shall see presently, appear to require that "community" be defined organically (though in social, ethical, and cultural terms), such that individuals are constituents of a given, constituted, and highly abstract order. In contrast to both, liberalism as a political philosophy is typically regarded as allowing that social interactions result from an apprehension of like interests, and so proceeds without the need for any communal sentiment; liberalism must thus claim a role for *community* while at the same time maintaining an *individualist* ontology. As the individual is granted central place, the social is defined, it is often claimed, only with respect to the person: the whole is identified through its constituent parts. It is here that a difficulty arises, *viz.*, if liberalism treats community as a *constructed* order as opposed to the predicate of the social order, can liberalism support any but the most tenuous value structure? To what extent, and by what mechanism, do competing *individual* values coalesce and give rise to *social* norms? On the other hand, if liberalism is said to embrace a concept of social order, must it, if only to ensure stability and cohesion, also hold that the individual is socially embedded? Must *individual* values be derivative of some transcendent *community* ethos or purpose? It is along these lines that liberalism is attacked by both conservative and communitarian critics. Yet despite the fact that both conservatism and communitarianism treat it as a foil, liberalism, we will argue here, acknowledges the importance for social cohesion of the community-oriented or other-regarding self; in point of fact, liberal political theory is fundamentally incoherent unless one accepts at the outset at least an implicit regard for this aspect of human nature.

The point of this chapter is to identify certain key elements of liberalism, communitarianism, and conservatism such as are necessary to the discussion to follow. As the focus of the book is an appreciation of liberalism and its development in the writings of some of its more ardent defenders, we will begin with an overview of that position, while covering in greater detail the conservative and communitarian perspectives.

Liberalism as foil

There is one thing upon which there seems to be agreement: there is no agreement on the essentials of liberalism. John Gray characterizes liberalism as individualist (and hence anti-collectivist); morally egalitarian, in so far as it "denies the relevance to legal or political order of differences in moral worth among human beings"; universalist, suggesting an affirmation of "the moral unity of the human species" as it accords "a secondary importance to specific historic associations and cultural forms"; and meliorist, maintaining "the corrigibility and improvability of all social institutions and political arrangements" (J. Gray 1995, p. xii). David Johnston identifies with the liberal philosophy the principles of the primacy of individuals, individual equality, and human agency (Johnston 1994, pp. 17–24). David Gauthier describes the liberal individual as an autonomous, rational, "active" being, with an "independent conception of the good." It is not necessary to advance a conception of the social good, for, as society is a "co-operative venture for mutual advantage," the free social affections of individuals are seen as sufficient to social cohesion and the maintenance of a just social order (Gauthier 1986, pp. 346–49). John Rawls, in his various efforts at delimiting political liberalism (without actually explicitly *defining* it), requires of a liberal society constitutional democracy (an enumeration of basic rights), common values (a prioritization of rights), and a moral nature, this last encompassing concepts of right and justice (Rawls 1999, pp. 14, 23–4).

The problem with such definitions is that they do not, in and of themselves, provide any but the most general insights into the nature of the liberal doctrine; they provide more a taxonomic than an analytical function. What is needed is a more concrete expression of the principal tenets of the philosophy, a task best accomplished through a comparison of alternatives. To this end, we may consider the presentations of Stephen Holmes. As Holmes defines it, liberalism strives for "psychological security and personal independence for all, legal impartiality within a single system of laws applied equally to all, the human diversity fostered by liberty, and collective self-rule through elected government and uncensored discussion" (S. Holmes 1995, p. 16). The "core" values of liberalism are then personal security, impartiality in respect of law, individual liberty, and democratic governance

(S. Holmes 1993, p. 4). In contrast to liberalism, Holmes presents anti-liberalism, an amorphous grouping of ideologies which nonetheless manifest a united front of opposition to liberal political philosophy. Anti-liberals of the non-Marxian variety – represented by, among others, Leo Strauss, Carl Schmitt, and Alasdair MacIntyre – are identified as antagonistic to the rationalism associated with the Enlightenment philosophy; they perceive social ills as the result of the success of liberalism in fostering an attitude of irreligious scientism which has served to erode the value-structures of the social order. While anti-liberals range over a host of political philosophies, they nonetheless have in common a general hostility to liberal principles. As Holmes defines it, anti-liberalism is not so much a definite political or philosophical conviction as it is a "mindset," a "sensibility as well as an argument." Its "enmity" to liberalism is evident in the denunciation of the "corrosive" influence of "individualism, rationalism, humanitarianism, rootlessness, permissiveness, universalism, materialism, skepticism, and cosmopolitanism" which they assert are the actual "core" values of the liberal creed (p. 5).

Consider only a few of the distinctions between these two opposing philosophies. To the liberal, authority as represented in government is "socially indispensable," with the proviso that it be so constituted as to be under the control of the governed (S. Holmes 1993, p. 201), while to the anti-liberal, authority is an essential force for the inculcation of standards of good and right (p. 94). To the liberal, the "common good" is represented in the constructs of "[j]ustice, self-rule, and the fruits of peaceful coexistence" (p. 200), in other words the general welfare or the public interest, while to the anti-liberal it appears more as an end to which all actions should be directed. To the liberal, rights are "facilitative," while to the anti-liberal "[r]ights are isolating, sacrifice self-development to self-protection, and elevate selfish concerns above social obligations" (p. 225).

Holmes does not see the need to divorce liberalism from either tradition or duty; he even quotes Adam Smith, approvingly: "'a sense of duty' is 'the only principle by which the bulk of mankind is capable of directing their actions'" (S. Holmes 1993, p. 228). Adherence to social norms, and an understanding of the difference between right and wrong actions, are seen by the liberal as indispensable to the functioning of a stable order. Liberals affirm a view of community and sociality, and do not, in fact cannot, be subjected to the criticism of atomism. Among the duties and obligations supported by liberals is, first and foremost, obedience to the law. The rationale behind this obedience, however, is not that it, in some manner, conduces to a moral order. Rather, the rationale is at once instrumental ("for the sake of the relatively civilized, just, cooperative, and free order it would help create") and conditional (as those in the society impose the laws and grant themselves the power to alter them, they must then themselves be obligated to obey) (pp. 228–9).

Communitarianism

Communitarians generally hold that the liberal school perceives the individual as antecedent to any social order, meaning that he is unencumbered by the influences of his community or his environment; as he is free to choose, he is also capable of situating himself as circumstances dictate. Man as a self-determinative, self-interpretive subject is relationally prior to purposes, so the right – defined to a large degree with respect to freedom of contract – is antecedent to the good, where the good is defined as an end to be pursued. As the individual is independent of social identity and can define the ends to be pursued – can question his very belief system – the liberal concern with right must be independent of any social conception of morality or ethics, which otherwise serve to define the good.

There remains the question of whether there is, in fact, any such thing as *a* communitarian position, i.e., whether the very term is simply a label applied to a group of philosophies that appear to be in general agreement as to certain political conclusions. It is by no means clear from what typically passes for communitarianism that agreement of even fundamentals has been reached. For example, Jeffrey Friedman (1994) classifies four types of communitarianism: Republican (associated with Charles Taylor), American (associated with Michael Sandel), Socialist (associated with Michael Walzer), and Premodern (associated with Alasdair MacIntyre). In addition, Stephen Gardbaum[1] observes that communitarianism makes not one, but three, separate claims of community. That the various strains of communitarian thought tend to be grouped together as representative of a coherent tradition is due to the fact that each employs a similar terminology. As one delves beneath the surface, however, the differences become obvious, and may be seen to be pronounced.

Consider the last contention in more detail. Gardbaum offers that communitarianism is a rubric covering claims as to the nature of individuality (as atomic or organic), the source of value (the recognition of a shared tradition), and the objects of value (the acknowledgment of the primacy of the social), each of which is independent of the others. The first two claims – of "antiatomism" and "metaethical communitarianism" – are quite consistent with classical liberalism – liberalism, after all, requires neither atomistic individuals nor extreme subjectivism, as these are (as Gardbaum rightly observes) methodological postures, distinct from any social philosophy. Liberals are quite prepared (as we shall see throughout) to acknowledge not only the social nature of man, but also the importance of shared values and traditions, indicative of a constitutive morality. They are, of course, not *required* to do so – the morality of Millian Utilitarianism is universal, i.e., autonomy is a universal value, independent of specific community values, while other conceptions treat the *individual* as the ultimate source of value; in liberalism, there appears to be either a single morality, or none at all, but one cannot identify the "liberal" position on this basis alone (Gardbaum 1992, p. 721). Only the third claim – "strong communitarianism" – is inconsistent with liberalism, and this claim is little more than "an *antimodern* critique of modernity" (p. 689; emphasis in original). The reason is quite simple: strong communitarianism demands a concept of substantive community, a single value or notion of the good, and so is opposed to all pluralistic theories. With these definitions in hand, Gardbaum identifies the "strong" communitarian position with Sandel and MacIntyre, as it posits a universal value of community, independent of the diversity of values found in particular communities. By contrast, the "weak" form, rejecting universalism in favor of particularism and pluralism, is evident in the works of Walzer and Taylor. In addition, the substantive community of strong communitarianism is consistent with the claims made by conservatism, republicanism, and communism, each making strong claims as to the nature of the good.

With this preface in mind, we turn now to an examination of the positions of two of the more important of the "strong" communitarian critics of liberalism, Alasdair MacIntyre and Michael Sandel, ending with a consideration of the "weak" communitarian views of Michael Walzer.

MacIntyre: the fundamentality of tradition

Alasdair MacIntyre, in *Whose Justice? Which Rationality?*, launches the onslaught against liberalism by exploring the significance of the ancient Greek ideals of community and the bases of order. MacIntyre argues that the modern conception of virtue inherent in liberalism has strayed significantly from its Greek roots. Specifically, he regards the modern understanding as representative of a shift away from the Greek perception of community and toward the notion of the centrality of the individual, which shift has been most profound in defining the modern ethos.

This is best understood by digressing to a brief review of the roots of MacIntyre's communalism. To MacIntyre, a tradition is defined simply as "an argument extended through time" (MacIntyre 1988, p. 12). Yet the concept of tradition is more complex. Tradition affords the basis for rational enquiry; there is no "neutral standing ground," no "locus of rationality as such," to which one can appeal as an independent source of enquiry into the practices of a tradition. Any attempt at a rational appraisal (let alone a deconstruction) of a tradition must be understood as taking place within some opposing tradition, comprised of its own accepted practices and norms governing argumentation. There exists no mechanism outside of tradition itself through which the practices of a society may be articulated or criticized, for the rules of engagement of such an enterprise are thoroughly encapsulated in the practices and principles therein. Each tradition has its own (to some extent unique) standards and practices, beliefs and background principles which, while providing the means for deliberation *within* the tradition, serve to limit the effectiveness of appraisal and hence criticism *between* traditions. It is in essence the tradition, then, which formalize enquiry: "To be outside all traditions is to be a stranger to enquiry; it is to be in a state of intellectual and moral destitution" (p. 367).

One should not then minimize the importance of tradition as a means for the preservation of the social or the intellectual order, for its function is to provide a means to the resolution of conflict in those situations in which "we cannot adequately identify either our own commitments or those of others in the argumentative conflicts of the present except by situating them within those histories which made them what they have now become" (MacIntyre 1988, p. 13). This is as true in respect of tradition writ large (those intellectual traditions of philosophical enquiry that animate arguments on the nature of the social order) as well as those traditions within which develop the perspectives unique to individual cultures.

Following Plato, Aristotle, and other Greek authorities, MacIntyre proceeds to dissect these early (and to him authoritative and even patristic) accounts of the relationship of the individual to the *polis*, "the institution whose concern was, not with this or that particular good, but with human good as such, and not with desert or achievement in respect of particular practices, but with desert and achievement as such." The *polis* represented, in effect, "the expression of a set of principles about how goods are to be ordered into a way of life" (MacIntyre 1988, p. 34). It was a community that recognized a standard of conduct to which could be compared individual achievements, so as to gauge individual merit and desert, allowing contributions to be recognized and appraised with reference to a fixed and accepted criterion. More emphatically, the Greek conception of the *telos* of the *polis*

> was the achievement of a structured communal life within which the goods of the other forms of activity were ordered, so that the peculiar *telos* of the *polis* was not this or that good, but *the good and the best* as such.
>
> (p. 44; emphasis in original)

As the individual relates to the *polis* as the parts to the whole of the body, the *polis* is then the "human community perfected and completed by achieving its *telos*" (p. 97). It is only when each member of the *polis* is perfected "in that form of activity for which his ... soul is peculiarly fitted" that the *polis* itself "is in good order" (p. 73).

Diké – justice stemming from an acknowledgment that the universe has "a single fundamental order, an order structuring both nature and society" (MacIntyre 1988, p. 14) – "is the ordering of the *polis*," and significantly "lacks application apart from the *polis*" (p. 97). (*Diké* "accords" with the requirements of *themis*, that which is "ordained" (p. 14).) It is in respect of *diké* and *dikaiosuné* (justice, in the sense of "the norm by which the *polis* is ordered") that the need for a community standard is most essential. Both *diké* (as a cosmic order) and *dikaiosuné* (as the practical norm of the *polis*), in order to be realized and to perform their structuring roles, must be predicated on such a standard. The individual *within* the *polis* is subjected to the stabilizing influence of these norms, while the norms themselves are so intimately tied to the structure of the *polis* that they cannot even be conceived apart from that context (p. 97).

In addition, one needs to consider in this argument the formative influence of virtue and practical reasoning. The possession of virtue (*areté*) is essential to right choice, while practical intelligence (*phronésis*) is the mechanism through which such actions are effectuated: virtue and practical reasoning are then interdependent, each a necessary condition for the existence of the other. But it is crucial to the argument that neither could develop in the absence of the order provided by the *polis*. In the absence of the influence of the *polis*, the individual is simply incapable of developing the "biologically given capacities" of *areté* and *phronésis*, and instead reverts to a feral nature (MacIntyre 1988, p. 97). Further, practical reasoning is a necessary requirement for the existence of the norm of justice (p. 123). The *polis*, then, provides the requisite structure of both virtue and practical reasoning, and lays the conditions for the development of a just order (pp. 97–8).

It is also within this structured whole that one sees the place of rational action. For MacIntyre, human beings and animals are distinguished by the fact that, for humans, "desires and dispositions ... are ordered to what they have truly judged to be their good, rather than by *epithumia* [desire] ungoverned by such judgment" (MacIntyre 1988, p. 130). The actual *desire* becomes the *affirmation* of the judgment of goodness. The process by which such reasoning occurs, and through which action is caused, begins with the "practical syllogism," consisting of a major or "initiating" premise and a minor or "secondary" premise. The initiating premise is declarative, as it stipulates for the individual "what good is at stake in his acting or not acting as he should," while the secondary premise is situational, as it seeks to specify "what the situation is in which, given that this good is at stake, action is required" (p. 129). Given knowledge of the good "at stake," and the situation in which action is needed, the conclusion – the form of the action required – can then be deduced.

Now each syllogism is peculiar both to the individual engaged in the process of rational deliberation and to the situation in which he is engaged: the "good" to be achieved is that particular "good" of the actor, and the conclusion will perforce be one pertinent to the immediate occasion. Here we are led to an appreciation of the "fully rational" individual. Rational deliberation is defined with respect to conformity to standards (MacIntyre 1988, p. 131). While the initiating premise stipulates a personal judgment of good, the initiating premise of the "fully rational" individual will affirm "a well-founded and true judgment," and "will only be effective in generating action if the individual's desires and dispositions are ordered accordingly" (p. 130). Rational deliberation dictates that, at each stage of the deliberation, one poses the question, "If such and such is the good which constitutes the *telos*, what means must I employ to achieve that good?" (p. 131). So the good as represented in the initiating premise "will be the immediate *arché* of his about-to-be-performed action," i.e., the complete specification of both the course and the subject of inquiry, and is such as "will provide his action with its immediate *telos*" (p. 130). Further, this specific concept of good will only be "genuine" for the individual if it is both consistent with and derivable from "the set of ultimate first principles and concepts [the *arché*], which specifies the good and the best for human beings as such" (p. 130).

Thus there is now no longer a need in contemplating a course of action to consider ends, as we need only contemplate "what conduces to ends," i.e., we need only consider means (MacIntyre 1988, p. 132). But this then requires that means and ends be ordered in such a way that we realize through a specific means the end to be achieved.

> The deliberative task of rational construction is then one which issues in an hierarchical ordering of means to their ends, in which the ultimate end is specified in a formulation which provides the first principle or principles from which are deduced statements of those subordinate ends which are means to the ultimate end.
>
> (MacIntyre 1988, p. 132)

Implicit, of course, in this account is the existence of a single, supreme good. Following Aristotle, MacIntyre rejects the notion that the individual antedates society, that his initial condition is as a solitary being unfettered by any commitment to others. Were the individual so situated he would be utterly incapable of choice, because he would be incapable of evaluating alternative desires in terms of a standard. It is only within the confines of the *polis* that the individual can develop the basic deliberative outfit, as it provides a forum through which his actions can be compared and evaluated. (MacIntyre goes so far as to define a rational individual as one who not merely participates in the activities of social life, but who strives to conform to the standards of the *polis* (MacIntyre 1988, p. 141).) Only in such a setting, in which there exists a ready means of evaluating rival goods and actions, can it be known whether any specific ideal is in fact *the* ideal – the "supreme good." But this alone is indicative of the fact that there actually *exists* some supreme good which, however complex, is nonetheless capable of being known (p. 134).

Liberalism, with its attachment to the primacy of rationality, rights, and the rule of law, must be recognized as but another tradition. Rationality and justice are not of themselves neutral, universal principles, but are contingent on the tradition inherent (but inadequately expressed) in the philosophy of liberalism. The principles of the liberal tradition that give rise to the particular practices of practical rationality and justice administered through the rule of law are themselves little more than attempts to "impose a particular conception of the good life, of practical reasoning, and of justice upon those who willingly or unwillingly accept the liberal procedures and the liberal terms of debate" (MacIntyre 1988, p. 345). For this reason, the good advanced by liberalism is no less contingent than the good advanced in any other tradition, as it represents "no more and no less than the continued sustenance of the liberal social and political order" (p. 345).

For MacIntyre, contemporary society is "emotivist" – moral questions are phrased in a rhetoric designed to give expression to *personal* standards and preferences; there is no objective morality, as morality, in congruence with preference, is relative. While emotivism denies the existence of an objective standard of moral reference, it nonetheless proceeds as if moral *language* were on the same plane as objective principles of moral *conduct*. Yet it is clear that statements of personal value are fundamentally different from statements of principle, for the latter derive from objective standards and are thus not subject to personal definition. To deny this is to deny any role whatever for statements respecting moral conduct, for such statements no longer have any meaning (MacIntyre 1984, pp. 19–20). This makes it impossible to *define* moral conduct, for the language cannot facilitate the expression of concepts of virtue.

To see why this is so, it is enough to concede that emotivist society gives central place to individual sentiment. The emotivist self is a moral agent in the sense that it is capable of detached judgment, i.e., it can arrive at moral judgments "from a purely universal and abstract point of view that is totally detached from all social particularity" (MacIntyre 1984, p. 32). So, to the extent that virtue is identified with sentiment, virtue is *ipso facto* divorced from any concept of the social good: it is the *personal* standard which motivates *moral* behavior. As there is no basis upon which to secure agreement as to *rules*, since the emotivist self has no value structure beyond preference, there is no basis for agreement as to *social virtues*. Virtue – which MacIntyre sees as important "in sustaining those traditions which provide both practices and individual lives with their necessary historical content" (p. 223) – becomes from the emotivist standpoint entirely instrumental.

In MacIntyre's communitarianism, social obligation requires a rejection of emotivism and a realization that human beings are first and foremost *social* agents. This requires in turn cognizance of a transcendent *telos*:

> unless there is a *telos* which transcends the limited goods of practices by constituting the good of a whole human life, the good of a human life conceived as a unity, it will *both* be the case that a certain subversive arbitrariness will invade the moral life *and* that we shall be unable to specify the context of certain virtues adequately.
>
> (MacIntyre 1984, p. 203; emphasis in original)

The problem lies in the unit of analysis. With the individual as subject, man is independent of his social and moral relationships. The common good is then constructed from individual preferences. With the community at the center, there is formed a bond, "a shared understanding both of the good for man and of the good of that community," so that "individuals identify their primary interests with reference to those goods" (MacIntyre 1984, p. 250). The common good is then the community standard through which preferences may be interpreted. It is through a combination of standards and rules, framing or boundary conditions, and inherited obligations (termed by MacIntyre practices, narrative unity, and tradition) that the individual is situated within a social frame of reference, and he thus is able to evaluate his preferences in terms of the community. Without such an appreciation of the way in which individuals are connected to social communities, and the way in which these connections affect choice, there can be no understanding of or regard for moral virtue. Yet it is important to remember that the good of the community is not simply the sum total of individual goods, since the community good must itself be internalized by its members. In addition, the good of each individual must be seen as comprising more than the common good.[2] It is the failure of liberalism to recognize and to embrace the inherent sociality of the individual as exemplified in these concepts that MacIntyre sees as its central flaw.

So for MacIntyre, while the idea of community is crucial to the ideal of the social good, moral virtue is central to the concept of community: "a community which envisages its life as directed toward a shared good which provides that community with its common tasks will need to articulate its moral life in terms *both* of the virtues *and* of law" (MacIntyre 1984, p. 169; emphasis in original). Without a clear awareness of the place of virtue in defining social morality, it is not possible to view the individual as situated in society, or to entertain any concept of the good.

Sandel: the unencumbered self

Michael Sandel, by contrast, places the emphasis on a broader notion of the social good, one influenced by Aristotle's conception of rights as redounding from "the moral importance of the ends they serve" (Sandel 1998, p. xi). As the community is the *subject* of human motivations, good must be antecedent to right, and society antecedent to the individual. Yet an important qualification is in order. Sandel does not suggest (as MacIntyre does) that shared values or shared understandings are sufficient to ground a theory of justice, for these values and understandings must themselves be judged in terms of moral import. The resort to a community standard as an objective moral criterion is flawed in that the criterion itself is contingent on the constitution of the community. One can only escape this trap by acknowledging that the moral criterion is independent of social preference, that the good life is somehow a transcendent value. Ends are constitutive, and so the good is a categorical imperative, not a contingent, socially prescribed goal.

With MacIntyre, Sandel considers the liberal notion of the individual (the "unencumbered self") – as purposeful, rational, deliberative, and independent – to be at the core of what he perceives as a perverse juxtaposition of right and good. Specifically, he opposes the philosophy of "deontological liberalism," which holds (1) that "society ... is best arranged when it is governed by principles that do not *themselves* presuppose any particular conception of the good," and (2) that these principles "conform to the concept of *right*, a moral category given prior to the good and independent of it" (Sandel 1998, p. 1; emphasis in original). This is somewhat different from Rawls's use of the term. Rawls defines a deontological theory as "one that either does not specify the good independently from the right, or does not interpret the right as maximizing the good"; deontological theories do not "characterize the rightness of institutions and acts independently from their consequences," as it is understood that "[a]ll ethical doctrines worth our attention take consequences into account in judging rightness" (Rawls 1971, p. 30).[3] In any event, deontological liberalism is non-act-consequentialist – "certain categorical duties and prohibitions ... take unqualified precedence over other moral and practical concerns" – and non-teleological – there is no presupposition of "any final human purposes or ends" (Sandel 1998, p. 3).[4] It is here that the conflict arises between Rawls and the communitarians as Rawls, in advancing a deontic theory, is accused of being anti-utilitarian (to the extent that Utilitarianism "denies the distinction between persons" and so seeks to establish a definition of the social good as a greater benefit, the provision of which requires individual sacrifice), focusing his attention on a "rights-based ethic," which treats individuals as separate and distinct. This impels him to "treat every person as an end and not merely as a means," and as a result to "seek principles of justice that embody it" (Sandel 1998, pp. 66–7).[5]

In Sandel's view, the "unencumbered self" at the center of the liberal position can feel a communal spirit only in the sense that he is free to associate with whomever he desires. This suggests that the moral choices of the individual arise from personal preferences and not from social attachments or the pressure of socially prescribed behavioral norms; ends can be ranked, their relative value determined not by any perfectionist standard but by own beliefs respecting moral choice. Objective, moral judgment has no place in such a rational order, as the right itself is paramount. Rights (such that promote freedom of choice) take precedence over the common good, and the principles necessary for the elucidation of those rights – typically subsumed under the banner of justice – are independent of any notion of the good. Since each member of the society is free to exercise his rights as he sees fit (subject to the proviso that this exercise does not pose a burden to or deny the rights of others), the ends should be interpreted neutrally. But the question arises, what of the *morality* of preferences? As Sandel argues, because (on the liberal argument) the individual has been situated relationally prior to his ends, rights become more significant than their moral content. As choice takes precedence over what is chosen, the individual is removed from any commitment to a larger conception of the good. In effect, a concern for basic individual liberties is granted precedence over moral obligation and moral virtue; rights need no justification beyond their inviolability. Thus, on the liberal model, nothing has any hold on the individual beyond the satisfaction of his own immediate wants (the good redounds to expressions of personal utility), and so nothing in his external relations can serve as binding constraints on these desires.[6]

By insisting on an entirely subjective self, given only to voluntary associations and so not bound to any social ends, liberalism (at least in the Rawlsian sense, the form explicitly condemned by Sandel) denies that the individual can be in any way shaped or influenced by his social ties or by shared moral understandings; the unencumbered self is by definition completely purposeful in *choosing* ends (so the end becomes the *object* of free choice), a profoundly Kantian notion.[7] Where ties of community and beneficence exist, they are made without reference to any antecedent value structure, the result of a choice among competing aims. But Sandel believes more is required:

> What is denied to the unencumbered self is the possibility of membership in any community bound by moral ties antecedent to choice; he cannot belong to any community where the self *itself* could be at stake. Such a community – call it constitutive as against merely cooperative – would engage the identity as well as the interests of the participants, and so implicate its members in a citizenship more thoroughgoing than the unencumbered self can know.
>
> (Sandel 1984, p. 87)

Sandel does therefore allow that liberalism can indeed support a theory of community, and even follows Rawls in identifying two: the instrumental (private society) and the sentimental (cooperative society). The instrumental community arises from cooperative arrangements designed in pursuit of selfish aims; it "is not held together by a public conviction that its basic arrangements are just and good in themselves, but by the calculations of everyone ... that any practicable changes would reduce the stock of means whereby they pursue their personal ends" (Rawls 1971, p. 522). The sentimental community (which Rawls favors), by contrast, allows the individuals comprising it to cooperate through a realization of mutual or shared benefit; those who constitute the community possess "shared final ends and … value their common institutions and activities as good in themselves" (p. 522). The sentimentalist approach to community precludes pure egoism, all the while sustaining the centrality of self. While the individual *can* make sacrifices for the benefit of others, he is under no obligation (as a matter of justice) to do so.

Yet while liberal theories of justice *can* support community, neither of these approaches suffices as the basis of the *communitarian* community, as they lack the necessary ontology. To the instrumentalist, "the good of community consists solely in the advantages individuals derive from co-operating in pursuit of their egoistic ends"; it is "wholly *external* to the aims and interests of the individuals who comprise it." To the sentimentalist, the individual is antecedent, and so "the good of community … consists not only in the direct benefits of social co-opera- tion but also in the quality of motivations and ties of sentiment that may attend this co-operation"; it "is partly *internal* to the subjects, in that it reaches the feel- ings and sentiments of those engaged in a co-operative scheme" (Sandel 1998, pp. 148–9; emphasis in original).

Still, Sandel finds both conceptions wanting, as both require the "antecedent individuation of the subject." His alternative views the community as both subject and object of motivations; it would retain Rawls's sentimentality, but would be radically different in that the idea of community "would describe not just a *feeling* but a mode of self-understanding partly constitutive of the agent's identity," so that identity follows from community (Sandel 1998, p. 150; emphasis in original).[8] Sandel thus argues that a theory of community must extend beyond an understanding of the social nature of the aims and value- structures of the individual members; the self and the ends pursued cannot be understood in isolation, as the former defines the latter. The community serves to inculcate in its members a respect for these standards of behavior and conduct, to forge a sense of obligation. It is not enough to accept that each member of a community is governed by feelings of a shared morality or shared sentiments, i.e., to insist that the popular will be indicative of community morality. A theory of community must also accept as a first condition that each individual *identifies himself with, and is only realized through,* his community relationships and the sense of moral obligation this embodies, i.e., that he perceives his *individual* identity in terms of the *social* identity; in G. W. F. Hegel's felicitous phrase, "[i]n furthering my end, I further the universal, and this in turn furthers my end" (Hegel 1821, §184 add.). In a sense, then, one cannot *choose* whether to belong, since then the community would be little more than the object of personal sentiment. Rather, the community itself defines choice, the "sense of community" being reflective of individual identity (Sandel, 1998, p. 150). One embarks on a journey of discovery, of self-knowledge, through which one succeeds in gauging one's constituent nature. The concept of community therefore becomes intimately tied to the very values of each individual comprising the society.

Thus the self is never truly unencumbered, for each member of the society must have knowledge of the existing social arrangements and institutional structures, and each must be cognizant of both his individual desires and the means to their attainment. This "encumbered self" is ultimately a moral creature, obligated to pursue ends not of his own choosing, ends grounded in virtue and stipulated by culture and tradition.[9]

Another communitarianism: Walzer

In sum, communitarians base their attacks on individualist theories of justice on the ontological foundations of those theories. They aim to replace the "thin" self of libertarianism with a "thick," socially embedded self. For some, such as MacIntyre, the community or society in which the individual functions, not the individual himself, determines in large measure his constitution. They do not deny that "individuals matter." Rather they stress that it is the social setting which identifies the individual and induces feelings of community and self. For others, such as Sandel, the right cannot be judged absent a moral judgment of the good. The moral claims of community cannot of themselves *declare* an end to be good, for then the end itself is derivative from preferences. Morality must be understood as distinct from preference, whether the preference of the individual or the preference of the community; it cannot be seen as derivative, but must be viewed as prior to any such judgment. In general, the communitarian message is that ends define conduct, but they are not themselves the objects of choice. As subject, the community is the basis of individual identity; as object, the individual is bound to the motives of the community. Thus the community (in terms of the social collective and the moral conscience) is not a mere voluntary association, but is a constitutive force defining individual purpose and existence. As Sandel phrases it:

> To imagine a person incapable of constitutive attachments such as these is not to conceive an ideally free and rational agent, but to imagine a person wholly without character, without moral depth. For to have character is to know that I move in a history I neither summon nor command, which carries consequences nonetheless for my choices and conduct.
>
> (Sandel 1984, p. 90)

In contrast to the declarations of the strong communitarian critics of liberalism, there is a communitarian strain that does not require such a strict universalism, a strain that instead acknowledges the importance of pluralism. This variant is exemplified in the work of Michael Walzer. Walzer distances himself from the demands of both MacIntyre and Sandel as regards the premises of the liberal theory. Specifically, he identifies two mutually inconsistent communitarian arguments against liberalism. The first (a Marxian account) accepts that liberal philosophy is consistent with what is perceived to be the constitution of liberal society: liberal philosophy takes seriously the notion of society as a Hobbesian order populated by egoistic individuals, divorced from any social consciousness, dedicated to the pursuit of personal ends, and in complete disregard of community affections and traditions (in effect, the classical economic man). The second argument denies the validity of the postulate of the unencumbered individual and instead holds liberalism at fault for perpetrating a deception as to the nature of society; it is the liberal ideology which is responsible for misrepresenting the communal nature of man, of ignoring the "deep structure" of community which defines the modern social order (Walzer 1990, pp. 9–11). Liberalism indeed acknowledges the value of "associative" and "dissociative" tendencies but, notes Walzer, insists upon regarding these tendencies as voluntary and even pragmatic, not as real and constitutive. It is this lack of any secure basis for community that Walzer believes animates the liberal perspective on the role of government, specifically the demand for neutrality in respect of individual liberties:

> [t]he standard liberal argument for neutrality is an induction from social fragmentation. Since dissociated individuals will never agree on the good life, the state must allow them to live as they think best ... without endorsing or sponsoring any particular understanding of what "best" means.
>
> (Walzer 1990, p. 16)

The truth, however, as Walzer sees it, is somewhere in between: the individual is indeed situated within a social order, even as he is fully cognizant of his individuality. Walzer thus disagrees with the notion that liberalism requires as a first condition an unencumbered self, arguing that "[c]ontemporary liberals are not committed to a presocial self, but only to a self capable of reflecting critically on the values that have governed its socialization" (Walzer 1990, p. 21).

For Walzer, the values of liberal society are not determined by atomistic, unencumbered individuals seeking to pursue personal ends; the values of the liberal society are, rather, *shared* values reflecting the traditions of the various communities of which the individuals are part. Individualism just happens to be *one* of these community values. The individual is indeed socially encumbered, as he is "capable of reflecting critically on the values that have governed his socialization". Liberalism is, then, at its core "a theory of relationship, which has voluntary association at its center and which understands voluntariness as the right of rupture or withdrawal" (Walzer 1990, p. 21).[10]

Conservatism

As with liberalism, conservatism as a political and social philosophy is difficult to define, due in large measure to the deformation of the concept in modern political discourse. As articulated in its most general form by Roger Scruton, conservatism "arises directly from the sense that one belongs to some continuing, and pre-existing social order" (Scruton 2002, p. 10), and so shares with communitarianism the notion of the encumbered individual: individuals are autonomous "only because they can first identify themselves as something greater – as members of a society, group, class, state or nation ..." (p. 24).

Conservatism is not to be construed as the philosophy of the market or of capitalism, although there are aspects of both which are accepted as necessary, not only to the flourishing of individual initiative but also to the stability of the social order. On the contrary, as David Reisman argues, conservatism is a political philosophy at times at war with the capitalist structure it is typically held to justify. Capitalism asserts an individual "not just as self-conscious and self-aware but also as goal-orientated, purposive and economical of scarce resources"; he is a "one-dimensional being," rational in his actions, seeking in all things to maximize his personal utility (Reisman 1999, p. 3). Conservatism, by contrast, is reflective of a social need for institutional stability; it is an organic philosophy of shared customs and conventions, of community morality, embracing the stability provided by the preservation of the status quo. Conservatism "assigns particular value to the shared, the continuing and the accepted," eschewing rational calculation in favor of reliance on custom, tradition, and non-rational motivation; eschewing risk-taking in favor of the comfort and security of stasis; eschewing the delimitation of individual spheres of action in favor of social obligation, duty, and the maintenance of social standards (p. 8).

In its most elementary form, conservatism (1) situates the individual within a constitutionally defined social order not of deliberate and rational design, as it (2) identifies in institutions a means to continuity and social stability. The conservative sees the existing institutional structures as essential to the preservation of the common weal, but at the same time is cognizant of the fact that such structures are not immune to change and even replacement; all that he is suggesting is that there be a reason behind any alteration in the basic framework, that change not be made merely for the sake of change. The conservative views the social order as natural and organic, not merely as an association of otherwise autonomous individuals dedicated to the furtherance of perceived common ends. The structures of that order reflect the historical development of those values and traditions that define a community. As such, these structures are not to be viewed in any instrumental sense but are to be understood as constitutive of the social whole; they are not amenable to rational deconstruction and reconstitution. As Edmund Burke proclaims, it would be folly for one to believe that society could be altered so as to bring it into conformity with the latest vogue; to attempt such an alteration would be to admit of nothing permanent, to allow that "[n]o one generation could link with the other." The following passage presents the case:

> Of course, no certain laws, establishing invariably grounds of hope and fear, would keep the actions of men in a certain course, or direct them to a certain end. Nothing stable in the modes of holding property, or exercising function, could form a solid ground on which any parent could speculate in the education of his offspring, or in a choice for their future establishment in the world. No principles would be early worked into the habits. As soon as the most able instructor had completed his laborious course of institution, instead of sending forth his pupil, accomplished in a virtuous discipline, fitted to procure him attention and respect, in his place in society, he would

find every thing altered; and that he had turned out a poor creature to the contempt and derision of the world, ignorant of the true grounds of estimation. Who would insure a tender and delicate sense of honour to beat almost with the first pulses of the heart, when no man could know what would be the test of honour in a nation, continually varying the standard of its coin? No part of life would retain its acquisitions. Barbarism with regard to science and literature, unskilfulness with regard to arts and manufactures, would infallibly succeed to the want of a steady education and settled principle; and thus the commonwealth itself would, in a few generations, crumble away, be disconnected into the dust and powder of individuality, and at length dispersed to all the winds of heaven.

(Burke 1790, pp. 193–4)

Societies must evolve in response to the needs of the individuals of which it is comprised. This no one denies. While change may be inevitable, we should, implores Burke, approach it with more than an element of caution. One must not proceed indiscriminately in deconstructing the institutions and value structures of a society without having an idea as to the consequences of such actions, and in the absence of a replacement. Before one seeks the replacement of "an edifice which has answered in any tolerable degree for ages the common purposes of society," it should be made abundantly clear precisely which "models and patterns of approved utility" one seeks to offer in its place (Burke 1790, p. 152).

To elucidate further on the form and substance of the conservative philosophy, we shall turn now to a presentation of its identifying traits as presented in the works of the philosophers Michael Oakeshott and John Kekes.

Oakeshott: tradition in the service of individuality

As defined by Michael Oakeshott, to be conservative[11]

is to prefer the familiar to the unknown, to prefer the tried to the untried, fact to mystery, the actual to the possible, the limited to the unbounded, the near to the distant, the sufficient to the superabundant, the convenient to the perfect, present laughter to utopian bliss.

(Oakeshott 1991, p. 408)

Conservatism implies an aversion to change, and yet at the same time it is a philosophy that realizes the importance of *accommodating* change. The conservative is apprehensive about change not because of fear or mistrust, or because of some misplaced longing for the past, but because he is aware of the nature of his environment and is committed to a particular way of life. Change for the sake of change is welcomed only by someone who is without social attachments or is apathetic in respect of the received tradition; change is "welcomed indiscriminately only by those who esteem nothing, whose attachments are fleeting and who are strangers to love and affection" (Oakeshott 1991, p. 409).

Such an attitude is foreign to the conservative disposition. Change represents for him a loss of the familiar, that which has always attended to feelings of happiness and comfort. In place of this realized quantity is submitted an unknown to which he has not developed any feeling or attachment. The change may indeed be an improvement over that which it supersedes. The problem, however, is that this cannot be known beforehand: any advantages that may be anticipated may not materialize, and the disadvantages and unintended negative consequences attending change are rarely perceived. This explains the need in the conservative for continuity, the fulfillment of expectations (Oakeshott 1991, pp. 409–11).

This is especially important in respect of social change. Changes affecting the institutional structures of a society may in fact be for the good, and are often advertised and promoted as instrumental in the advancement of the overall good of the society. Only social betterment can result from the alteration of the contemporary social condition, and accordingly the proposed transformation must be seen as desirable to the prevailing state of affairs. Yet this conviction ignores the essential nature of tradition and institutional structure. Traditions and stable social structures are indispensable to the functioning of any community, as they assist in the creation of an atmosphere of solidarity and fellowship, which are essential to the maintenance of civil society; the very existence of such relationships is secured by the continuity evinced in these social arrangements. In seeking to replace tradition with novelty, the process succeeds only in destroying the bonds of community that are themselves the result of identification with a commonly held set of beliefs and values.

This emphasis on the importance of tradition and habit recurs as Oakeshott considers the question of the more appropriate of two forms of moral life. The first he terms "habit of affection and behaviour," defined as conduct initiated "without reflection" (Oakeshott 1991, pp. 467–8). Such conduct requires no introspection, no calculation of net benefit, no consideration of alternative courses of action. It is but the "unreflective following of a tradition of conduct," best described as "moral habit," a reflexive response to "the emergencies of life." This is conduct that is for the most part acquired in the same way as language, and is equally as habitually practiced (p. 468).

This form of moral life is coextensive with neither the moral sense nor the moral conscience, since there is involved no appeal to authority (in any sense of the term); nor does it demand an obedience to prescribed rules of conduct (although such rules may be formulated *ex post*, in attempting to justify such actions), since the knowledge or understanding of such rules is not important in the formation or acquisition of the moral habits. It is at once plastic (i.e., susceptible to and accepting of significant alteration), yet stable, continually changing but only incrementally and for the most part imperceptibly. The moral habit is then best described as imitative behavior that "continues as selective conformity to a rich variety of customary behaviour" (Oakeshott 1991, p. 469). It is this form of moral life which is essential to the stability of the community, precisely because of its role in the continuation of tradition and custom, aspects of a culture which are of immense significance to its survival.

The second form of moral life Oakeshott considers is "the reflective application of a moral criterion," composed of "the selfconscious pursuit of moral ideals," and "the reflective observance of moral rules" (Oakeshott 1991, p. 472). In contrast to moral habit, this form of moral life *requires* the application of a rule of behavior, typically in the nature of an abstract principle or "moral aspiration," a standard of perfection, as justification for conduct. The rule is formulated for the express purpose of achieving some desired end result, its necessity derived from the need to make absolutely clear the type of conduct allowed (and, perhaps more importantly, conduct not allowed). The fact of the moral rule itself is often not to motivate action but to instill "the right moral ideal," to foster a moral attitude commensurate with the rule as opposed to compelling behavior (although the mere expression of the ideal itself may be sufficient to lead to conduct consistent with the ideal as represented by the rule).

It is to this, the second form of moral life, that education is most important. Education provides the necessary training in the recognition and the internalization of the moral ideal, as the ideal is often imperfectly expressed and so imperfectly appreciated and understood (Oakeshott 1991, p. 474). The task of the educational system, then, becomes more extensive than mere training in necessary skills such as reading, writing, mathematics, and the sciences. It is seen as the forum in which the inculcation of moral ideals is best discharged. In accomplishing this task, education provides the additional service of creating within individuals the capacity to become members of a cohesive community (p. 475).

Unlike moral habit, moral rules are not plastic. They are designed with constancy in mind. While the rules are susceptible to interpretation (necessary as society evolves), they are not readily given to wholesale alteration, except in those extreme circumstances wherein they become so oppressive in their operation as to foment revolution (and even then are altered only with great trepidation).

Oakeshott does not, however, consider either of these two extremes to be alone capable of acting as a guide to the moral life. Moral habit, because it is divorced from moral reflection, is inconsistent with self-criticism and easily converted to superstition (Oakeshott 1991, p. 471). Moral rules often involve conflicting ideals which are "dangerous in an individual and disastrous in a society" (p. 476). This leaves open the question of the proper mix. In a society in which moral habit is supplemented by moral rules, the rules serve to ameliorate the problem of the unknown ideal. Reflexive behavior still dominates, but it is tempered by reflection: free action can be undertaken with little need to pause and ponder the motivations behind it, while at the same time one is aware of the potential of reflective criticism of any action taken in conflict with the ideal, criticism which may lead to a change of the tradition itself. The advantage is that any criticism generated by perceived deviations from the rules is not threatening to habitual moral behavior (p. 477).

A society in which moral rules dominate moral habit, however, may produce negative consequences. Instead of assisting in the formation of moral habit, the rules actually lead to a self-conscious critical evaluation of all conduct. Habit becomes subordinate to a need for self-examination in light of the prevailing ideology, with constancy and ideological consistency taking precedence over the plasticity and spontaneity of tradition (Oakeshott 1991, p. 478). This rationalistic morality "is the morality of the self-conscious pursuit of moral ideals," its continuity guaranteed "by training in an ideology rather than an education in behaviour" (p. 40). It seeks the destruction of tradition and custom, replacing them with moral technique. This admixture then results in the "denial of the poetic character of all human activity" (p. 479). As in poetry the idea and the presentation of the idea are one and the same, so in morals the feeling and the conduct are coextensive, with reflection providing the justification and the means for later refinement or reconsideration (pp. 479–80). In placing the ideal (in the guise of a moral rule) above habit, this connection is broken, as the dominance of reflection destroys the creativity inherent in habit.

In the opinion of Oakeshott, moral conduct can be equated with behaving as we should, "of approving and of doing what is approved" (Oakeshott 1991, p. 296). This is inextricably tied to our sense of our own nature, to the identification of our actions and our desires with our identity, so that "what we ought to do is unavoidably connected with what in fact we are" (p. 296). To explicate this assertion, he then proceeds to identify three "idioms of moral conduct," these being communalism, individualism, and the common good. To the first of these idioms, communalism, individual choice has no meaning. Prescribed conduct is ritualized in furtherance of a communal will, the remnant of some past experience (in short, tradition), with members of the community unaware even of the existence of alternatives to that will. Here the good is "understood as appropriate participation in the unvarying activities of a community" (p. 296). To the second, individualism – "the morality of self and other selves" – each person is accorded "separate and sovereign" status, allowing each to engage "in an enterprise of give and take ... accommodating themselves to one another as best they can" (p. 297). This idiom declares that happiness is reflected in the pursuit of personal, not community or collective, choice. To the third, common good, individuality is recognized, but is tempered by the understanding that the interests of the society take precedence over those of the individual. Pursuit of the "social good" dictates "a single approved condition of circumstance" for each member of the society, with social good having acquired a meaning far different from that which might be understood by those in the society (p. 297).

Of interest in Oakeshott's presentation is the way in which he employs these categories in analyzing, through the evolution of European culture, the advent of the "mass man," a quite loathsome creature who epitomizes the degradation of social life and ultimately portends the destruction of individuality. In encapsulated form, individualism issued as a reaction to the constraints on behavior, condition, and choice endemic in the communalism of the medieval period. Communalism – through which the individual was defined by self and others with respect to his position in and relationship to the specific groups of which he was part, be they family, occupation, social class, nationality, clan, etc. – gradually gave way to individualism, as a realm of private activity was acknowledged as presenting a viable alternative to the existing closed social (and principally agrarian) structures. This affirmation of a separate sphere of private activity made anachronistic the command arrangements and the collectivist morality of the previous age. Recognition of a domain within which the individual was free to seek his own happiness and to be responsible for his own fate meant that aspirations could be realized, unfettered by the need to consider choice as bound by the constraints of a communal will (Oakeshott 1991, pp. 368–70).

Yet the flourishing of individuality would ultimately sow seeds of disaffection. The pursuit of individual happiness manifested in a freedom of choice led to a wholesale transformation of culture and society. Those prepared to exercise this choice – to take advantage of the new-found freedom to act unfettered by the restrictions of social, moral, and cultural bonds – found immeasurable opportunities for the expression of creativity and individual will, a freedom that resulted in revolutionary change not only in science and the arts but in political, social, and economic relations as well. The material success, however, came at a high price, as the radical alteration of the social relationships led to the dissolution of the old order and the stability it represented to large segments of the society. For each winner, so it was thought, there could be shown to be someone who had been sacrificed to the new cause of individualism. "The familiar anonymity of communal life was replaced by a personal identity which was burdensome to those who could not transform it into an individuality" (Oakeshott 1991, p. 371).

This feeling of disaffection led to the appearance of what Oakeshott terms the "individual *manqué*", the "failed individual," a "modern character" for whom the very notion of individualism represented a threat, and to whom economic, cultural, and political "progress" seemed to represent not social advancement and the promise of enlightenment, but little more than moral and civil decay (Oakeshott 1991, p. 371). The old moral order of communalism had of necessity given way to a base morality of individualism; the individual *manqué*, to preserve those ideals he held dear, felt no recourse but to turn "anti-individual." As he came to recognize others in the same predicament – to identify with the mass of the dispossessed – he and others in this "new class" came to appreciate the possibilities to be derived from political action. Specifically, he recognized in this new collective the possibility of imposing on the society as a whole "a uniformity of belief and conduct that leaves no room for either the pains or the pleasures of choice" (p. 373). The problem, however, was that, comprised of "feelings rather than thoughts, impulses rather than opinions, inabilities rather than passions," he was utterly incapable of acting to achieve his ends and so resigned himself to the need for a dominating, as opposed to a directing, governing power.

While failing as an individual, the individual *manqué* nonetheless had the capacities necessary to the success of a mass movement. This movement thrived under the banner of re-establishing the old order, seeking to re-energize the old feelings of community and social oneness with calls for a return to solidarity and social and political equality, for a need to reassert standards conducive to the social good. Yet behind this façade was "a new morality," one "calling for the establishment of a new condition of human circumstance reflecting the aspirations of the 'anti-individual'" (Oakeshott 1991, p. 375). This "new morality" revolved around the pursuit of an organic concept of the "common good," a new spirit which would replace the egoism of individualism with the ethos of community. To desire to further the common good, though, necessitated the deprecation of those rights that had been secured by the individual in support of his freedom of choice, and their rational and purposeful redirection in support of the betterment of society; government could be employed as the agent through which the necessary social engineering could be accomplished. The rights which had been applied to the end of the *pursuit* of happiness became instead reoriented to the *enjoyment* of happiness, individual choice being superseded by "the right to enjoy a substantive condition of human circumstance in which he would not be asked to make choices for himself" (p. 378).

This, in a nutshell, then, is an explanation of the shift in meaning of the notion of community, from one based on a "natural" order in human relations to one arising from design. Whether or not it is historically accurate is beside the point; its import here is to demonstrate the divergence in meaning as between the conservative and some forms of communitarian visions.

Kekes: the character of the good society

Taking his cue from, for him, the three most influential philosophers of liberalism – John Locke, Immanuel Kant, and John Stuart Mill – John Kekes identifies among key liberal ideals the need to protect life, liberty, and property, ensured through the guarantees of the rule of law; the need to secure some large measure of individual autonomy, the ability on the part of individuals to make rational choices unfettered by external or internal influences; and the need to protect against interference in those personal actions that pose no external consequence (Kekes 1997, pp. 2–3). With the additional support of modern liberals such as John Rawls and William Galston, Kekes then distills what he takes to be "basic liberal values." These values, assumptions upon which he presumes many (but not all) interpretations of liberalism are grounded, are "pluralism, freedom, rights, equality, and distributive justice," ideals which are enabling of an autonomous life (p. 4).[12]

It is important to characterize each of these elements as they are presented. Pluralism implies the existence of competing values, each of which leads to a different evaluation of a "good" life. In setting the rules through which society regulates conduct among its members, the liberal opts for neutrality in respect of the good, insisting instead on the protection of individual rights, the existence of which is seen as enabling of good lives. Freedom (political liberty) is a necessary condition, which acts to facilitate choice, not merely in the securing of economic (physical) goods but also in the securing of values and conceptions of the good. Freedom is not, however, to be understood as boundless, as it is restricted to actions that do not adversely affect others. (It remains an open question as to the *degree* of the restrictions.) Rights refer to universal human rights, those essential to individual welfare and, of course, to the preservation of autonomy. They are not to be interpreted narrowly as claims on the "social product" or as guarantees of a minimum level of welfare, but rather are to be appreciated as basic conditions of human existence. Equality implies equal treatment, typically understood as equal treatment *under the laws*, but as employed by Kekes means equal protection of basic human rights. Finally, distributive justice regards it as essential that, to realize the good life, all must be guaranteed access to those "social" goods which attend to that realization. This need not take the form of redistributive politics or rampant egalitarianism; Kekes requires only the provision of the minimum demands (Kekes 1997, pp. 6–12).

A problem arises when it comes to implementing these five value forms, as not all are consistent with every form of liberalism; the list itself actually comprises an antinomy. For instance, to promote distributive justice so as to enable choice actually means interfering with freedom of individual choice; to the extent that it also abrogates the rights of some so that others may enjoy an "equal share" in the gains of the society, such promotion leads to a violation of neutrality. The autonomy inherent in the values of freedom and pluralism likewise may conflict with the values of equality and distributive justice, and even the extension of rights from the political to the economic.

This inconsistency Kekes takes to be destructive of liberalism. The very values that are said to be essential to the maintenance of good lives may actually produce negative results, to wit, a greater degree of "evil." While he may have set up a "straw man" argument, there is nevertheless some validity to the claims advanced, that, to some degree at least, each of the values depicted is represented in the various portrayals of liberalism.

With these preliminaries thus established, Kekes depicts the alternative, the political morality of conservatism, as "skeptical, pluralistic, and traditionalist," a philosophy lending support to limited government. The primary aspiration of this philosophy is "to enable people to live as they please, rather than to force them to live in a particular way" (Kekes 1998, p. 41). Implicit in this characterization is what Kekes regards as conservatism's primary concern: identification of "the political arrangements that make a society good" (p. 45).

We need at this juncture to clarify certain concepts. The first is the idea of a "good" life. As employed by Kekes, the "good" life is not to be confused with the "moral" life, for good lives "require a coherent ordering of both moral and nonmoral values" (Kekes 1998, p. 50). In short, good lives are those which are personally satisfying, while at the same time being outwardly beneficial (p. 49).

Second, it is necessary at this juncture to distinguish between primary and secondary values. Primary values are universal (objective) attributes of all good lives, their particulars derived from a basic understanding of human nature. Within the general category of primary values are primary goods and primary evils. Primary goods are those goods that serve to establish the basic requirements of good lives, and include goods of "the self, intimacy [relations with others], and social order"; primary evils "are the frustration of those needs and the injury of the capacities required for satisfying them" (Kekes 1998, p. 53). Primary goods are always to be desired, primary evils always avoided. (Kekes seems at times to equate primary values and primary goods, and so we will do the same.)

Secondary values relate to the specific *forms* of good lives, and so are context-dependent. They are amorphous, not readily defined in any strict sense since their status as values depends on the specific cultural and social contexts, as well as the historical epoch in which they are set. Further, they are tradition-bound, and so they are not merely competing with the values of other traditions in a pluralistic society, but are also given to change as the tradition itself changes (Kekes 1998, p. 66).

We are now ready to proceed to the core of the argument. To animate his discussion, Kekes offers a conception of political morality constructed on three levels: the universal, the social, and the individual, the protection of each of which forms the good society. The universal level treats of limitations seen as essential to all societies seeking to promote the good. At its most basic, the universal level concerns the protection of the most primary values of moral society, those most critical in forming the good self. Specifically, the good society must, at the universal level, secure both the primary values and the accompanying required conventions, defined as those that "derive from the minimum requirements of all good lives" (Kekes 1998, p. 94). It is in the defense of these primary values, and in the safeguarding of these requirements, that society is justified in seeking to enforce morality; it is important to establish at the outset that such enforcement is not justified on any level other than the universal.

To the conservative (as defined by Kekes), it is not arguable that the morality of a society should be enforced. It is essential if society is to retain its cohesion that "a common morality" be observed, including in the calculus a general feeling of moral reprobation. In all societies, in order to maintain a sense of order and cohesiveness, it must be accepted that there is a prescribed level of tolerance for certain actions beyond which it is necessary to express moral reprehension, i.e., "at any given time in a good society there must be acts that people who are not depraved would find disgusting" (Kekes 1998, p. 99), acts that violate the core values and required conventions "in a gross, flamboyant, flagrant, and contemptuous manner," demonstrating nothing less than a "contempt for morality" (p. 105). Lack of disgust at the violation of the conventions implies "no strong commitment [of those in the society] to protecting the minimum requirements of good lives," and ultimately causes the society to degrade (p. 99). It is for this very reason that Kekes insists that society is justified in seeking to enforce the required conventions, for doing so perpetuates and strengthens the universal level of morality.

The second and third levels relate to "secondary" values and "variable" conventions, not subject to the strict demands of the primary values and required conventions. On the social level are those "traditional limits and possibilities that define the moral identity" of those in a society (Kekes 1998, p. 92). The moral tradition is defined as "the substratum of the evaluative dimension of people's lives," the purpose of which is to serve as a standard of conduct to which members of the society may appeal in gauging moral reason and defining "the acceptable possibilities of life" (p. 130). Unlike the values and conventions associated with the universal level, at the social level moral identities are variable across societies, cultures, and traditions. In Kekes' view, "[a] convention is moral if its primary purpose is to secure the conditions required by good lives" (p. 111). Such a definition poses no problem when dealing with required conventions supporting primary values, since the values protected are "universal and minimum conditions of good lives" (p. 111). However, when dealing with variable conventions in support of secondary values, the situation is more problematic, as not all variable conventions can be equated with moral conventions. Further, the distinction is difficult at best owing to different values held by different cultures at different times. To simplify matters, then, Kekes offers a test related to consequences, to wit, that "if a variable convention is treated as moral, then its justification must exhibit its effects on the goodness of lives" (p. 111).

It is important to note that the variable conventions need not be explicitly stated or recognized to be followed, but rather often take the form of custom and habit. Knowledge of the convention frequently is made when it is violated, the conventions being for the most part not something of which individuals are consciously aware; being "the evaluative background of the conduct of its members," violations are seen by others in the society as "moral lapses," adherence (in the sense of abiding conduct) seen as conformity to social and hence moral values (Kekes 1998, p. 112). These traditions, in other words, channel conduct to morally right behavior without *requiring* specific acts; they "are enabling rather than productive; defensive rather than venturesome; regulative rather than goal-directed," readily learned yet practiced as though innately understood (pp. 113–14). Traditions exist precisely because they are apprehended by those living under them to provide acceptable means to the preservation of the society.

It is the moral *traditions* of a society which act to forge a moral identity, as they confer on members "a common way of interpreting and responding to the world" (Kekes 1998, p. 116). Traditions (a composite including "authority, institutions, conventions, and rules") "impose restrictions on what their adherents can do and provide forms for doing what they want and society allows"; they "establish moral possibilities and moral limits" (p. 52). It is in this context that we see the significance of intuition. As Kekes employs the term, intuition does not mean guidance by the moral sense, conscience, or "inner voice," for such concepts he views as "dogmatic and obscurantist" (p. 118). Rather, following W. D. Ross (and consistent with the expression of Oakeshott), he ascribes to intuition the perspective of routine: as circumstances present themselves, one sees immediately, without the need for reflection (in the sense of pattern recognition), the moral significance of the situation and is impelled to action accordingly (pp. 119–20).[13] Two qualifications are important in understanding intuitions as they relate to moral values. The first goes to the fact that intuitions apply only to those routine events which, taken as a whole, reflect "the morality of everyday life" (p. 123). This suggests that the events to which intuition applies are themselves simple enough to require little or no need for contemplation. As such, they are readily seen as being understood by all in the community as being valid responses to circumstances.

Second, and this relates to the first, as each member of the community understands and accepts the intuitions as valid, they form a ready standard by which to assess conduct. To the extent that one's intuitions are in agreement with the intuitions of others, they are reinforced; to the extent that they are in opposition, there is reason for suspecting a need for reassessment (Kekes 1998, p. 124).

In any event, the ubiquity of such intuitions is evidence of shared moral conventions, and conduct in accordance with such conventions serves to promote secondary values. While inculcated through education, they are fundamentally different from other traditions in which individuals may be trained, the primary difference being that moral intuitions embody traditions that "enable people who participate in them to make good lives for themselves" (Kekes 1998, p. 124). To the extent that this is indeed achieved, the intuitions are valued; to the extent that they fail to act as appropriate guides to moral behavior, they are seen as irrelevant and in need of refinement or replacement (p. 124).

The third level encompasses those constraints on individuals that impel them to participation in social activities, constraints that "are set by the need for moral authority" (Kekes 1998, p. 137). Moral authorities serve to provide counsel in those instances in which the moral tradition itself is silent or provides insufficient guidance to the problem at hand, or in circumstances in which the individuals involved have only vague or limited knowledge of the tradition; the complexities inherent in the situation make it difficult for the individual to trust his own understanding. Here the intuition is unable to offer the necessary support (p. 145). In order to rectify the situation, to re-establish the ability to evaluate actions, it becomes necessary to look for a guide to assist in judgment. To provide the necessary countenance, the designated moral authority must possess five essential qualities: (1) knowledge of the required and variable conventions, including experience in evaluating the conventions and the moral tradition; (2) commitment to that tradition; (3) "reflectiveness," a desire and capability to delve into the very nature of the conventions upon which the tradition is grounded; (4) the ability to articulate their reflections; and (5) trustworthiness, established through an "exemplary life" (pp. 147–52). It is only through possession of these qualities that the authority is capable of clarifying to others the moral value of the traditions, allowing others the possibility of internalizing them (pp. 150–1).

This is not to suggest that the moral authority is in fact a single person, for Kekes insists that the conservative thesis admits pluralism. Each person may have for himself a moral authority to whom he turns for direction and judgment (and so even moral authorities may feel the need for moral authorities). The "authority relations," then, "depend on the respective qualifications of the people who participate in them," the mutuality of allegiance providing "an objective standard of evaluation" (Kekes 1998, p. 154).[14]

It is also not to deny the place of individual autonomy in the characterization of the good life. Kekes denies both the liberal attitude – that of individual autonomy – and the absolutist/communitarian attitude – that social arrangements must be given overwhelming importance. The deontological liberal view identifies autonomy with the good life, while authority (usually held to be coincident with the institutional setting) is perceived as the center of any evil (thus denying the possibility of "autonomous evil"); the absolutist/communitarian view (including within its realm "absolutist" conservatives and Marxists) envisions the good society as shaped by the imposition by a central authority of its will over individual wills, enforcing its prescriptions for the maintenance of good lives through the suppression of any autonomous action (Kekes 1998, pp. 36–8). Yet Kekes argues that the conservative thesis maintains that both autonomy and authority are essential to the structure and the preservation of good lives. To aim for one or the other is to choose among the conditions of good lives, bestowing preference to some at the expense of others. Instead, he proposes a third alternative. Both individual autonomy and social authority are essential to fashioning good lives, with tradition – "a set of customary beliefs, practices, and actions that has endured from the past to the present and attracted the allegiance of people so that they wish to perpetuate it" – being the conjoining mechanism: individual free choice is exercised within the framework of the authority of the social (moral) tradition (pp. 38–9). This is of critical importance in understanding the conservative position. The good life and the good society are simply inseparable conceptually: "[t]he goodness of a society just is the social dimension of good lives" (p. 164).

Thus we see the integrated workings of the universal, the social, and the individual levels of morality: the universal and the social levels establish "possibilities and limits," allowing individuals within the community to "form and conduct themselves according to conceptions of a good life that they derive from their moral tradition and adapt to their own characters and circumstances" (Kekes 1998, p. 158). The conservative philosophy does not, then, demand adherence to a single, "true" morality. Beyond the need to defend the minimum arrangements of a good society, social traditions can take on any number of forms (p. 165).

Cooperation and conflict in community

We have identified with communitarianism an overarching concern with the need for structures designed to mold individuals into communal beings, to replace the ethos of the individual with an ethos of community. What is to be argued here is that the liberal philosophies that are the focus of this attack are immune from such criticism for one very important reason: they already accept as an initial premise that individuals are socially embedded, their beliefs forming and being formed by the social institutional structures within which they function. Man is not by nature a solitary creature, for whom social union represents a means of forestalling the *bellum omnium contra omnes*. He is instead very much the product of his milieux and of the social practices of which they are constituted.

Bernard Yack offers an interpretation of Aristotle's political philosophy consistent with this view, identifying with Aristotle a portrayal of community more sympathetic to the classical liberal orthodoxy. This reading thus serves as a counter to MacIntyre's claim of the mantle of Aristotle in support of a communitarian ethic as narrowly defined. It is to a brief examination of Yack's thesis that we now turn.

On Yack's reading of Aristotle, the political community is "a conflict-ridden reality," and not "a vision of lost or future harmony" (Yack 1993, p. 2). The very concept of community – *koinōnia* – refers to the most basic of social groupings, be they the household, the village, or the State (p. 28). The Aristotelian community is comprised of heterogeneous individuals who nonetheless exhibit a shared identity or set of common values. It is this heterogeneity which is critical to Aristotle's social philosophy, in that the multiplicity of individual identities promotes a "creative – and sometimes destructive – tension" that "is one of the most important features of community" (p. 30). This is in direct opposition to the communitarian belief that the shared values of the political community are a prescription for social consonance and social cohesion, and as such should be not only cultivated but inculcated, for such a position ignores the fact that these same factors are productive of an opposing tendency to conflict. Aristotle's political community allows that "[s]elf-serving actions, just as much as self-sacrificing actions, can express the shared expectations and identity" inherent in community (p. 10). The difficulties associated with "political life" are in no way the result of the collapse of feelings of commonality or belonging, but rather are inherent in the very idea of the political community (p. 2).

To suggest, then, as does MacIntyre, that a solution to the problems besetting modern societies is a return to the Aristotelian conception of community is to misunderstand the very idea of community as defined by Aristotle. Yack insists that, while it is essential that the notion of "political community" be apprehended before one can begin to understand the sources of political conflict, it is equally true that "we need to understand political conflicts in order to identify and explain the nature of the good life as actually led" (Yack 1993, p. 3). This requires attention be paid to the constitutive nature of social structures. To insist that political theory can be divorced from ethical considerations is to engage in a fruitless quest, making an artificial distinction between interdependent activities. This Aristotle would reject. One simply cannot legitimately claim that ethics and politics are distinct domains, political arrangements being mere mechanisms designed as constraints on conduct, for such a distinction ignores the essential social and political contexts within which ethical norms develop (p. 4).

In contrast to much of political and ethical philosophy that has developed along lines established by Hobbes, Kant, and Rousseau, Yack argues that the Greek conception of community is too complex a concept to be identified with any conscious effort to counter the base elements of human nature. It is not to be construed (as it has consistently been) as identical with institutional forms but is, rather, inseparable from the nature of human activity. While of course the institutions of law and education, for example., are essential to the development and to the maintenance of the virtuous life, as they serve to inculcate within the citizenry those traits that allow interaction in civil society, it is equally true that these arrangements are not to be regarded as merely regulative of animalistic tendencies in man. The institutions of civil society serve to "draw out and build on human beings' natural capacities and natural impulses for communal living," i.e., they are effective in engendering feelings of mutual obligation from which derive conceptions of justice and right, critical to the maintenance of the community. They are thus facilitative, and so cannot be construed as mechanisms "to transform naturally self-regarding beings into other-regarding citizens" (Yack 1993, p. 15).

The tendency to communal living is pre-existent; it does not need to be imposed from without. The mere fact that Aristotle assigns priority to the social over the individual – as communitarians insist is essential to the existence and maintenance of the virtuous civil polity – does not imply that he somehow seeks a society in which the cohesion of community follows from the acceptance of a collective ethos, that homogeneity and cooperation toward a common end must be fostered against heterogeneity and competition. Aristotle does not fall into the communitarian trap of defining community as somehow coterminous with communion, i.e., of equating the *circumstance* of belonging with a *sense* of belonging. He does not demand of those in a community that they reject individual identity in favor of collective identity, that a prerequisite for membership in a community is a submersion of distinction and a heightened awareness of commonality (Yack 1993, pp. 31–3). Rather, Aristotle maintains precisely the opposite view, *viz.*, that "community is a structural feature of everyday social interactions rather than an ideal of solidarity and harmonious living" (p. 33). On this reading, community reflects the fact that mutual interests and shared values serve an integrative function, that a community comprised of free-acting individuals with shared identities is preferable to one in which a collective identity is defined and the members of the collective molded to its form. Moreover, he argues that efforts at promoting such solidarity and harmony, at forging a sense of communion, will have disastrous consequences, noting "that the elimination of social heterogeneity threatens to eliminate political community itself" (p. 15). To insist on the need to forge a collective identity by directing individual identities to the common good may actually be counterproductive and even destabilizing. For Aristotle, "the nature of a state is to be a plurality," a community "not made up only of so many men, but of different kinds of men; for similars do not constitute a state." The common good can best be advanced, not through direction, but through the choices made and the actions taken by individuals in pursuit of personal ends. The shared identity is sufficient to bring about the common good (Yack 1993, p. 31).

Thus the very definition of community in Aristotle is to a certain extent antithetical to a communitarian reading: the Aristotelian community is not reflective of a common understanding of the qualities of virtue and the good life, or the need to strive toward some common goal, but is based upon "a combination, a sharing and differentiation" (Yack 1993, p. 15). Aristotle indeed holds that individuality is socially constructed, as evidenced in his depiction of community, while at the same time demonstrating an acute awareness of the superficiality of such concepts as social harmony and the need to fashion a more highly developed moral consciousness (p. 16). Interpreted in this way, Aristotle represents a political philosophy consistent with liberalism and its celebration of differences among individuals, his communitarianism capable of acknowledging the importance of conflict and cooperation in the community.[15]

The argument to come

The discussion above serves to identify three major and often opposing philosophical approaches to the organization of society: the liberal, the communitarian, and the conservative. While there are clear differences among them, each embraces the need for acceptance of community and the social nature of man in addressing the problems of the polity.

The point to be made in the present work is that this concern with the nature of the individual with respect to the community is one which has motivated some of the most notable of political philosophers. As suggested earlier, this theme has been explored at some length by Stephen Holmes in his dissection of the "anti-liberal" critics of liberalism, but there the exposition is more thematic. In what follows we will examine the place of community in the social philosophies of just six of the more significant liberal social theorists of the past 150 years: John Stuart Mill, James Fitzjames Stephen, Herbert Spencer, William Graham Sumner, Ludwig von Mises, and Friedrich A. von Hayek. The selection of these six figures as somehow representative may seem a bit idiosyncratic, and indeed it is. With the exception of Mill and, to a lesser extent, Hayek, this is not a group that springs to mind when one proceeds to a review of the political philosophy of liberalism. However, there is a logic to the choice. Mill and Stephen, it will be seen, both committed to Utilitarianism, represent a clear delineation of two strains of the liberal philosophy, *viz.*, "libertarian" and "conservative" liberalism, respectively, and especially in respect of the social dimension of individualism. Mill is generally acknowledged as the quintessential libertarian liberal, and so any attempt to distill the essential elements of the doctrine must account for his definitions and his characterization of its scope and limitations; Stephen, a self-defined liberal, is taken as representative of a more conservative variant, typically seen as standing in opposition to Millian liberalism in a demand for obedience to law and social norms as essential to the well-being of the community, and it is in his works that we are presented with (perhaps) the most well-thought-out exposition of the Victorian social philosophy that defined the period.

In Spencer and Sumner we see attempts to rationalize the structure of social relationships, arguing from the anthropological record that man can only be understood as a social being, but that nonetheless it is the protection of his individuality which is of the utmost importance to society at large. Spencer the polymath continues the utilitarian traditions of both Mill and Stephen, but goes much farther than either in his desire to fashion liberal principles of morality on a firm scientific foundation; Sumner the erstwhile disciple brings to the Spencerian argument the rigor of the economist and the passion of the preacher.

In Mises and Hayek we find a distinction between an almost anarchic libertarianism and a more conservative liberalism, alongside a clash between Utilitarianism and anti-Utilitarianism. Here we see a resurrection of the argument that surfaced in the Mill–Stephen "debate," as Mises the rational utilitarian in a sense expands upon the Millian social philosophy (in its severest form), and Hayek, with his focus on rules as coordinating mechanisms, is given to restate after a fashion (although not necessarily consistently) the position of Stephen. More significantly, we see a difference as to the nature of the individualist ontology itself: must individuals be so construed as to preclude statements with respect to the social complex, or is it yet possible to admit of competing interests within the social whole?

In all, despite what may be perceived as the efforts at transmuting the liberal philosophy, each of our selected protagonists will be seen to have held as core beliefs an individualist ontology and a conviction of man as a social being, incapable of definition apart from his community affiliations. In the end, liberalism – as least so far as it is identified in the writings of the six figures here offered for consideration – is much richer as a political philosophy than its detractors may be willing to acknowledge, as it is capable of incorporating those very elements of community said to be essential on the conservative and communitarian views to the existence of the good society.

Notes

1   I am indebted to an anonymous reader of an early draft for pointing out this important essay.
2   This position is explored at length in MacIntyre (1999).
3   Note also the following from Jürgen Habermas:

> Deontological approaches ... rightly insist that one would misunderstand the meaning of the moral "ought" if one saw it only as expressing the attractive character of certain goods. We 'ought' to obey moral precepts, because we know they are right and not because we hope to realize certain ends by doing so – even if the end were that of the highest personal happiness or the collective weal.
>
> (Habermas 1998, p. 153)

4   Sandel points to Kant as the chief exponent of this position.
5   As Will Kymlicka (1988) argues, Rawls seems to equate Utilitarianism with teleology, but does so by "misdescribing" Utilitarianism. Indeed, *if* Utilitarianism places the good over the right, as would be the case were it teleological, it would no longer be a *moral* theory at all.
6   No commitment could grip me so deeply that I could not understand myself without it. No transformation of life purposes and plans could be so unsettling as to disrupt the contours of my identity. No project could be so essential that turning away from it would call into question the person I am. Given my independence from the values I have, I can always stand apart from them; my public identity as a moral person "is not affected by changes over time" in my conception of the good.
> (Sandel 1998, p. 62)

7   As Kant observes, "I can never be constrained by others *to have an end*: only I myself can *make* something my end" (Kant 1797, p. 146; emphasis in original).
8   For them [the individual members of the community], community describes not just what they *have* as fellow citizens but also what they *are*, not a relationship they choose (as in a voluntary association) but an attachment they discover, not merely an attribute but a constituent of their identity.
> (Sandel 1998, p. 150; emphasis in original)

9   Although Sandel does admit to the need for "a conception in which the subject is empowered to participate in the constitution of its identity" (Sandel 1998, p. 152), an admission that seems to suggest a nascent liberalism.

10   A noncommunitarian anti-liberal, Roberto Unger, reaches a similar conclusion which must be acknowledged here, as he employs in his argument (such as it is) the language of communitarianism: To Unger,

> [t]he political doctrine of liberalism does not acknowledge communal values. To recognize their existence, it would be necessary to begin with a vision of the basic circumstances of social life that took groups rather than individuals as the intelligible and primary units of social life. The individuality of values is the very basis of personal identity in liberal thought, a basis the communal conception of value destroys.
>
> (Unger 1975, p. 76)

11   Some have suggested that Oakeshott is actually a representative of the liberal tradition. See particularly Wendell John Coats (1985) and Paul Franco (1990).

12   The litany of political programs said to be favored by liberals (the American variant), however, would suggest that Kekes's version of liberalism is left-liberalism, or egalitarianism. This, in the American case at least, is liberalism in its popular, as opposed to its philosophical, understanding.

13   The intuitive knowledge of the moral significance of simple situations may then be said to have the following characteristics. It is immediate. There is no conscious inference, reflection, or thought involved in recognizing their moral significance. People spontaneously perceive them that way. As soon as the facts present themselves, they fall into a pattern. And the pattern is normally the same for all normal adults who belong to a moral tradition.

> (Kekes 1998, p. 120)

14   The standard is objective in the sense that how closely lives and conduct approximate it is a factual question whose answer is independent of what anyone thinks, feels, hopes, or fears. The standard is not objective in the sense that any reasonable person would have to accept it ... What cannot be done without the loss of reason and objectivity is to make a commitment to a particular conception and then refuse to recognize it as a standard of moral evaluation that applies to all those who are similarly committed.

> (Kekes 1998, p. 155)

15   Robert Goodin (1998) offers a defense of Enlightenment philosophy against communitarian criticism along similar lines. For Goodin, the Enlightenment philosophy *can* accept many different forms of community, including communities of generation (families), meaning (language), experience (social relations and interactions), regard (reference groups), and subsumption ("total" institutions).

2 Mill and libertarian liberalism

John Stuart Mill (1806–73) – variously political philosopher, logician, economist, politician – established the terms upon which has emerged the modern understanding of liberalism. The son of James Mill and amanuensis to Jeremy Bentham, two of the more conspicuous of the Philosophic Radicals who propounded the doctrine of Utilitarianism, he was exposed early to the various philosophies upon which liberalism was formed, as he was personally acquainted with many of those whose inquiries served to provide it the requisite structure. In his essays *On Liberty* (1859) and *Utilitarianism* (1861), and his posthumously published *Chapters on Socialism* (1879), to name but the more significant (for present purposes) of his voluminous writings, Mill defined for many the nature of obligation, justice, and duty, the role of the individual in society, and the proper function of the State in relation to the individual. As it is with Mill that much of our current understanding of the nature of a liberal political order derives, it is only natural that any discussion begin with an overview of his contributions.

Requirements for political society

Before entering into the fray, we must begin by asking: What are the conditions necessary to the establishment of political society? In his essay on Samuel Taylor Coleridge (Mill 1840),[1] Mill identifies from the historical record three principles essential to any society desiring to impose on its citizens the institutions of law and government, while at the same time preserving individualism and the freedom of action. These are (1) the establishment of a system for instilling discipline, (2) the promotion of allegiances or loyalties, and (3) the maintenance of social cohesion. None of these principles can be dispensed with if order is to be preserved, as each is necessary to the others. Consider each in its turn. Education is of the utmost importance in fostering discipline, in compelling the members of the community to conform in ways conducive to order. Its primary service to the stability of political society is

> [t]o train the human being in the habit, and thence the power, of subordinating his personal impulses and aims, to what were considered the ends of society; of adhering, against all temptation, to the course of conduct which those ends prescribed; of controlling in himself all the feelings which were

liable to militate against those ends, and encouraging all such as tended towards them.

(Mill 1840, p. 193)

Likewise, allegiance or loyalty to a group, or to an idea, or to an ideal is indispensable to the preservation of society, in that it provides a "fixed point" upon which each member may focus with assurance. Such allegiances may be to a person, to a religious belief, to an institution, to a principle, or to a code of conduct. All that matters is that, for those in the society, there is agreement that *something* is so sacred, so constitutive of the order, that its removal or attempted replacement is unthinkable. Whatever other disagreements there may be, whatever conflicts may erupt among the populace, these differences must not be allowed to affect the character or the integrity of those underlying principles that bind together the social union.

The principle of allegiance, then, forms the basis for the third condition, this being cohesion fostered by feelings of sympathy and common interest. Here is the single most clearly stated expression of Mill's commitment to community and of liberalism's commitment to the encumbered self. It is this condition of sympathy and belonging which is responsible for sustaining community. It is absolutely essential, for men to exist in any social union, that each regard himself as part of the whole, "that one part of the community do not consider themselves as foreigners with regard to another part," that each places such a premium on his connectedness with others that living outside the bounds of the community cannot be contemplated for long; those within the community "do not desire selfishly to free themselves from their share of any common inconvenience by severing the connection" (Mill 1840, pp. 195–6). No community can long exist in the absence of such a commitment to others in similar circumstance. The very idea of unencumbered selves, each pursuing his own personal happiness, without any concern in their actions for the welfare of others, may be seen as anathema to Mill, and to his version of the liberal and the utilitarian philosophies, as it runs counter to the very claims he makes with respect to those expressly detailed principles of social and political union.

These principles of belonging must thus be seen as informing Mill's later writings: even when not explicitly referred to, one nevertheless must be aware that Mill's social philosophy is unsustainable without them. With this in mind, we turn now to an exposition of critical elements in Mill's social thought.

Utility, morality, obligation, and duty

The standard of utility

To begin any discussion of Mill's liberalism, one needs to understand that Mill accepts Bentham's notion of consequentialism, wherein morality redounds to the consequences of actions. The foundation of Bentham's ethics – hedonistic Utilitarianism – is the pleasure–pain principle, the most basic of "sovereign masters." The combined influences of pleasure and pain are sufficient "to point out what we ought to do, as well as to determine what we shall do" (Bentham 1988, p. 1). So important are these influences, in fact, that Bentham attributes to them the status of objective moral standards.[2]

With these standards thus established, Bentham defines the principle of utility as "that principle which approves or disapproves of every action whatsoever, according to the tendency which it appears to have to augment or diminish the happiness of the party whose interest is in question," with utility itself being

> that property in any object, whereby it tends to produce benefit, advantage, pleasure, good, or happiness, (all this in the present case comes to the same thing) or … to prevent the happening of mischief, pain, evil, or unhappiness to the party whose interest is considered.
>
> (Bentham 1988, p. 2).

The "party whose interest is in question," Bentham quickly notes, may be the individual or the community; the difference is insubstantial, since the community interest – where community is defined as "a fictitious *body*, composed of the individual persons who are considered as constituting as it were its *members*" – is no more than the sum of individual interests (p. 3; emphasis in original). Now, as Frederick Copleston notes, since the community interest and the individual interests are coextensive, the pursuit of *individual* happiness or good must lead to a commensurate increase in *social* happiness or good. But this implies that the individual can only be understood as a social being, "and that his happiness is a constituent element in an organic whole" (Copleston 1994, p. 33), an understanding inadequately expressed and greatly under-appreciated in Bentham's work and misconstrued in other similar expositions of hedonistic Utilitarianism.

It is Mill who actually perceives that the difficulty in Bentham is his failure to provide an adequate characterization of man as a social being. Mill does of course accept Bentham's maxim that actions are to be viewed as "right in proportion as they tend to promote happiness, wrong as they tend to produce the reverse of happiness" (Mill 1861, p. 394). The question then centers on the extent to which this utilitarian maxim is adequate as a first principle, i.e., whether it is sufficient to the task. In confronting this problem, so as to prepare the ground for his own version of Utilitarianism, Mill first considers the complications inherent in those moral philosophies that assert the existence of a moral sense. The chief difficulty with theories of intuitive ethics is that, as they are "a branch of our reason, not of our sensitive faculty" (p. 392), they supply merely general principles of morality. Such theories maintain no first principle of conduct, and offer no premises from which may be deduced such principles, and so they are insufficient in application to particular ethical questions. Morality for the intuitionist is little more than "the application of a law to an individual case," the ultimate principle being alleged *a priori* known and thus, on this basis alone, authoritative in the guidance of conduct (p. 392). The deficiency of such a view, according to Mill, lies in its demand for a standard of conduct which itself cannot be explicitly stated but only tacitly recognized (as if self-evident). Compounding this deficiency is the reliance on circular logic, the intuitionist maintaining in the face of reason that morality and law derive from and conform to one another, that there is no priority.[3] Mill demands more, and specifically an explicit basis upon which to derive moral principles. As "[a]ll action is for the sake of some end, and rules of action ... must take their whole character and colour from the end to which they are subservient" (pp. 391–2), so in the realm of morals some identifiable benchmark – a "test of right and wrong" – is necessary to the ascertainment of moral beliefs.

For Mill the utilitarian, such a standard is evident in utility, although he in fact holds that *any* end principle will suffice.[4] Utility is "the ultimate appeal on all ethical questions," and so Mill is led to reject the notion of an "abstract right, as a thing *independent* of utility" (Mill 1859, p. 14; emphasis added). Indeed, in general, as "the ultimate end ... is an existence exempt as far as possible from pain, and as rich as possible in enjoyments," it must be the case, by extension, that this serves as "the standard of morality" (Mill 1861, pp. 397–8). As if to stress the point yet further, he later insists that happiness "is the sole end of human action, and the promotion of it the test by which to judge of all human conduct," and so again one sees, by extension, that happiness is "the criterion of morality" (p. 533). Yet Mill is not ready to accept Bentham's position that "all right thinking on the details of morals depends on its [the utility principle's] express assertion" (Mill 1838, p. 170). Clearly it is not the case, for Mill, that an act must produce the greatest happiness to be regarded as good. Utility is simply the *standard*. As the standard, one must accept, with John Gray, that utility is not itself an ethical principle, since it serves to *assess* conduct, while not *enjoining* conduct; as utility is the standard (a consistency principle by which conduct may be evaluated), "it cannot by itself impose obligations or yield judgments about right action," which would require a principle of action or consequence (J. Gray 1996, p. 22). Mill concedes as much in his qualifications to the principle:

> We think utility, or happiness, much too complex and indefinite an end to be sought except through the medium of various secondary ends ... Those who adopt utility as a standard can seldom apply it truly except through the secondary principles ...
>
> (Mill 1838, p. 170)

> To give a clear view of the moral standard set up by the theory [of utility], much more requires to be said; in particular, what things it includes in the ideas of pain and pleasure; and to what extent this is left an open question.
>
> (Mill 1861, p. 394)

Finally, we must consider here an objection to Mill's Utilitarianism raised by G. E. Moore. Moore accuses Mill of having based his utilitarian ethics on the "Hedonistic principle," which is "that pleasure is the only thing at which we ought to aim, the only thing that is good as an end and for its own sake" (Moore 1903, p. 116). Mill, concludes Moore, conflates pleasure and happiness as *desires* with pleasure and happiness as *goods*, as ends to be pursued. In doing so he commits the "naturalistic fallacy," granting to the indefinable analytic concept "good" qualities that pertain only to synthetic notions of "the good." "Good" in Moore's sense is "that quality which we assert to belong to a thing, when we say that the thing is good," whereas "the good" is merely "the substantive to which the adjective 'good' will apply" (p. 61). "Good" for Mill, according to Moore, means "desirable," and this is to be ascertained by inquiring as to "what is actually desired" (p. 118).

However, Moore notes that Mill's use of the term actually represents a misapprehension of a key distinction: that which is *capable* of being desired cannot be taken as equivalent to that which *should* be desired, where this latter is taken as the literal meaning of "desirable," or that which "is good to desire" (Moore 1903, p. 119). If in fact it is granted that "desirable" is equivalent to "that which ought to be desired," then it can only apply to the good (for the bad is clearly not desirable). Mill's insistence that we are motivated to pursue those actions that lead to the good, and that we actually desire that which is desirable, is inconsistent with his acknowledgment that we may pursue desires of greater or lesser value, that the objects of desire somehow fall along a continuum of more and less good. Likewise, if by "desirable" Mill means that which *ought* to be desired, and not that which *is* desired, he would not have expended so much effort at conjuring up motives behind good actions, for "if the desired is *ipso facto* the good; then the good is *ipso facto* the motive of our actions" (p. 119). To Moore, the conclusion is obvious, that "the first step by which Mill has attempted to establish his Hedonism is simply fallacious," for (1) if "desirable" means "desired," Mill's later discussion is contradictory, and (2) if "desirable" means "good," then this first premise is insufficient" (p. 119).

Second, even if we grant Mill's primary premise that "desirable" is equivalent to "desired," and so is identical with "the good," one *still* finds a contradiction. The desirable is that which is desired, and so that which is good. In addition, pleasure is offered as the *sole* good. It remains to prove that pleasure is the only thing to be desired, which would serve to complete the syllogism. But, notes Moore, Mill does not hold this second premise to be true, as he considers objects of desire other than pleasure, such as virtue and even pecuniary gain. Mill thus conflates ends and means, by considering *both* pleasure and other objects as desired and hence desirable.

Moore offers an explanation. To Moore, an *idea* (a mental image of some object or event) is sufficient to stimulate pleasure, which in turn stimulates desire; pleasure is not, then, in itself good. To Mill (in Moore's view), an *abstract pleasure* is the idea which stimulates the desire, not any object from which pleasure may derive. If this is so, then pleasure cannot be an object of desire, for it would antedate desire, and so would not be a good (Moore 1903, pp. 121–3). Thus once again Mill has failed to provide a grounding for his Hedonism.

Utilitarian ethics and the general interest

While Mill does not believe that moral feelings are innate qualities of human beings, he does concede that they are "a natural outgrowth" of our constitution

(Mill 1861, p. 528); indeed, while it is true that we are not yet (in our current state of development) capable of pronouncing "that entireness of sympathy with all others," it is nonetheless true that we cannot completely regard others as "struggling rivals … for the means of happiness" (p. 529). It is the hallmark of an evolved civilization that its members recognize a fellow-feeling, a sympathy with others in the society. This realization that the promotion of the general happiness *is* the ethical standard establishes the foundation of Utilitarianism (at least the variant pursued by Mill). Hence the utilitarian morality requires that man be viewed as a social creature, not as an isolated individual who seeks only the fulfillment of his own pleasure.

> The social state is at once so natural, so necessary, and so habitual to man, that, except in some unusual circumstances or by an effort of voluntary abstraction, he never conceives himself otherwise than as a member of a body …. Any condition, therefore, which is essential to a state of society, becomes more and more an inseparable part of every person's conception of the state of things which he is born into, and which is the destiny of a human being.
>
> (Mill 1861, p. 528)

That we are incapable of perceiving ourselves outside of society reinforces a capacity for social interaction, compelling us to identify our own ends with the ends of others in the community. It is this perception, borne of civilization, that leads to mutual cooperation and to the formation of a collective interest, which in turn leads to an identification of individual interest with social welfare, to the point of forming in the individual an almost instinctive feeling of sympathy and regard for others (Mill 1861, pp. 528–9). Indeed, "intuitive ethics" (which appeals to a moral sense) coincides with "utilitarian ethics" if one accepts that the defining principle is a "regard to the pleasures and pains of others" (p. 527), for this criterion provides an objective rationale for action absent from ethical theories founded upon sentiments.[5] Bentham himself opines "that the dictates of this principle [of 'sympathy and antipathy'] will frequently coincide with those of utility, though perhaps without intending any such thing" (Bentham 1988, pp. 18–19), and Mill follows suit, suggesting that Bentham's principle "has had a large share in forming the moral doctrines even of those who most scornfully reject its authority" (Mill 1861, p. 392).[6]

But Mill also notes that his proposal is for a utility "in the largest sense, grounded on the permanent interests of man as a progressive being" (Mill 1859, p. 14), suggesting that the principle of utility is itself an axiological principle, a general ethical principle of value which, by its very nature, requires subsidiary principles in application to social questions.[7] To Mill, a chief problem with utilitarian ethics up to his time is the absence of any appreciation of individual morality and a sense of community, and their connection to the employment of the "higher faculties." He actually laments "that utilitarian writers in general have placed the superiority of mental over bodily pleasures chiefly in the greater permanency, safety, uncostliness, &c., of the former – that is, in their circumstantial advantages rather that in their intrinsic nature" (Mill 1861, p. 395), and thereby appear to ignore the significance of those "elevated" faculties, the gratification of which is essential to human fulfillment. These writers may very well, admits Mill, have reached the same conclusions had they been cognizant of "the fact, that some *kinds* of pleasure are more desirable and more valuable than others" (p. 395; emphasis in original). One must, in attempting to establish a framework for a theory of moral obligation, account for the intrinsic value of actions (and individuals) and not look merely to extrinsic ones. As J. J. C. Smart observes in his defense of utilitarian ethics, the statement of preference for a dissatisfied Socrates over a satisfied fool represents for Bentham a calculation of social utility (Socrates would provide a greater level of social usefulness than would the fool) and so the choice represents a consideration of extrinsic value, while for Mill the fact of *being* Socrates – its intrinsic value – is enough to substantiate the preference (Smart 1973, pp. 15–16).

So, despite his acceptance of the general course of Bentham's doctrine – that "right" implies the promotion of pleasure, "wrong" the denial of pleasure – Mill is not prepared to argue that action is dictated by a mere calculation of pleasure over pain, as he actually inquires as to the *quality* of the pleasure, where quality is a comparative relation, such that, "[o]f two pleasures, if there be one to which all or almost all who have experience of both give a decided preference, irrespective of any feeling of moral obligation to prefer it, that is the more desirable pleasure" (Mill 1861, p. 395). Further, Mill believes it possible actually to judge objectively of pleasures, the basis for such judgment being knowledge of (or acquaintance with) the pleasures themselves; after all, is there any other manner "of determining which is the acutest of two pains, or the intensest of two pleasurable sensations, except the general suffrage of those who are familiar with both?" (p. 397). This judgment deems those "pleasures derived from the higher faculties" to be of the utmost importance, such pleasures esteemed "as being a necessary part of a perfectly just conception of Utility or Happiness" (p. 397). Yet such an understanding of the necessary *components* of utility is not sufficient to the general acceptance of the *standard* of happiness, since the standard is the Benthamite one of the greatest happiness of the greatest number, and not the personal fulfillment of each individual in isolation. To make the extension from personal fulfillment to the acceptance of the moral standard by society requires the further step of realizing that nobility of character is itself socially virtuous, for whether or not any single person is happier because of it, "there can be no doubt that it [a noble character] makes other people happier, and that the world in general is immensely a gainer by it" (p. 397). Accordingly, the end pursued by the utilitarian, itself a moral standard, can only be fostered "by the general cultivation of nobleness of character, even if each individual were only benefited by the nobleness of others, and his own, so far as happiness is concerned, were a sheer deduction from the benefit" (p. 397).

In *Considerations on Representative Government*, Mill extends this position, and even argues that it is the social function itself which is important in shaping character and instilling within individuals a necessary discipline. The form of the social function is rather immaterial. Mere service on a jury or other such public act is significant in itself in developing in the individual the social faculties, including the moral. In undertaking these civic charges,

> [h]e is called upon ... to weigh interests not his own; to be guided, in case of conflicting claims, by another rule than his private partialities; to apply, at every turn, principles and maxims which have for their reason of existence the common good: and he usually finds associated with him in the same work minds more familiarized than his own with these ideas and operations, whose study it will be to supply reasons to his understanding, and stimulation to his feeling for the general interest. He is made to feel himself one of the public, and whatever is for their benefit to be for his benefit.
>
> (Mill 1865, p. 412)

It the absence of these feelings for the general interest, this "school of public spirit," that leads one to reject any commitment to society beyond the mere observance of law; the only interest then is the personal or the family interest. To Mill this represents a coarsening of the society, a diminution of private morality and the death of public morality (Mill 1865, p. 412).[8]

Mill's utilitarianism: act or rule?

Having reviewed the necessary conditions underlying the concept, there is still the question of the *form* of Mill's Utilitarianism. It seems to be clear that Mill cannot be identified with act-Utilitarianism, since such a position requires that actions be evaluated on the basis of their consequences, and so utility considerations alone allow judgments of right and wrong, the very thing Mill denies. On David Lyons's interpretation, Mill is only *committed* to utility-preference rankings of acts in terms of beneficence, and is not willing to extend this principle to identify failures to maximize utility with moral wrongness (Lyons 1994, p. 50). Even considering Smart's interpretation of act-Utilitarianism as consistent with rule-following (wherein the rules are taken to be "rough guides" to action, to be employed "when there is no time to think" and hence ruling out any moral basis for such actions), it is still inconsistent with Mill's position (Smart 1973, p. 42).

As to rule-utilitarianism, while John Gray dismisses the possibility that Mill can be so classified with the claim that it places an "unacceptably restrictive emphasis on the institution of social rules in the production of good consequences" and so cannot handle Mill's identification of an "area of moral indifference – an area where moral right and wrong are simply inapplicable" (J. Gray 1996, p. 32), this is nonetheless not fatal to the rule-utilitarian interpretation. As Richard Brandt observes, Mill intends his moral theory to relate not to *acts*, but to *act-types*, the difference being that particular acts are defined with reference to particular situations, while act-types, being more general, can serve as the basis for delimiting moral obligation (Brandt 1992, p. 129).[9] Thus, instead of assessing the consequences of each individual act, the moral agent must be mindful of the *general type* of action and, if the *type* is deemed morally wrong, must refrain from such actions as fit the type, despite the fact that the consequences of the individual action may lead to the promotion of personal gratification or gain. On this reading, one may conclude that Mill actually adheres to a version of the Ideal Moral Code theory, a form of rule-utilitarianism whereby

> [a]n act is right if and only if it would not be prohibited by the moral code ideal for the society; and an agent is morally blameworthy (praiseworthy) for an act if, and to the degree that, the moral code ideal in that society would condemn (praise) him for it.
>
> (pp. 119–20)

In terms of Mill's Utilitarianism, a right act-type "is fixed by the content of the moral system with maximum utility," and so an appeal to utility as a first principle may be made as justification for an action that is itself "fully interiorized" within the moral system (p. 130).

Duty, obligation, and justice

Here we come to consider in somewhat more detail the concept of duty as moral obligation. In his 1869 essay, "Thornton on Labour and Its Claims," Mill insists that duty and virtue, while distinct, still inhere within the domain of utilitarian morality: both social virtue and moral duty are predicated on the utilitarian standard of the promotion of the general happiness or the general interest. This is evident in the need to promote the common good, the well-being of the community. It is in this context that duty gains its standing. So necessary to the stability of the community are certain "acts, and a still greater number of forbearances," that members of the community may be compelled as a price of membership – "either by law or by social pressure" – to submit to their authority (Mill 1869, pp. 650–1). The realm of virtue or merit then is reserved to those acts or forbearances that cannot be regarded as essential to the welfare of the community. While they may have negative effects, it is better for the whole that they be encouraged or discouraged by other means. (This will be discussed further on pp. 47–58.)

Duty for Mill is an "internal sanction," "the essence of Conscience" (Mill 1861, p. 526). It "is a thing which may be *exacted* from a person, as one exacts a debt" (p. 663; emphasis in original), even while it "consists in the existence of a mass of feeling which must be broken through in order to do what violates our standard of right" (p. 526). More forcefully, a duty cannot be so defined unless such exaction can be conceived as compulsory, i.e., unless it is perceived as a moral obligation, such that failure to perform would invite punishment; duties then arise as certain rules are granted obligatory status – they are held to be essential to the well-being of the community – and this obligation is not necessarily confined to actions that the individual would perform of his own accord.[10]

Mill goes further, as he connects right and wrong to considerations of justice in his differentiation of morality and justice (the latter being a specific category of the former) from "Expediency" and "Worthiness": an action is wrong "according as we think that the person ought, or ought not, to be punished for it," while an action is right (or "desirable or laudable") "according as we would wish to see the person whom it concerns, compelled, or only persuaded and exhorted, to act in that manner" (Mill 1861, p. 664).[11] This of course suggests that an action may be inexpedient or inappropriate without necessarily being condemned as wrong, as it falls beyond the boundaries of moral consideration; it would then not be subject to punishment or other sanction. More precisely, "duties of perfect obligation" (the domain of justice as moral obligation) require the definition of a "correlative" right, while "duties of imperfect obligation" (which includes "the other obligations of morality" exclusive of justice) are those for which no such right is maintained (p. 664).[12] One may then agree with J. O. Urmson that the received reading of Mill is erroneous: the rightness or wrongness of an action is not defined with respect to the ultimate end, but rather is so designated as it is or is not in accordance with a moral rule, that this moral rule serves an instrumental need in promoting the end, that the rule is itself justified only in cases "in which the general welfare is more than negligibly affected," and in instances in which the rule does not apply, some other principle of judging actions must be employed (Urmson 1953, p. 35). One may also, then, rightly conclude, with Brandt, that Mill's concept of duty is inconsistent with the utility-maximization inherent in Benthamite ethics (in its hedonistic, act-utilitarian guise), in that duty is not wholly derivative from utility maximization, but rather conforms "to the *requirements* ... of an *optimal* moral system" (Brandt 1992, p. 142; emphasis in original).[13]

From an understanding of duty derives the idea of justice. Justice is "only a particular kind or branch of general utility" (Mill 1861, p. 660), and in its most elementary form "implies something which it is not only right to do, and wrong not to do, but which some individual person can claim from us as his moral right" (p. 664). More correctly, it "is a name for certain classes of moral rules, which concern the essentials of human well-being more nearly, and are therefore of more absolute obligation, than any other rules for the guidance of life"; it is "the chief part, and incomparably the most sacred and binding part, of all morality" (p. 670), to be "distinguished from the milder feeling which attaches to the mere idea of promoting human pleasure or convenience, at once by the more definite nature of its commands, and by the sterner character of its sanctions" (p. 673). As a type of moral rule, justice is fundamentally different from beneficence, and that difference lies in the equation of justice with right and moral obligation, a distinction that goes well beyond the simple requirement of virtue that supports beneficence. It is the existence of moral rules which ensures the continued existence of society: "they are the main element in determining the whole of the social feelings of mankind" (p. 670). Moral rules "which compose the obligations of justice" are those "which protect every individual from being harmed by others, either directly or by being hindered in his freedom of pursuing his own good." These rules and obligations are of such great importance that observance serves as a test of one's "fitness to exist as one of the fellowship of human beings" (p. 671).

Still, while maintaining that justice as a type of moral requirement "stand[s] higher in the scale of social utility" than other moral requirements (Mill 1861, p.

673), Mill does concede that a conflicting "social duty" may "overrule" the general maxims governing it. Here Mill engages in what he himself describes as a "useful accommodation of language," when he justifies committing an illegal or an immoral act in the service of another social duty: it is not the case that justice has been, for the sake of expediency, disregarded, but rather "that what is just in ordinary cases is, by reason of that other principle, not just in the particular case" (p. 673).[14] (Although it would seem to be the other way round, that what would be *unjust* in general becomes *just* in the particular case.) It is in this regard that Sandel holds that Mill cannot be classified as a true deontological liberal, for, although he is non-act-consequentialist, he is too willing to concede that justice is not granted complete primacy, and even to accept that other concerns may indeed override it in importance (Sandel 1998, p. 5).[15]

The necessity for rules governing conduct

Society and the individual

As we have seen, of special import to Mill's individualism is the place of morals in society, and specifically the function of rules as a means to their fulfillment. In *Utilitarianism*, Mill motivates the discussion of the place of rules in a utilitarian framework, connecting them to considerations of obligation and justice. Yet while Mill focuses in *Utilitarianism* on the ethical foundations of *society*, the important discussion of the scope and limits of social action as they relate to the *individual* are most clearly expressed in his companion essay, *On Liberty*.[16] Here he promotes his claim that all human faculties – including "perception, judgment, discriminative feeling, mental activity, and even moral preference" – are derivative of individual initiative expressed through free choice (Mill 1859, p. 59). Indeed, "the free development of individuality is one of the leading essentials of well-being" (p. 57). It is only through the promotion of individuality, in the face of demands for uniformity, that society as a whole will flourish. Only by embracing individuality, "by cultivating it and calling it forth, within the limits imposed by the rights and interests of others," do we see that "each person becomes more valuable to himself, and is therefore capable of being more valuable to others" (p. 63).

Mill's stated objective in *On Liberty*, then, is "to assert one very simple principle" – a principle of liberty denoted the "harm principle" by Joel Feinberg (1973) – governing the imposition of rules in society:[17]

That principle is, that the sole end for which mankind are warranted, individually or collectively, in interfering with the liberty of action of any of their number, is self-protection. That the only purpose for which power can be rightfully exercised over any member of a civilised community, against his will, is to prevent harm to others. His own good, either physical or moral, is not a sufficient warrant. He cannot rightfully be compelled to do or forbear because it will be better for him to do so, because it will make him happier, because, in the opinion of others, to do so would be wise, or even right.

(Mill 1859, p. 13)

This principle Mill sums up in two maxims: given a person of the age of majority, in full possession of his faculties, fully competent and capable of rational deliberation,[18] (1) "the individual is not accountable to society for his actions, in so far as these concern the interests of no one person but himself," and (2) "for such actions as are prejudicial to the interests of others, the individual is accountable, and may be subjected either to social or to legal punishment, if society is of opinion that the one or the other is requisite for its protection" (Mill 1859, p. 94). To the extent that actions affect only the individual responsible, i.e., so long as the acts are purely self-regarding, he is to be left to his own devices; society as a whole has no justifiable role respecting intrusion in individual affairs, nor in imposing a right of duty, in those instances in which actions have no external consequences. The self-regarding actions may be classed into three categories: (1) "the inward domain of unconsciousness," encompassing freedom of conscience, opinion, thought, and sentiment; (2) "liberty of tastes and pursuits," which allows us the freedom of "framing the plan of our life to suit our own character," encompassing the freedom to do as we wish so long as we refrain from causing external harm and are willing to accept the personal consequences; and (3) freedom of combination "for any purpose not involving harm to others" (pp. 15–16). While Mill admits that one may, for the good of another, advance sufficient warrant to remonstrate, reason, persuade, or entreat, he nonetheless argues that it is illegitimate to *compel* action, unless "the conduct from which it is desired to deter him, must be calculated to produce evil to some one else" (p. 13). The interests of mankind "authorise the subjection of individual spontaneity to external control, only in respect to those actions of each, which concern the interest of other people," i.e., individual actions may only be restricted to the extent that they are other-regarding (p. 14).

Custom and tradition

In seeking to promote individuality, Mill is adamant in his demands for protections against the "tyranny of the majority," a phrase in need of some elucidation. This tyranny of which he writes is not confined merely to acts of public officials or to the fancies of the ruling parties or dominant power elites; it is not a fear that the majority will enact legislation that serves to keep in a servile state some identifiable minority group. The tyranny against which Mill rages is much more ubiquitous (and potentially more insidious), as it involves the "collective will" of the society, the prevailing attitudes, customs, social practices that taken together define social convention. In attempting to define it, or at least to give it more precision, one may adopt Mill's characterization as:

the tendency of society to impose, by other means than civil penalties, its own ideas and practices as rules of conduct on those who dissent from them;

to fetter the development, and, if possible, prevent the formation, of any individuality not in harmony with its ways, and compel all characters to fashion themselves upon the model of its own.

(Mill 1859, p. 8)

It is in the nature of the majority to advance the prevailing conventions as truth. Attempts by minorities to supplant these received truths are typically viewed as dangerous and even seditious; the position of the majority appears as a result of such challenges to be threatened, and the very rationale for its existence is placed in question. Thus Mill evinces a suspicion of popular democracy, as he warns of the potential of the majority to regard the stability of the status quo as more significant than the prerogative of its members to address concerns in respect of the conventional order; as unconventional behavior, attitudes, ideas are potentially disruptive of the current state of affairs, limitations on deviations from social norms may come to be seen as essential to social stability and, by extension, to the attainment of the social good. This imposition of a majority will Mill sees as especially insidious, "a social tyranny more formidable than many kinds of political oppression, since ... it leaves fewer means of escape, penetrating much more deeply into the details of life, and enslaving the soul itself" (p. 8).

The need to cultivate individuality suggests itself in the need to promote "experiments in living," to determine empirically and through trial and error which social arrangements are most conducive to the development of the individual (Mill 1859, p. 57). It is in this context that Mill broaches the subject of the influence of tradition and custom. Mill expresses alarm at the very real possibility that, in desiring to improve the moral standards of the community, i.e., to promote a "regularity of conduct" through the "discouragement of excesses," it may be that the "public" feel compelled "to prescribe general rules of conduct, and endeavour to make every one conform to the approved standard" (p. 69). The great danger he sees in this eventuality is that such conformity produces little more than "weak feelings and weak energies," diminishing the vitality of the population by compelling behavior to the traditional and the small, producing mediocrity by reducing the creative will of the individual to the mundane and contented existence of the collective. The machinery responsible for this state of affairs is tradition and custom, "everywhere the standing hindrance to human advancement" (p. 70). Custom, of course, can be useful as a means for appraising conduct, and even Mill accepts the socially stabilizing effects it offers. Still, it is the pernicious influence of custom which is anathema to "the spirit of liberty, or that of progress or improvement," the latter impossible to achieve without the former; Mill goes so far as to equate societal backwardness with a blind appeal to custom, as it destroys all originality and individuality upon which progress depends. This he holds to be the fate of all societies seeking to govern conduct by rules having as their end the formation of a uniform and homogeneous population. Once this is achieved, the degradation of the society begins.[19]

Mill thus follows Wilhelm von Humboldt in insisting that individuality is only encouraged through the exercise of "freedom, and variety of situations," leading as it were to a blossoming of "originality" (Mill 1859, p. 58).[20] The blind and even unconscious following of customs and traditions, by contrast, extinguishes the essence of individuality indispensable to original thinking; no one could possibly argue, then, that this mere imitative behavior could in any way lead to "excellence."

Yet tradition and custom are of service: if nothing else they provide a yard-stick by which one may evaluate the relative values of modes of conduct and of arrangements for living. The past provides the means for appraising the actions of the present and serves an essential function in planning for the future. The difficulty arises when custom is applied in areas beyond its legitimacy. Customs and traditions may have been too narrowly construed, or may be ill-suited to the purpose at hand. Worse, unthinking adherence dulls the abilities essential to the very act of choosing: "perception, judgment, discriminative feeling, mental activity, and even moral preference" have meaning only in the context of free choice; following tradition or habit limits the exercise of these faculties (Mill 1859, p. 59). Thus does Mill conclude that

> in things which do not primarily concern others, individuality should assert itself. Where, not the person's own character, but the traditions or customs of other people are the rule of conduct, there is wanting one of the prin-ciple ingredients of human happiness, and quite the chief ingredient of individual and social progress.
>
> (p. 57)

If only this were understood, "there would be no danger that liberty should be undervalued, and the adjustment of the boundaries between it and social control would present no extraordinary difficulty" (p. 57). Society will progress only so long as this fundamental notion is understood; society will cease to progress "[w]hen it ceases to possess individuality" (p. 71).

Limits on individual action

This fear of such a force for constraint compels Mill to attempt to discover the "limit to the legitimate interference of collective opinion with individual inde-pendence" (Mill 1859, pp. 8–9). To this end, he seeks to answer three questions: "What, then, is the rightful limit to the sovereignty of the individual over himself? Where does the authority of society begin? How much of human life should be assigned to individuality, and how much to society?" (p. 75). Note here that Mill explicitly refers to the imposition of "ideas and practices as rules of conduct" introduced by "society," as he declares his intention to analyze the doctrine of Social Liberty, "the nature and limits of the power which can be legitimately exercised by society over the individual" (p. 5). He is not prepared to limit the possibility of tyrannical imposition to governments alone, but rather feels the need to extend the scope of his definition to include society as a collec-tive, in an effort to discern the limitations of "the legitimate interference of collective opinion with individual independence" and to promote the means of maintaining these limitations (pp. 8–9).

It is in attempting to discern such a limitation that Mill is led to expand upon the importance of rules in society such as may serve to shape expectations as to conduct, a category that includes not merely legal restrictions but also public opinion "on many things which are not fit subjects for the operation of law" (Mill 1859, p. 9). Standards are thus an essential ingredient in Mill's attempt to advance an ethical theory, standards being, on H. L. A. Hart's definition, coincident with *social* morality and so in contrast to those ideals that serve to govern the actions of an *individual* (Hart 1994, p. 69); an appeal to pragmatism in such matters will not suffice. While Mill in fact holds that man has some control over his actions, he nevertheless is not willing to concede that he has any control over the *consequences* of those actions. This suggests a need for rules of behavior, which serve to channel those attributes regarded most highly by society in terms of their utility-enhancement. Mill accepts the premise that membership in a society requires that "each should be bound to observe a certain line of conduct towards the rest," a position not dramatically different from that of the social contract theorists (Mill 1859, p. 75). Conduct conducive to a moral order consists of (1) refraining from usurping the rights and interests of others (whether these interests are defined by "express legal provision" or merely "by tacit understanding"), and (2) bearing one's "share (to be fixed on some equitable principle) of the labours and sacrifices incurred for defending the society or its members from injury and molestation" (p. 75), both of which are obligations that society may demand from its members and may exact under threat of penalty. In addition, society may seek redress for "hurtful" actions which, while not violative of another's rights or person, are nonetheless serious enough to warrant some expression of social disdain; the conduct may be outside the bounds of legal punishment, but it may yet still be subject to the strictures of public opinion. This is far from a libertarianism that stresses egoism as the primary motive, and Mill explicitly rejects the charge that his philosophy promotes "selfish indifference, which pretends that human beings have no business with each other's conduct in life" (p. 76). He even goes so far as to place priority on the social virtues.

Yet this is not to be understood as limiting social restraint to the consequences of action alone, as one's *inaction* may also lead to harmful outcomes for which one need be held to account. Acts directly harmful to others are punishable by law or "general approbation," as they are by definition other-regarding, but Mill goes further, and offers that society may compel individuals to perform "positive acts for the benefit of others ... necessary to the interest of the society of which he enjoys the protection," such as military service and jury duty, as well as "acts of individual beneficence ... things which whenever it is obviously a man's duty to do, he may rightfully be made responsible to society for not doing," such as coming to the assistance of a drowning man (Mill 1859, p. 14). In each case, the social obligation outweighs any individual advantage one could gain by failing to perform. Mill expresses this attitude succinctly: "In all things which regard the external relations of the individual, he is *de jure* amenable to those whose interests are concerned, and if need be, to society as their protector" (pp. 14–15).[21] The failure to act, as much as acting to cause injury, is itself subject to "moral reprobation, and, in grave cases, of moral retribution and punishment" (p. 78).

Even in those instances in which legal enforcement is impractical, "the conscience of the agent himself should step into the vacant judgment seat, and protect those interests of others which have no external protection" (Mill 1859, p. 15). Yet the *dispositions* that may lead to such offenses, while moral vices, are nonetheless beyond *public* censure, even though they may be morally reprehensible; for Mill, moral censure may only be invoked in the case of a breach of duty to others. This is not to imply that individuals may not express disdain and even disgust for a person "grossly deficient" in those qualities "which conduce to his own good" (p. 77). Such a person of "lowness or depravation of taste" may indeed by regarded with contempt by those with whom he comes into contact, and this is a perfectly legitimate expression of individual opinion, as each of us has the right "to act upon our unfavourable opinion of any one, not to the oppression of his individuality, but in the exercise of ours" (pp. 77–8). Accordingly, Mill sees the usefulness of opinion as a form of moral persuasion, even suggesting that it would be of benefit "if this good office were much more freely rendered than the common notions of politeness at present permit" (p. 77). He even goes so far as to suggest that "it may be our duty, to caution others against him, if we think his example or conversation likely to have a pernicious effect on those with whom he associates" (p. 78), and the subject of such cautions "has no right to complain" (although Mill qualifies this by offering that "special excellence in his social relations" may provide merit which overwhelms the demerit of the personal behavior: one may be as disgusting as one wishes, provided one is "connected").[22]

Although an expression of personal disgust is legitimate, and one may take actions designed to actualize that opinion (including the granting of preference to others "in optional good offices"), it is manifestly (as we have seen) illegitimate to extend this expression of feeling to actions designed to inflict harm (broadly defined), for then one infringes on a protected sphere. Mill sees this as especially problematic as regards the notion of social rights, a category that includes a "primary right of security," a "right of equality," and a "right to free moral and intellectual development" (Mill 1859, p. 89). As Mill defines it, a theory of social rights must admit

> that it is the absolute social right of every individual, that every other individual shall act in every respect exactly as he ought; that whosoever fails thereof in the smallest particular, violates my social right, and entitles me to demand from the legislature the removal of the grievance.
>
> (p. 89)

Social rights are thus not ideal moral codes, since any utility gain realized by one protected group is offset (or may be offset) by a utility loss to another. Such a principle *compelling* behavior in accordance with certain group-acceptable mores (redefined as social norms) Mill finds "monstrous," proclaiming it so pernicious that "there is no violation of liberty which it would not justify". It would in effect prohibit (or generate such a climate of fear, loathing, and apprehension that one would *de facto* be prohibited from) any freedom of action and expression, "except perhaps to that of holding opinions in secret, without ever disclosing them" (p. 89). The very notion compels each member of the society to manifest a concern with every other member, not merely a concern with his overall well-being (which concern may be indicative of a communitarian ethic), but with a greater concern that individual standards of moral behavior comport with the subjective standards of a specific group, and that these subjective standards be given an absolute standing; it "ascribes to all mankind a vested interest in each other's moral, intellectual, and even physical perfection, to be defined by each claimant according to his own standard" (p. 90).

Mill himself provides examples of such attempts at defining social rights, including temperance laws, Sabbatarian legislation, and restrictions on the practices of Mormonism, each of which represents an attempt to impose moral rules upon private actions. We will focus for the present on the first of these three.[23] Mill's expressed objection to the institution of temperance laws is that their sponsors assume a division of acts into those relating to opinion and conscience, and those definable as social acts, the first, not being properly acts but rather ideas, defined as being outside the bounds of legislation, the second, to the extent that they are manifest in behavior to which some may take offense, defined as being within the purview of the State. The specific claim on the issue at hand is that intemperance violates social rights to the extent that it leads to social disorder (and so affects the right of security), compels the temperate to submit to a tax for its support (and so affects the right of equality), and fosters the degradation of society (and so affects free moral and intellectual development).[24] In making such a distinction, says Mill, those advocating such constraints ignore a third class of acts, a class of overwhelming significance, *viz.*, those acts the consequences of which fall only on the individual engaged in the activity (Mill 1859, pp. 89–90). While the community may indeed have a legitimate concern in promoting social betterment, this concern cannot be allowed to override the primary concern with protecting the liberty of the individual to engage in self-regarding acts.[25]

In this same vein, one must consider restrictions on trade, in which the buyer's freedom to purchase a good or service is infringed, subject to intrusion by the machinery of the State on the pretense of protecting him from harm. While Mill accepts that there is a sphere of trade into which the State may legitimately interfere, especially in regard to the *seller*, an area that includes protection against fraud and the insurance of workplace safety (the two that Mill himself mentions), the State has no right to interfere in the activities of the *buyer*. Consider the sale and purchase of poisons as an example of a controlled substance. It is not the function of the State to prohibit the purchase of any commodity for which there is only a possibility (or even a probability) of its misuse. If the only use for a substance such as a poison is in the commission of a crime, the State could indeed restrict or prohibit its sale and use and even its manufacture, for then the State would be acting responsibly in its protective function. But barring a certainty of social danger or even personal danger resulting from misuse of the product, in those instances in which there is "only a danger of mischief," the State simply has no role; as "no one but the person himself can judge of the sufficiency of the motive which may prompt him to incur the risk" it follows that, being warned of the possible dangers associated with the product, he should not be prevented from purchasing it (Mill 1859, pp. 96–7). Even given Mill's qualifications, Hart, who otherwise agrees with Mill, expresses disagreement with this "extreme fear of paternalism," noting that we have as a society come to be aware

> of a great range of factors which diminish the significance to be attached to an apparently free choice or to consent. Choices may be made or consent given without adequate reflection or appreciation of the consequences; or in pursuit of merely transitory desires; or in various predicaments when the judgment is likely to be clouded; or under inner psychological compulsion; or under pressure by others of a kind too subtle to be susceptible of proof in a law court.
>
> (Hart, 1963, p. 33)

Despite his protestations against sanctions applied to self-regarding acts, Mill is prepared to allow that certain legislative and juridical interferences may in fact be legitimate. Take the issue of intoxication. That a person may, of his own choice and even in the confines of his own home, over-imbibe on occasion is a matter beyond the scope of State interference, as the act, while perhaps offensive, is not in and of itself other-regarding; the consequences (not confined to hangovers and even pauperhood) fall solely on the person committing the act. However, suppose that the inebriated individual, as a result of his condition, commits an act of violence or vandalism for which he is convicted. In this instance, what had been merely self-regarding conduct has produced external consequences which compel public action. It is then perfectly reasonable that the person may henceforth

> be placed under a special legal restriction ... that if he were afterwards found drunk, he should be liable to a penalty, and that if when in that state he committed another offence, the punishment to which he would be liable ... should be increased in severity.
>
> (Mill 1859, p. 98)

(The same reasoning applies to the case of a person who chooses to be idle: to the extent that his idleness affects only himself, he should be left alone; to the extent that his action affects others, e.g., by causing hardship to his family, he may be compelled to seek employment.) The criterion for social action, then, is whether the consequence of the otherwise self-regarding action is "a violation of good manners," a category that includes "offences against decency" (p. 98).[26]

In sum, Mill is not advocating that the individual should be completely free to act as he wishes, to pursue vices in the purported furtherance of public benefit. As we have seen, Mill certainly accepts the need for restrictions on individual actions that may cause harm to others and, even in those instances in which no external consequences are forthcoming, it is clear that he sees merit in compulsory adherence to rules governing behavior. Such rules are critical in promoting a better, more congenial social intercourse, as such compulsory adherence "developes [sic] the feelings and capacities which have the good of others for their object" (Mill 1859, p. 63); the educative function is expressly designed to inculcate such values in the population. What Mill objects to are those rules having as their object the restriction of private behavior of which others, while not directly affected by such actions, may nonetheless take offense, a direct punitive action extending well beyond the bounds of moral persuasion or education as shapers of social values. While he acknowledges that "it is necessary that general rules should for the most part be observed, in order that people may know what they have to expect," it is yet still imperative that "in each person's own concerns, his individual spontaneity is entitled to free exercise" (p. 77).[27] He phrases it quite well in *Principles of Political Economy*, where, in a recapitulation of his principle of liberty, he maintains that

> there is a circle around every individual human being which no government, be it that of one, of a few, or of the many, ought to be permitted to over-step: there is a part of the life of every person who has come to years of discretion, within which the individuality of that person ought to reign uncontrolled either by any other individual or by the public collectively.
>
> (Mill 1871, p. 943)

The end of such restrictions can only be a loss of individuality, and by extension a diminution of the society.

Paternalism

While one may wish one's subjects to exhibit a consistency of thought, it is undeniably often the case that deviations appear which threaten to blemish an otherwise glorious façade. So it is with Mill's statement of individualism. In spite of his best efforts to construct a principle by which individual liberty might be protected from the unwarranted intrusion of the State, Mill does allow a place for social interference in self-regarding conduct, and does so not merely for the enhancement of the social good but, importantly and expressly, for the good of the individual as well; in so doing, he opens himself to a charge of promoting paternalism. Specifically, Mill accepts that the State may be justified in preventing any person from entering into a contract that is ultimately injurious to himself, such as a contract placing him into lifelong servitude or slavery.

Why this restriction? What is it in the nature of such a contract that is so profoundly different from any other arrangement into which the person enters freely and without compulsion? Mill sees a fundamental distinction: an acceptable contract is one conducive to an individual's good, one that does not place an undue restraint on his liberty, including his freedom to act autonomously in the future. In an acceptable contract, the individual's "voluntary choice is evidence that what he so chooses is desirable, or at the least endurable, to him, and his good is on the whole best provided for by allowing him to take his own means of pursuing it" (Mill 1859, p. 103). Competent, rational adults, knowledgeable of the consequences of their conduct (or capable of making themselves aware of such consequences), must be allowed the greatest freedom of action. As the principle of liberty demands noninterference in actions having no external consequences, there is no moral basis for pre-empting anyone from engaging in such activity, even if performance of the act itself ultimately has a negative impact on his well-being. A voluntary slavery contract, however, violates one of the most fundamental tenets of liberty. Should a person choose freely to place himself in a condition of slavery, voluntary, free choice ceases to exist; in entering into such an agreement, the individual "abdicates his liberty," as he "foregoes any future use of it beyond that single act" (p. 103). The individual is then no longer autonomous, as by the very act of entering into the contract he is no longer capable of free choice in future actions on the basis of self-interest. Again, Mill relies on the authority of Humboldt, who opines:

> [T]he restraint which every engagement imposes is only just and salutary, when, firstly, the implied limitation extends only to him who enters into it; and secondly, when he has in general, and at the time of the engagement, acted with a proper capacity for reflection, and of his own free will. Wherever this is not the case, coercion is as unjust in principle as it is pernicious in its effects.
>
> (Humboldt 1791/2, p. 95)

Given this understanding, the State is well within its bounds in refusing

> the support of the law to such engagements as are contrary to justice, and to take all necessary precautions consistent with the security of property to prevent a moment's want of reflection from curtailing such restrictions on a man as to retard or prevent his own perfect development.
>
> (Humboldt 1791/2, p. 95)

Within these parameters, the State is justified in preventing any person from contracting to place himself in slavery.

Gerald Dworkin has taken this example as evidence of a paternalistic strain in Mill's thought. As Dworkin defines the term, paternalism is "the interference with a person's liberty of action justified by reasons referring exclusively to the welfare, good, happiness, needs, interests or values of the person being coerced" (Dworkin 1971, p. 108). Alternatively, it may be characterized as "the use of coercion to achieve a good which is not recognized as such by those persons for whom the good is intended" (p. 112). For Mill, the utmost value is freedom of action, the freedom to choose that which he desires simply because he desires it. To have such freedom requires autonomy. If indeed autonomy and freedom of choice are the highest values, Mill's restriction can be justified only by insisting that such a restriction expands the domain of individual liberty.[28]

For instance, would Mill accept the validity of a slavery contract that stipulated a time period of servitude, or that granted the "slave" party legal recourse should the "master" violate the strict terms of the agreement? Clearly, in this case, a contract would provide the person placing himself in servitude options to regain his freedom and to reclaim his autonomy. If one answers in the negative, the question, then, would appear to revolve around the primacy of liberty: if freedom and liberty and the need to preserve personal autonomy are indeed inviolable, then it would appear as though even this contingent claim would and indeed must provoke Mill's disgust. Second, one must consider whether Mill would be opposed to the proposition that a person has a right to sign away his rights, which would place in jeopardy the universal nature of the principle of liberty, or merely be opposed to State *enforcement* of such a contract. For Mill to be consistent, he must allow any competent and rational person, fully informed, the right to surrender his rights, unless freedom and autonomy are taken to be, in and of themselves, of paramount moral value. Allowing to the individual such a freedom of contract, there is a *social* interest which still must be taken into account. If any society deems slavery – as involuntary servitude – to be so morally reprehensible that its formal and absolute abolition is essential to the maintenance of the social good, then this society must not give sanction to any agreement, even if freely negotiated, which could be construed as placing qualifications on such restrictions. While the State may acquiesce in the *signing* of the contract, it could intervene should the "slave" party decide, for whatever reason, to nullify it. The fact of the contract being freely entered into, even if with the complete knowledge of the consequences for future actions, is irrelevant, as society places a premium value on freedom from servitude.[29]

Liberty and utility

To end this section, it is instructive to compare the positions advanced by Mill in *Utilitarianism* and *On Liberty*, especially in respect of a question that arises which has been examined by, among others, John Gray. It is said by critics of Mill that his moral theory as presented in *On Liberty* conflicts with his general principle of utility. Specifically, it is maintained that the principle of liberty – the "harm principle" – diverges from the utility principle, as the principle of liberty actually acts "as an absolute bar against many utility-promoting policies" (J. Gray 1996, p. 3). In terms of the critics, what should be a principle justified by considerations of utility becomes in effect a competing ethical principle.

As noted above, the principle of utility and the principle of liberty cannot be in conflict because the former is not a moral principle and so cannot by itself inform judgments of right and wrong. The principle of utility is the standard, "a general principle of valuation," "an axiological principle specifying that happiness and that alone has intrinsic goodness," which is of no import to questions of morality (or of action, for that matter) without the aid of some additional postulates that serve to its implementation. We saw above Mill's assertion of just this point, *viz.*, of the need for secondary ends, agreement on which is much more forthcoming than is agreement on the ultimate standard. Thus, in his argument in *Utilitarianism*, Mill supplements the utility principle with a principle of expediency, "a consequentialist principle specifying that that act is maximally expedient and ought to be done which has the best consequences" (J. Gray 1996, pp. 11–12). As the principle of expediency is a necessary supplement to the principle of utility in the utilitarian theory of action, so the principle of liberty is a necessary supplement to the principle of utility in a (Millian) utilitarian moral theory: in both cases, the supplemental postulates allow the application of the general principle, which otherwise is little more that a vacuous maxim. In terms of the general procedure, Mill seems to concur:

> It is when two or more of the secondary principles conflict, that a direct appeal to some first principle becomes necessary; and then commences the practical importance of the utilitarian controversy; which is, in other respects, a question of arrangement and logical subordination rather than of practice; important principally in a purely scientific point of view, for the sake of the systematic unity and coherency of ethical philosophy.
>
> (Mill 1838, pp. 170–1)

(This explains Gray's preference for the term "indirect utilitarianism" as descriptive of Mill's approach, as opposed to the less informative "act" or "rule" utilitarianism.) So, in Gray's estimation, "Mill argues for the adoption of his Principle of Liberty, in effect, in virtue of its being that utility-barring maxim whose observance will have the best utility-promoting effects" (J. Gray 1996, p. 16).

The role of the State

The need for a common ethic

While Mill holds that society should not attempt to exact a punishment for actions the consequences of which fall on the individual himself, but rather should be concerned with only those areas of conduct upon which the actions have external consequences, his belief in the perfectibility of man leads him to entertain the notion that a liberal polity formed along utilitarian lines must, in pursuit of a common good, undertake to promote in its citizens a common ethic. Very early on, Mill sees a positive role for State action to this general end: "Government exists for all purposes whatever that are for man's good: and the highest & most important of these purposes is the improvement of man himself as a moral and intelligent being" (Mill 1829, p. 36). We have had a glimpse of his position on this matter in respect of the concept of social rights. The State cannot legitimately intrude into "that portion of a person's life and conduct which affects only himself, or if it also affects others, only with their free, voluntary, and undeceived consent and participation" (Mill 1859, p. 15). On the other hand, the State is not to be neutral with respect to questions of right and the good. Mill is especially clear on this point in *Considerations on Representative Government*. Observing that "[t]he first element of good government" is "the virtue and intelligence of the human beings composing the community, the most important point of excellence which any form of government can possess is to promote the virtue and intelligence of the people themselves." The principal function of any political or social institution is "to foster in the members of the community the various desirable qualities, moral and intellectual"; that government that succeeds in this task "has every likelihood of being the best in all other respects, since it is on these qualities, so far as they exist in the people, that all possibility of goodness in the practical operations of the government depends" (Mill 1865, p. 390).

Limits of State intervention

It is in the context of objections to government interference that Mill identifies two types of governmental intervention: the *authoritative* and the *advisory* (Mill 1871, pp. 941–2). Authoritative interference seeks to prevent through restrictive enactments or prescriptive edicts the free exercise of individual liberty; it is coercive in that it demands strict adherence to the laws. The authoritative form of interference, being restrictive, Mill finds limited in its legitimacy, and so its use demands strong justification, if only because it has the potential of demanding too severe a restriction of liberty, and especially of individuality, as the government may seek to exercise functions it was never intended to possess. Specifically, Mill is concerned (as throughout his writings) with the intrusion of governmental authority into the private realm, that protected sphere "within which the individuality of that person ought to reign uncontrolled either by any other individual or by the public collectively." It ought always to be the obligation of the government to justify any proposed infringement on this sphere, and "constructive or presumptive injury to others" is insufficient in this regard (p. 943).

The advisory role is more acceptable from the perspective of the protection of individual rights, because it does not require oppressive legislation. The advisory role requires positive reinforcement, and involves only the setting of limitations on behavior, not proscriptions on actions. In performing this role, the government can legitimately establish rules as to the constitution of acceptable behavior, so long as it does not interfere with the ability of others in the provision of these same services. This Mill sums up as follows:

> When a government provides means for fulfilling a certain end, leaving individuals free to avail themselves of different means if in their opinion preferable, there is no infringement of liberty, no irksome or degrading restraint. One of the principal objections to government interference is then absent.
>
> (Mill 1871, p. 944)

In sum, Mill advises that a *laissez-faire* approach "should be the general practice," and that "every departure from it, unless required by some great good, is a certain evil" (Mill 1871, p. 950). This follows from Mill's general rule: "the business of life is better performed when those who have an immediate interest in it are left to take their own course, uncontrolled either by the mandate of the law or by the meddling of any public functionary" (p. 952). He who is most directly affected is best able to ascertain the appropriate mode of action.

Legitimate areas of State action

Mill considers that one of the most important and enduring social questions revolves around the legitimate areas of State action. *Some* form of State intervention, even in a society governed by the principle of liberty, is essential to social order. The central point of contention is between those who "are under a constant temptation to stretch the province of government beyond due bounds," and those who, having become disillusioned by legislators who engage in actions "for purposes other than the public good," or who are "under an erroneous conception of what that good requires," have developed "a spirit of resistance *in limine* to the interference of government" and so are disposed "to restrict its sphere of action within the narrowest bounds" (Mill 1871, p. 795).

In the most general terms, Mill offers three objections to government interference: (1) individuals are likely to perform tasks more efficiently than is government, since "there is no one so fit to conduct any business, or to determine how or by whom it shall be conducted, as those who are personally interested in it"; (2) individuals should exercise their own judgment "as a means to their own mental education," instead of relying on the judgments of others; and (3) government should be restricted in its scope as a matter of course, so as to avoid increasing unnecessarily its power (Mill 1859, pp. 109–10). The first of these objections is prompted by the belief that government should interfere to the least extent possible in the workings of business and the economy. The second objection goes to the heart of the argument in *On Liberty*. It is only through the free exercise of individual judgment that one develops the faculties necessary to forming that judgment. The State tends to the promotion of uniformity; a free and dynamic society, on the other hand, requires individuals constantly engaged in experimentation, constantly offering new approaches of which the State could never have conceived. The third objection relates to Mill's belief that centralized power is itself a "great evil."

> Every function superadded to those already exercised by the government, causes its influence over hopes and fears to be more widely diffused, and converts, more and more, the active and ambitious part of the public into hangers-on of the government, or of some party which aims at becoming the government.
>
> (p. 110)

Moreover, the more efficient the government becomes, the more pervasive is its control: the bureaucracy becomes the instrument in which power is vested, and the bureaucracy is liable to little external control.

While preferring to restrict the legitimate areas of State interference to the protection of public safety, the resolution of disputes, and the enforcement of contracts, Mill is acutely aware of the fact that "the admitted functions of government embrace a much wider field than can easily be included within the ring-fence of any restrictive definition." Unable to provide any clear-cut ethical justification, he is left to consider that the proper and legitimate scope of State action is determined by "general expediency," the only real limitation being "that it should never be admitted but when the case of expediency is strong" (Mill 1871, p. 800).

Mill, especially in *Principles of Political Economy*, spends considerable effort in examining the public finance functions of government, and expounds as well on those "ordinary" functions, such as the administration of justice and economic regulation. Yet, even in *On Liberty*, he acknowledges that there are areas in which the State has a legitimate duty in interfering with individual conduct. For instance, laws regulating marriage and even procreation to those able to support a family and so not tax the resources of the society are legitimate in that they serve to prevent acts "injurious to others, which ought to be a subject of reprobation, and social stigma" (Mill 1859, p. 108). While government has an important role to play as an agent of acculturation, it should not be forgotten that it is a necessary evil. There is no reason to believe that the government is any better equipped to impose moral and ethical systems of conduct on the populace than the people themselves can devise. While social reformers may desire governmental action on the ground that it is more immediate to the solution of social problems than, for instance, education could be in altering attitudes and behaviors, and inculcating a proper sense of morality, it should never be forgotten that the public has become wary of government intrusion in their lives and so in most instances profoundly seek to resist it.[30]

One institution for which Mill reserves the most attention is that of public education, or rather the public educative function. To Mill, education is the measure of moral worth: the more educated the person, the more intrinsically valuable he is. Through education, society (in the guise of the State) has the potentiality of "bettering" the population, inculcating standards of behavior and a sense of social purpose, arming its citizens with the ability to make moral decisions. Education and "the ascendancy which the authority of a received opinion always exercises over the minds who are least fitted to judge for themselves," as well as the "*natural* penalties which cannot be prevented from falling on those who incur the distaste or the contempt of those who know them," are sufficient as mechanisms to promote social cohesion (Mill 1859, pp. 82–3; emphasis in original). The State, therefore, in asserting the necessity of an educated citizenry, accepts also its sufficiency as a means of acculturation, suggesting that the educative function is sufficient to form the means of obedience to social norms.[31] At the same time, Mill recognizes a negative side to education, as it has the potential of destroying individuality and, with it, creativity. A universal system of education "brings people under common influences, and gives them access to the general stock of facts and sentiments," leading in the end to an assimilation of the individual to the whole. The result is a tendency "to raise the low and to lower the high" (p. 73).

Mill is perfectly willing to limit the government role to *requiring* education, but is unwilling to entertain extensions of that authority to *providing* education: "objections which are urged with reason against State education, do not apply to the enforcement of education by the State, but to the State's taking upon itself to direct that education" (Mill 1859, p. 106). Again, the reason relates to his position as explained above. In order that individuality may flourish, it is essential that the self-regarding virtues be cultivated along with the social. The problem arises when, in promoting the educative function, the State places reliance on the compulsory role at the expense of the persuasive. It is altogether fitting and proper that society strive to instill in its members the self-regarding virtues, stimulating to the greatest possible extent the "higher faculties." It is, however, wholly improper that the State should direct curricula with the end of producing a population of uniform intellects cast in the mold of the dominant governing authority, however enlightened that authority may be; it is not the function of the State to instill right values or to impose conceptions of moral goodness, for this is ultimately destructive not only of individuality but also the cohesiveness of the family unit (p. 106). The educative role is ultimately to rest with the parents, and is to be regarded as properly their moral (and legal) obligation.

Another legitimate area of State action explicitly mentioned by Mill is birth control, specifically the right of the State to intervene so as to prevent procreation. At first blush, this may seem a direct contradiction of the principle of liberty: after all, is not the right to reproduce one of the most basic of all human rights? Mill does not regard it as thus, and grants that the State may act to prevent procreation in three important instances: (1) where the child may reasonably be expected to be born deformed or otherwise incapable of living a "desirable" existence; (2) where the parents can be shown to be incapable of providing adequate support to a family; (3) to prevent social harm to the society (to wit, to the workers) that may result from an overabundance of labor (Mill 1859, p. 108). Given Mill's vehemence with respect to State intrusion into personal conduct, what is his justification for such interference? Very simply, he defines procreation as outside the bounds of moral rights, and equates it with other-regarding acts against which the State may legitimately intrude.

Mill thus allows that abortion, population policies, and even eugenic controls are consistent with an overall concern for the preservation of individual liberty and the need for protection of individual rights and individual liberty from a potentially coercive State, but he can do so only by radically reinterpreting other-regarding conduct. Here, as we saw in the discussion of paternalism, it is evident that the principle of *utility* trumps the principle of *liberty*, and the social welfare is given priority over individual rights and liberties.[32] Perhaps, then, Rawls is correct in his estimation that coercive State action is inevitable in any society predicated on a comprehensive doctrine such as Utilitarianism, if only to maintain the legitimacy of that moral view (Rawls 2001, p. 34). For Mill, the social repercussions from allowing personal choice to dictate in these matters are simply too great to leave this activity to individual choice. The State may, and indeed in the final instance *must*, intervene to ensure an outcome consistent with some measure of social good. Thus one sees that Justice Oliver Wendell Holmes, Jr., may well have employed Mill's argument to buttress his opinion regarding forced sterilization in the case of *Buck v. Bell* (247 US 200, 1927) – his argument ultimately resting on his belief that "three generations of imbeciles are enough," instead of relying on other, less pragmatic means for justification.

The *Chapters on Socialism*

One may see Mill's stance on individualism reflected in his critical look at Socialism. The posthumously published *Chapters on Socialism* represents an application of Mill's utility and freedom principles to his understanding of the mechanisms of social organization as manifest in the socialist and communist movements of his time.

Mill begins by noting that, with the inevitability of universal suffrage, a paramount concern would be the distribution of wealth, especially the position in society of the right of property and individual ownership. The impecunious would, as a matter of course, most certainly not be mollified by arguments for the protection of a right to individual ownership of something to which there is a *social* benefit. As they have, as a class, little or no property of their own, but rather are dependent upon the wages received for their labor services, which wages are meager at best, sufficient to keep them just at the level of poverty, one can only assume open hostility to the existing private property arrangements and the purported inequalities to which these arrangements are associated. Granted the suffrage, it seems obvious that they would insist on a reconsideration of the very notion of private property as the center of the social relationship, and would almost certainly be disposed to accept any solution that has as its central tenet communal ownership.

So it is that those "classes who have next to no property of their own, and are only interested in the institution so far as it is a public benefit ... will not allow anything to be taken for granted – certainly not the principle of private property." If anything, it is true that they

> will certainly demand that the subject, in all its parts, shall be reconsidered from the foundation; that all proposals for doing without the institution, and all modes of modifying it which have the appearance of being favourable to the interest of the working classes, shall receive the fullest consideration and discussion.
>
> (Mill 1879, p. 220)

Withal, it is the Socialists who are the most vocal proponents of such a dramatic reappraisal of the institutional relations engendered by the framework of private property. Property relations, they argue, an argument the laboring classes seem quite prepared to accept, reflect merely another obstacle on the road to a more complete political and economic freedom: the working classes have achieved some measure of *political* rights, but yet are denied many *economic* rights, without which they are effectively prohibited from an equal place in the social order. They are in effect

> chained to a place, to an occupation, and to conformity with the will of an employer, and debarred by the accident of birth both from the enjoyments, and from the mental and moral advantages, which others inherit without exertion and independently of desert.
>
> (Mill 1879, p. 222)

Given the historical chronicle of the continued extension of the franchises to the laboring classes, one should not find it extraordinary that they would feel "entitled to claim that the whole field of social institutions should be re-examined, and every question considered as if it now arose for the first time" (p. 222). It is here that Mill asserts a Rawlsian prescription:

> It should be the object to ascertain what institutions of property would be established by an unprejudiced legislator, absolutely impartial between the possessors of property and the non-possessors; and to defend and justify them by the reasons which would really influence such a legislator, and not by such as have the appearance of being got up to make out a case for what already exists.
>
> (Mill 1879, p. 223)

Mill notes several socialist objections to the structure of a property-based order. First, the Socialists contend, property as an institution "is upheld and commended principally as being the means by which labour and frugality are insured their reward, and mankind enabled to emerge from indigence" (Mill 1879, p. 224). The problem, as they perceive it, is that, in this regard, private ownership has failed as a means of reducing poverty, the "[f]irst among existing social evils": the population has simply not received any substantial benefits from the current distribution. The mantra – that those best fit for the challenge will survive, and those unfit to the challenge will perish – is not a philosophy worthy of an enlightened people; indeed, it may be offered that

> if there be any who suffer physical privation or moral degradation, whose bodily necessities are either not satisfied or satisfied in a manner which only brutish creatures can be content with, this, though not necessarily the crime of society, is *pro tanto* a failure of the social arrangements.
>
> (p. 225)

In the "right state," the prosperous would take the initiative in insisting that, in exchange for the continuance of their prosperity, those in their charge would be granted an opportunity of "obtaining a desirable existence" and would thereby reject any notion that one's lot is the result of personal fortune or misfortune (p. 225) (although it seems as though the Socialists may still insist on the *guarantee* of a desirable outcome.)

The ideal state would be that which recognized the importance of desert, i.e., as each derives benefit from his own labor and from personal abstinence, then it follows that "every one who was willing to undergo a fair share of this labour and abstinence could attain a fair share of the fruits" (Mill 1879, p. 226). That this does not occur, say the Socialists, that the vast majority suffer the hardest labor but receive the least benefit of the fruits of that labor, is further evidence of the bankruptcy of the existing social and economic structure. While reward is not entirely divorced from ability and effort, it is nonetheless the case that nothing even remotely identified with distributive justice can be seen in the circumstances of the time. The existing property arrangement, including the "evil" inherent in those institutions underlying inheritance, only succeeds in separating reward from effort.

The second failure of the existing arrangement is "human misconduct," including "crime, vice, and folly, with all the sufferings which follow in their train" (Mill 1879, p. 227). To the Socialists, these "failures" are the result of poverty, idleness, and "bad" education. Poverty and idleness are "failures in the social arrangements," while "bad" education is "the fault of those arrangements – it may almost be said the crime" (p. 227). At fault, we are told, is the entire structure of society, including the structure of production, which "is essentially vicious and anti-social." Specifically, the culprits are individualism and competitive self-interest, both of which are anathema to the moral structure of the community and the moral fiber of its individual members as they are productive of a "vicious and anti-social" morality:

> It is the principle of individualism, competition, each one for himself and against all the rest. It is grounded on opposition of interests, not harmony of interests, and under it every one is required to find his place by a struggle, by pushing others back or being pushed back by them. Socialists consider this system of private war (as it may be termed) between every one and every one, especially fatal in an economical point of view and in a moral. Morally considered, its evils are obvious. It is the parent of envy, hatred, and all uncharitableness; it makes every one the natural enemy of all others who cross his path, and every one's path is constantly liable to be crossed. Under the present system hardly any one can gain except by the loss or disappointment of one or of many others.
>
> (Mill 1879, p. 227)

The socialist "solution" contemplates a complete reconfiguration of the social structure to ensure a community of interests derived from a community of feeling: "In a well-constituted community every one would be a gainer by every other person's successful exertions" (Mill 1879, pp. 227–228). The principle of individualism upon which the capitalist order is based has resulted in a competitive order conducive not to the *betterment* of the whole, but to its *coarsening* and *decay*; labor competition has produced low wages and miserable working and living conditions, staggering poverty, and social deprivation, while market competition has driven the small producers to bankruptcy and has resulted in the formation of conglomerates and restricted competition, productive only of gross inequalities of wealth and power. The result, in short, has been little beyond a resurgent feudalism (p. 228).

Yet, observes Mill, the socialist diagnosis of the problem, and their prescription for its amelioration, are both in error. Far from causing an immiseration of the condition of the working class, the capitalist organization of society and the individualism at its core have resulted in *increasing* the wages of labor and in *bettering* the lives of those in the labouring classes, as it has improved the general conditions of society. The decrease witnessed in the rate of poverty, despite the countervailing force of increasing population, is evidence of the efficacy of the capitalist mode of production, contrary to the pronouncements of the critics. The system that emphasizes individual initiative and free choice will continue with such improvements, but only to the extent that "bad laws do not interfere with it" (Mill 1879, p. 375).

In the end, while defending the role in which the capitalist mode of productive relations has played in the transformation of society, Mill does not in these ruminations dispute the *practicability* of Socialism: under the socialist organization of society, ownership of consumables and individual plots of land (residential property) is to be allowed, with the means of production being common property (the idea of the State as a community of communal villages). Mill's objection is to the attempt to engineer the workings of the entire national economy through a State bureaucratic organization, a prospect that would place severe restrictions on individual liberty and limit individual initiative, and so would run counter to his commitment as expressed in *On Liberty*.[33] Even from an efficiency standpoint, he questions whether State bureaucratic management would ever realize the efficiencies of private enterprise. The motivation to succeed under free enterprise is paramount; under Socialism, there is no such motivation, as the proceeds are divided equally irrespective of merit or desert. Exhortations to public spirit and social consciousness, while viewed by the Socialists as rewards, seem to Mill to serve a "restraining," not an "impelling" role (Mill 1879, p. 516). Under free enterprise, the desire for personal gain is the prime motivation; under Socialism, performance is raised to the standard of social duty, subject to sanctions for failure to perform, every act reducible to its most elementary form, such that it may be made subject to measurement and strict assessment. The regime of free enterprise fosters creativity and independent thought and action, as it promotes autonomy, the very elements stifled under socialist arrangements. Mill concludes with a less-than-hopeful assessment as to the prospects of the socialist model:

> We must therefore expect, unless we are operating upon a select portion of the population, that personal interest will for a long time be a more effective stimulus to the most vigorous and careful conduct of the industrial business of society than motives of a higher character.
>
> (Mill 1879, p. 516)

Thus, for Mill, the most important element in favor of free enterprise is the central place it affords to the exercise of individual human freedom ("experiments in living"), an element sorely lacking in socialist attempts at social and economic organization.

> The obstacles to human progression are always great, and require a concurrence of favourable circumstances to overcome them; but an indispensable condition of their being overcome is, that human nature should have freedom to expand spontaneously in various directions, both in thought and practice; that people should both think for themselves and try experiments for themselves, and should not resign into the hands of rulers, whether acting in the name of a few or of the majority, the business of thinking for them, and of prescribing how they shall act. But in Communist associations private life would be brought in a most unexampled degree within the dominion of public authority, and there would be less scope for the develop-

ment of individual character and individual preferences than has hitherto existed among the full citizens of any state belonging to the progressive branches of the human family. Already in all societies the compression of individuality by the majority is a great and growing evil; it would probably be much greater under Communism, except so far as it might be in the power of individuals to set bounds to it by selecting to belong to a community of persons like-minded with themselves.

(Mill 1879, p. 522)

Remarks

Mill is perhaps the single most important expositor of the principles of a liberal society, and this is the prime reason for beginning such a discussion with a review of his works. The defining character of liberalism is evident throughout his writings; what followed in the evolution of liberal political thought seems at times little more than an effort to expand upon or to delimit the principles he set forth.

But Mill's liberalism is open to caricature and misrepresentation; it is quite easy to read into a work understandings the author never intended, especially for those engaged in far-flung hermeneutical delusions. One may, of course, find in *On Liberty* and *Utilitarianism* what appear to be defenses of the unencumbered self, a person seeking to satisfy selfish desires, subject only to the proviso that he not harm others. The State and even the community thus have little justification to interfere with personal actions having no discernible negative social repercussions. This would establish Mill not only as a liberal, but as a *libertarian*. Such a reading, however, conflicts with Mill's expressed intention, as it neglects the critical place in individual motivation of community and belonging, of sympathy and allegiance, those critical principles set forth in his early essay on Coleridge. Such a reading also minimizes the significance of those paternalistic elements in Mill's thought, through which the social good is to be *imposed* if not otherwise advanced. It is this apprehension of social encumbrance that must be part of any effort to appreciate the full measure of Mill's political philosophy.

Mill is also important in the present context for another reason. His writings, especially *On Liberty*, had the effect of forcing his critics to confront his position directly, and so to provide the very justifications for community interference and State action that Mill demanded. Perhaps the most significant of these confrontations was that of the noted jurist and legal authority James Fitzjames Stephen, with whose contributions we shall deal in the next chapter.

Notes

1 Coleridge, poet, literary critic, and philosopher, planned to found a utopian socialist society in Pennsylvania – a pantisocracy, a perfectly democratic community of complete equality – with the assistance of his friend and fellow-poet, Robert Southey. Needless to say, the plan never came to fruition.
2 "On the one hand the standard of right and wrong, on the other the chain of causes and effects, are fastened to their throne" (Bentham 1988, p. 1).

3   Mill is especially clear on this point in his attack on the moral philosophy of William Whewell (Mill 1852, pp. 234–7).

4   "Whether happiness be or be not the end to which morality should be referred – that it be referred to an *end* of some sort, and not left in the dominion of vague feeling or inexplicable internal conviction, that it be made a matter of reason and calculation, and not merely of sentiment, is essential to the very idea of moral philosophy ..." (Mill 1838, p. 171; emphasis in original).

5   In his essay "Whewell on Moral Philosophy," Mill takes Whewell to task for not recognizing that he, while dismissive of Utilitarianism, actually derives his secondary principles from the utilitarian principle of happiness (Mill 1852, p. 261).

6   Rawls notes that in these passages Mill expresses agreement with the social contract view and justice as fairness. "With the constant assurance expressed by these principles, persons will develop a secure sense of their own worth that forms the basis for the love of humankind" (Rawls 1971, p. 501). He further suggests that, in Mill's portrayal of a harmony of feelings, he demonstrates a "desire to act upon the difference principle (or some similar criterion), and not a desire to act on the principle of utility" (p. 502).

7   This point is made by John Gray (1996). Also see p. 57–8.

8   Regarding Mill on this question, Rawls concludes that "equal political liberty is not solely a means. These freedoms strengthen men's sense of their own worth, enlarge their intellectual and moral sensibilities, and lay the basis for a sense of duty and obligation upon which the stability of just institutions depends" (Rawls 1971, p. 234).

9   Lyons (1994, p. 77) makes a similar argument.

10 Cf. Habermas: "'Obligation' presupposes the intersubjective recognition of moral norms or customary practices that lay down for a community *in a convincing manner* what actors are obliged to do and what they can expect from one another" (Habermas 1998, p. 3; emphasis in original).

11 As represented by H. L. A. Hart, rules impose obligations "when the general demand for conformity is insistent and the social pressure brought to bear upon those who deviate or threaten to deviate is great" (Hart 1994, p. 86). If the sanction for violating a specific rule is confined to social pressure (ostracism, or "verbal manifestations of disapproval," etc.), the rule is taken to be "part of the morality of the social group and the obligation under the rules as moral obligation," while in those instances in which sanctions involve physical punishment, the rule may be classified as a "rudimentary form of law" (p. 86).

12 As Brandt phrases it: "The moral motivations of a *group* 'require' a certain action in certain circumstances if they are for it, would register guilt if an act of their own were not of this sort, and disapprove/be indignant at anyone else whose act was not such" (Brandt 1992, p. 139; emphasis in original).

13 Although Brandt is not prepared to say that Mill's concept of duty is non-act-utilitarian. See Brandt, 1992, p. 142. Lyons, however, goes further, stating that "the very distinction between morality and expediency indicates that Mill is not an act-utilitarian" (Lyons 1994, p. 50).

14 Cf. Hart: "Laws may be condemned as morally bad simply because they require men to do particular actions which morality forbids individuals to do, or because they require men to abstain from doing those which are morally obligatory" (Hart 1994, p. 168).

15 Sandel also proclaims that Mill's liberalism is teleological, since the ultimate aim is happiness.

16 Richard Posner observes that Mill's libertarianism in *On Liberty* is actually independent of his moral theory as presented in *Utilitarianism*. The moral theory of *On Liberty*, Posner alleges, is pragmatic. See Posner 2003, pp. 384–5.

17 Robert Bork decries Mill's principle of liberty as "impossible and empty." Social relations cannot be encapsulated in a single, simple rule (impossibility), and Mill's desire to equate the moral concerns of all with his own is illegitimate (emptiness). See Bork 1996, pp. 59–60.

18 Interestingly, Mill also excludes from consideration "those backward states of society in which the race itself may be considered as in its nonage" (Mill 1859, p. 13).

19 Note the similarity of Mill's position with that of Carl Jung: "The hypnotic power of tradition still holds us in thrall, and out of cowardice and thoughtlessness the herd goes trudging along the same old path" (Jung 1966, p. 261).

20 "Joy is greatest in those moments in which man is aware that his individuality and creative energy are at their highest pitch" (Humboldt 1791/2, p. 31).

21 Although Mill concedes that compulsion may not be demanded in the case in which the individual "is on the whole likely to act better, when left to his own discretion, than when controlled in any way in which society have it in their power to control him; or because the attempt to exercise control would produce other evils, greater than those which it would prevent" (Mill 1859, p. 15).

22 Cf. Mill on this point with Mandeville: "It is incredible how necessary an Ingredient Shame is to make us sociable; it is a Frailty in our Nature; all the World, whenever it affects them, submit to it with Regret, and would prevent it if they could; yet the Happiness of Conversation depends upon it, and no Society could be polish'd, if the Generality of Mankind were not subject to it" (Mandeville 1732, I, p. 68).

23 Mill's objection to Sabbatarian legislation is that, while a one-day-per-week break from one's occupational labors may indeed be to the benefit of all, the legislation of such a custom is illegitimate in so far as it extends the authority of the State into promoting a religious-bound custom. His objection to laws pertaining to Mormon practices such as polygamy is that the practice, and indeed membership in the movement, is voluntary and not coerced.

24 Such is the opinion of T. H. Green:

> It used to be the fashion to look on drunkenness as a vice which was the concern only of the person who fell into it, so long as it did not lead him to commit an assault on his neighbours. No thoughtful man any longer looks on it this way.... Here then is a wide-spreading social evil, of which society may, if it will, by a restraining law, to a great extent, rid itself, to the infinite enhancement of the positive freedom enjoyed by its members.
>
> (Green 1881, p. 210)

25 Green's "response" is that the "essential condition" of individual liberty is "that the allowance of that liberty is not, as a rule, and on the whole, an impediment to social good" (Green 1881, pp. 210–11).

26 It would seem as though Mill's criterion would apply equally to the problem of pornography. However, some have argued that, taken in conjunction with his stance in *The Subjection of Women*, Mill would hold that pornography is by its very nature other-regarding and so should be banned. On this issue see especially David Dyzenhaus (1992), Robert Skipper (1993), and Richard Vernon (1996).

27 Thus Mill seems to be making the distinction between norms and values, favoring the former. This distinction is made again by Habermas:

> Recognized norms impose equal and exceptionless obligations on their addressees, while values express the preferability of goods that are striven for by particular groups. Whereas norms are observed in the sense of a fulfillment of generalized behavioral expectations, values or goods can be realized or acquired only by purposive action
>
> (Habermas 1998, p. 55).

28 David Archard (1990) disagrees with Dworkin, arguing that *freedom*, not *autonomy*, is the important principle.

29 Posner also notes this aspect of Mill's moral theory. While the slavery contract is not inconsistent with the argument in *On Liberty*, it is nonetheless contrary to both mid-nineteenth-century British morality and Mill's own moral sense (Posner 1999, pp. 65–7).

30 On this, see especially Mill 1871, Bk. V, Ch. I, sec. 1, p. 795.

31 This provides the rationale for Mill's proposal for proportional voting. While the suffrage would be universal, greater consideration would be given to the more educated in the society, as a means to prevent the uneducated, whom Mill regards as generally incapable of making informed, intelligent choices, from overwhelming the more intellectual and cultured elements. Depending on the profession of the voter – taken as a proxy for level of education – he may be allowed two, three, or more votes, as a reflection of his superior station in society.

32 H. J. McCloskey holds that Mill's purpose in *On Liberty* is to address the question of the proper functions of the State, not with that of the promotion of liberty. Thus Mill provides in this essay a justification for moral legislation so as "to secure and promote goods such as happiness, truth, rational belief, self-perfection, self-direction, moral character, and culture," even at the expense of liberty (McCloskey 1963, p. 155). Alan Ryan upholds the received view, insisting that Mill is concerned with "the individual against all forms of social pressure" (Ryan 1964, p. 254). See also McCloskey's rejoinder (1966).

33 As Nadia Urbinati phrases it, Mill "interpreted socialism as an extension of self-government in the social realm to break the chain of fear and poverty that prevented individuals belonging to 'the subordinated classes' from enjoying liberty as both security and autonomy" (Urbinati 2002, p. 190).

3 Stephen and conservative liberalism

Mill's interpretation of the liberal philosophy has been taken as the fundamental statement of the position as it developed in importance in the mid-nineteenth century, defining the terms of the debate and establishing the conditions for the discussions that followed. Virtually all inquiries into the nature of liberalism over the past century have seen the need to confront Mill's definitions, reconsider his premises, explain his oversights and misconceptions, and re-examine his contradictions and paradoxes.

Yet for all its pretense, the position set forth in *On Liberty* and *Utilitarianism* did not go without comment, even in Mill's time; the prevailing Victorian morality seemed to deny the very points Mill attempted to offer, and those keen on preserving that morality felt compelled to enter the fray. Of all the contemporary critiques of Mill's ethical theory, perhaps the most trenchant is that of Sir James Fitzjames Stephen, Baronet (1829–94),[1] lawyer, legal theorist, noted essayist, Cambridge Apostle, and Judge of the High Court of Justice, Queen's Bench. A pre-eminent legal scholar – his *General View of the Criminal Law* (1863) and *History of the Criminal Law* (1883) are regarded as among the outstanding legal texts of the nineteenth century – Stephen was also a most controversial intellectual whose journalistic output touched on many of the major issues of the day.

In the main, Stephen, despite his objections to Mill's moral philosophy, may be regarded as the quintessential *Victorian* liberal, to the extent that the term Victorian represents not merely a historical epoch, but a perspective on social values and morality. Quite willing to accept the social and political reforms that had transformed British society, he nonetheless became disenchanted with the decline of the culture brought about, in his estimation, by such reforms, as he became apprehensive about the consequences of too great an extension of popular democracy.

What sets Stephen apart from the others with whom we shall deal is his condemnation of the moral relativism he perceived to be inherent in the emerging restatements of both the classical liberal philosophy and the utilitarianism of Bentham. An avowed utilitarian and lifelong liberal – he stood (unsuccessfully) for Parliament as a member of the Liberal Party, and even rejected advances from the Conservative Party, when such an alliance might have gained for him the seat he coveted – he perceived himself as of the old school, much as Burke had perceived himself an old Whig seeking to return the new generation to the right path. Mill and others had diminished the liberal philosophy by minimizing the significance of morality, culture, and religion, and had cheapened the utilitarian doctrine by eliminating those elements explicitly recognized by earlier writers as conducive to social cohesion. Bentham had been altered almost beyond all recognition, his philosophy reinterpreted to give substance to positions which he would never have countenanced. Someone had to set the record right, and Stephen took up the task.

It is to an examination of Stephen's reconstituted liberalism and Utilitarianism that we now turn.

Society defined

As with Mill, we must begin our investigation into the social philosophy of Stephen by inquiring as to the circumstances by which men enter into social relations. This requires an examination of the notion of society. It is here that we see two apparently discordant philosophies reconciled. In Stephen's understanding of the concept, society is "the name of men considered in their social relations to each other" (Stephen 1863a, p. 34) or, alternatively, "the name of men as they stand related to each other by the benevolent affections" (p. 39). "Society" is then nominal, not real. In its characterization as a product of the benevolent affections, we see shades of the moral philosophers of the Scottish Enlightenment, especially of David Hume and Adam Smith. Social relations are positive in nature and as such are to be distinguished from those duties, "founded partly on fear, partly on respect for superiors, and partly on all the various feelings which are included under the word self-interest," especially as self-interest is taken to apply to "the wish, which every one ought to feel, to see his own character developed upon as large and good a scale as possible" (p. 35). These contrary duties – moral, legal, and religious – are negative in character, and so adherence to them may be enforced by the recognized dominant authority. The function of society as indicative of positive social relations is merely to act in concert with and as a complement to the institutional arrangements – religion, law, science, government – so as "to do so much of what they leave undone as will not interfere with their being efficiently conducted" (p. 39).

While sympathetic to the perspectives of Smith and Hume, Stephen evinces as well a solidarity with the moral philosophy of Hobbes. It is through his reading of Hobbes that Stephen comes to his views on the nature of man and society. Society does not emerge as the result of mutual cooperation through a realization of common bonds of sympathy and benevolence, but through an understanding that rules governing conduct are essential to the maintenance of social order and to the preservation of individual liberty. Specifically, with Hobbes, Stephen holds liberty to be a "negative idea," i.e., it is defined not with respect to enumerated rights, but rather emerges as the absence of restraint: justice inheres in the fulfillment of the law, and so one is free to engage in a particular course of conduct only so long as and to the extent that the State does not expressly prohibit the acts in question from being taken. Liberty is defined with respect to this understanding.[2] It is law which sets the parameters to individual liberty. As with Hobbes, Stephen sees these restrictions as essential to order, and even views such restrictions not as destructive of liberty and individual rights, but as supportive and affirming.

The errors of Mill

Mill's "dogma" of liberty

Stephen, in spite of what will be seen as his evident disagreement with Mill's refinement of liberalism and Utilitarianism, does not find distasteful the whole of Mill's philosophy. There is in fact much in Mill to admire, much in his analysis of individual liberty and social structure that is appealing. In his 1859 review of *On Liberty*, Stephen actually appraises the book on the whole quite charitably:

> Our agreement with the general tone of the book is so complete, and it coincides so entirely with the temper of mind in respect to political institutions and to customary social law which we have uniformly advocated, that we feel disposed rather to congratulate ourselves on being able to claim the sanction of so great a name for opinions which we have maintained in such various forms, and with reference to so many different subjects, than to praise the wisdom or the truth of the opinions themselves.
>
> (Stephen 1859, p. 186)

By the time he comes to prepare *Liberty, Equality, Fraternity* (1873; 2nd edn 1874), however, Stephen changes his perspective on Mill, at least with respect to certain *details* of his philosophy. Here he comes to consider the full range of Mill's work, and finds it wanting. While he expresses his agreement with "the greater part of the contents" of Mill's *A System of Logic* and *Principles of Political Economy*, esteeming them as efforts of great note, all the while Stephen feels the need "to dissent in the strongest way from the view of human nature and human affairs" that he finds in *On Liberty, Utilitarianism*, and *The Subjection of Women* (Stephen 1874, pp. 53–4). The early works – being more polished treatises – present a perfectly adequate explication of the liberal position as they account for the place of the individual in society; the latter works – more in the nature of essays than formal discourses – represent a strident defense of a reconstituted and morally neutral liberal ethos, in Stephen's estimation so thoroughly at odds with the reasoned positions of Mill's earlier statements of liberal principles, as to "afford excellent illustrations of the forms of the doctrines of equality and fraternity to which I object" (p. 54).[3]

The specific target of Stephen's attack on Mill is what he perceives as Mill's "religious dogma of liberty" (Stephen 1874, p. 54). Mill's system is inherently flawed because he insists upon arguing not by proof but by assertion: he seeks not to *derive* his principle of liberty, but finds it reasonable to *assert* it as an axiom upon which the rest of his political and moral philosophy must rest. Stephen will have none of this dogmatic formulation, and desires to demonstrate the validity of his own view by offering just such a demonstrative proof. In an attempt to define liberty (or at least to discern some necessary principles which underlie the concept) and to delineate certain commonalities between his understanding of the term and Mill's, Stephen submits that all "voluntary" actions are at bottom motivated by "hope and fear, pleasure and pain." Those acts motivated by hope are free acts, those motivated by fear are compulsory and, further, all morality is merely an appeal to these motivations (p. 57). Liberty in the sense of Mill is reflected only in those free acts motivated by hope and pleasure, and not in those acts motivated by fear and pain. Given this characterization of liberty, which Stephen insists is accepted by Mill, it then follows that no person may attempt to affect the conduct of another by appealing to his fears "except for the sake of self-protection" and, in the more general case, society may not similarly employ such tactics in an attempt to promote the general happiness (p. 57). To do so would violate individual liberty, as it would compel action and not allow it to be taken freely.

Yet Stephen sees in this (to him) somewhat peculiar depiction of liberty a striking and disturbing paradox, to wit, that morality is nothing if not "an appeal either to hope or fear" with an end to affecting conduct, "an engine of prohibition" far more important and wide-ranging than even the criminal law (Stephen 1874, p. 57). Mill's definition relies only on the *positive* motivations, clearly not as efficacious in affecting the conduct as are the *negative* motivations. The moral sanction (fear of disapprobation), the religious sanction ("fear of punishment in a future state of existence"), and the "conscientious" sanction (a combination of the moral and religious sanctions, the appeal to one's own conscience) all serve as restraints on actions far more powerful in their effect than any criminal sanctions, and thus obviously influence conduct to a much greater extent than a mere allowance of positive excitations (p. 57). More importantly, these sanctions are independent of the self-protection exemption, as they demonstrate "in the highest degree" an overall intolerance of evil (p. 58).

Now, according to Stephen, Mill seems to dismiss such devices as "essentially immoral and mischievous" (or at least the general tenor of his remarks would indicate a predisposition to such an attitude); Mill's standard would deny "that there are a court and a judge in which, and before whom, every man must give an account of every work done in the body, whether self-regarding or not," and by extension would label as a tyrant the God who sought to punish "except for the purpose of protecting others" (Stephen 1874, p. 58). Thus Stephen suggests that, in his articulation in *On Liberty* of the liberty principle – which Stephen sums up in the phrase "Let every man please himself without hurting his neighbour" – Mill in effect advances a doctrine that, if followed as a general guide to conduct, would lead to the rejection of all systems of morality. Morality – "positive morality" – Stephen asserts "is nothing but a body of principles and rules more or less vaguely expressed, and more or less left to be understood, by which certain lines of conduct are forbidden under the penalty of general disapprobation," and this principle is valid "quite irrespectively of self-protection" (p. 58). Before we assign praise or blame to any action, we must be assured that the action is taken willingly and is not simply an "occurrence" or a response to threat. If the act is taken willingly and without coercion, we may then assign the appropriate measure of approbation or disapprobation (Stephen 1861, pp. 677–8).

With this conception of morality Stephen admits Mill is in substantial agreement, except in so far as constraint enters into the formula. As we have seen, Mill is concerned to establish a protective sphere for that personal conduct having no external consequence, and so it is critical to the advancement of the individual that he be, to the greatest extent possible, free of restraint in those actions that affect him alone. By contrast, Stephen is adamant about the need for some sort of sanction for conduct deemed beyond the bounds of acceptability. In his view, as "morality is and must be a prohibitive system," it is essential that the moral code "impose upon every one a standard of conduct and of sentiment to which few persons would conform if it were not for the constraint thus put upon them," a constraint "far beyond anything that can be described as the purposes of self-protection" (Stephen 1874, p. 59). Mill's mistake is in not perceiving that his very approach "is violated not only by every system of theology which concerns itself with morals, and by every known system of positive morality, but by the constitution of human nature itself" (p. 59). Stephen is thus not prepared to limit the efficacy of constraint to other-regarding acts, for to do so would commit him to accept Mill's limited approach. Rather, he desires its general application to the promotion of the overall moral betterment of society. He regards it as essential to the life of the individual that he "be restrained and compelled by circumstances in nearly every action," a conclusion derived from his belief that "good" habits can only be "acquired by a series of more or less painful and laborious acts" (p. 59). There are no self-regarding acts; every individual action has *some* external consequence, even if that consequence is merely an affront to the socially accepted morality. To insist, then, as does Mill, that certain acts having no external consequences should be viewed differently from acts for which such consequences are manifest, is to make a distinction without a difference, a distinction between what Mill himself refers to as mere "inconveniences which are strictly inseparable from the unfavourable judgment of others," and those actions "organized, defined, and inflicted upon proof that the circumstances which call for their infliction exist" (p. 59).

It is of course true and well-established "that the restraint which the fear of the disapprobation of others imposes on our conduct is the part of the constitution of nature which we could least afford to dispense with," and to this extent Mill may be correct to focus attention on this aspect of moral coercion (Stephen 1874, p. 60). But, notes Stephen, by drawing a line between conduct the consequences of which redound only to the individual, and conduct having external consequences, Mill is unduly treating "the penal consequences of disapprobation as things to be minimized and restrained within the narrowest limits." In so doing, Mill seeks, perhaps unwittingly, "to diminish very greatly the inconveniences in question," all in the name of protecting and expanding the domain of liberty and freedom. The question, then, in Stephen's mind, is where do we draw this line?

> Strenuously preach and rigorously practise the doctrine that our neighbour's private character is nothing to us, and the number of unfavourable judgments formed, and therefore the number of inconveniences inflicted by them, can be reduced as much as we please, and the province of liberty can be enlarged in a corresponding ratio.
>
> (Stephen 1874, p. 60)

The result of such an extension of private conduct would be "gross licentiousness, monstrous extravagance, ridiculous vanity," in short a coarsening of society, all in the name of furthering "liberty" (Stephen 1874, p. 60).

Human nature

In order better to comprehend Stephen's attitude to Mill, it is necessary to understand his interpretation of Mill's theses. In Stephen's estimation, Mill (in *Utilitarianism*) adopts a principle of morality predicated on the idea of man as a "noble" being, for whom the happiness of others is as important as is his own. After all, Mill himself avers that the utilitarian doctrine, in seeking to promote the general happiness, demands of the individual that he "be as strictly impartial as a disinterested and benevolent spectator," the "ideal perfection of utilitarian morality" being encapsulated in the mantra "To do as you would be done by, and to love your neighbour as yourself" (Mill 1861, p. 401; quoted in Stephen 1874, p. 222). Further, Mill affirms that the foundation of utilitarian morality "is that of the social feelings of mankind – the desire to be in unity with our fellow-creatures," this social feeling being a motivating force

> which tend[s] to become stronger without express inculcation from the influences of advancing civilization. This state is "natural," "necessary," and "habitual to man," "essential to a state of society," "an inseparable part of every person's conception of the state of things which he is born into, and which is the destiny of a human being."
>
> (p. 223)

And so, each member of the society must in his own dealings, by his very nature, take account of the interests of all others.

It is in this context that Stephen articulates his most emphatic disagreement with Mill, as he accuses him of having a too-idealized view of human nature, one predicated on a universally accepted sociality, a sentiment akin to a religious belief. Mill, says Stephen, proceeds on the assumption that the unfettered individual (in some sense akin to Sandel's unencumbered self, with the understanding that Mill actually accepts the social nature of man) is the most capable of advancement in all areas of his existence; he "appears to believe that if men are all freed from restraints and put, as far as possible, on an equal footing, they will naturally trust each other as brothers, and work harmoniously for the common good" (Stephen 1874, p. 226). It is in the very nature of man to seek cooperation, not competition and conflict, to seek the common good, not to seek personal gain at the expense of others.

Such an opinion of human nature demands a sentimentalism not unlike that found in religious doctrines, for it presupposes a "natural feeling for oneself and one's friends," a feeling "sublimated into a general love for the human race" (Stephen 1874, p. 232). On this understanding, man is an inherently virtuous creature, willing at all turns to submerge his egoistic tendencies to the promotion of the social good. Stephen will have none of this utopian sentimentalism, and expresses his disagreement on very Hobbesian terms: "I believe that many men are bad, a vast majority of men indifferent, and many good, and that the great mass of indifferent people sway this way or that according to circumstances" (p. 226). Even those who are good "often are compelled to treat each other as enemies either by the existence of conflicting interests which bring them into collision, or by their different ways of conceiving goodness" (p. 226). Conflict is the natural order in human affairs, part of the very constitution of man. The impulse to society is not a natural one; man is not gregarious and encumbered, but is fundamentally self-interested and in need of external influences to compel him to behave socially. It is this understanding of the nature of man that motivates Stephen's desire to fashion institutional structures essential to the preservation of the social order.

The enforcement of morality

The need for coercion

It is because human nature is of such a Hobbesian character that "every emotion has to be regulated with reference to all the rest, if it is to be beneficial." Why must this be so? Stephen offers three reasons: (1) emotions are "painful or pleasant," (2) the experience of certain emotions "produces permanent secondary effects on the character," and (3) the emotions themselves may be so overwhelming in their influence as actually to determine conduct. So significant are the emotions in informing conduct that, in Stephen's view, all other influences – "reason, habits, laws, religious, moral and social checks" – act merely as restraints on conduct (Stephen 1864, pp. 69–70). Thus we see Hume's well-worn dictum – "Reason is, and ought only to be the slave of the passions, and can never pretend to any other office than to serve and obey them" (Hume 1739/40, p. 462) – resurrected in support of a moral philosophy justifying external restraints on conduct.

Morality is not manifest in a moral sense, but "is a system of rules affecting human conduct," its object being the furtherance of the general happiness (Stephen 1867, p. 502). The community has a direct interest in elevating virtuous conduct by insuring that the emotions of the individuals comprising it are held in check by appropriate means.[4] More importantly, the community has an interest in seeing to the overall development of the moral character of its members. The question then revolves around the most appropriate means to this development. For Stephen, the answer lies in the unceasing stimulation of "exertion" or perseverance in the face of adversity and restraint, which is itself "the greatest of all invigorators of character" (Stephen 1874, p. 81). Exertion promotes those virtues essential to the maintenance of a moral society, as each member is driven to overcome obstacles in the way of his objectives, and by so doing is in his character shaped and molded by the process. The greater the degree of exertion, the greater will be the extent of the character development; as exertion is lessened, as complacency and safety become the norm, so there results a diminution in "originality and resource" (p. 81). Mill's desire to remove all obstacles to human development as a means to the formation of moral character may thus be seen as leading as an unintended consequence to the moral disintegration of the society. It seems, then, that pluralism alone is enough to guarantee the failure of Mill's utopia.

This appreciation of the need for coercion is key to an understanding of the general tenor of Stephen's disagreement with Mill. Stephen's issue with Mill on the question of the need for coercion in pursuit of liberty and individual (and hence social) happiness rests on the *meaning* of coercion. Mill insists, says Stephen, that it has been the case throughout history that the wise must rise to accept their roles in ministering to the mediocre elements in the society. With this view Stephen agrees. Yet he cannot accept Mill's argument that this ministering role should be confined to mere guidance and persuasion, and not extended to compulsory obedience for the betterment of these elements and for the betterment of the community. To achieve the desired end of a moral order, compulsion must be allowed legitimacy as a means: so long as "the good obtained overbalances the inconvenience of the compulsion itself," even Mill's Utilitarianism would justify its use (Stephen 1874, pp. 85–6).

Custom and morality as coercive mechanisms

Stephen declares that the primary distinction between Mill's theory of liberty and his own relates to the fact that, while both "agree that the minority are wise and the majority foolish," Mill is unwilling to accept "that the wise minority are ever justified in coercing the foolish majority for their own good" (Stephen 1874, p. 32). Mill advocates popular government through majority rule, as he cautions against the real danger that the majority may seek to impose its will on the minority – this is one of the prime reasons behind his derision of custom, and a chief motivation behind the principle of liberty. Yet he is also aware that the governing class – those controlling wealth and power, those intellectual, religious, and cultural elites considered (by themselves and others) to be the font of social morality – are a privileged minority seeking to impose their norms on the society at large. For Mill, they represent a potential danger to the vast and unenlightened majority, who may be easily manipulated to accept restraints on their liberties to some professed better good.

For Stephen, this position represents one of Mill's most glaring errors. It is precisely because of their positions in society that the religious and cultural elites must exercise an influence over the majority. The wise *must* endeavor to rule, if need be "by persuading an efficient minority to coerce an indifferent and self-indulgent majority" (Stephen 1874, p. 83). Acceptance of this truth is essential if civilization is to continue. The elites are the protectors of the culture and of the social morality, and require the means to ensure the preservation of the culture and the moral code. These means cannot be limited to persuasion alone, if only because of the limitations involved: what is persuasive to some may not be persuasive to others, what persuades in one era may fail to do so in another. Some more restrictive methods may be needed to ensure compliance and continued social cohesion, methods which may interfere with the freedom advocated by Mill, if the social fabric is to remain intact. After all, it is obvious that "restraints on immorality are the main safeguards of society against influences which might be fatal to it," and so they should be embraced, not reviled (p. 60). From this it follows that "religion and morality are and always must be essentially coercive systems" (p. 62).

At this point, it may be instructive to contrast two positions respecting the enforcement of morality, positions addressed by Hart. The first, the "instrumental thesis," is identified with the jurist Patrick Devlin. This "weak" version maintains that the preservation through the law of a shared social morality is essential to the maintenance of an ordered society. The very idea of a social community is unsustainable in the absence of a mechanism to further the recognition of moral codes. Each member of the society may be compelled to adhere to certain standards of behavior; society is, after all, "a community of ideas, not political ideas alone but also ideas about the way its members should behave and govern their lives" (Devlin 1965, p. 89). It is absolutely essential to the maintenance of the social order that its members conform to such standards. This makes it imperative that, as a means to the enforcement of the shared morality, we recognize the importance of "intolerance, indignation, and disgust," as these "are the forces behind the moral law." So significant are these forces "that if they or something like them are not present, the feelings of society cannot be weighty enough to deprive the individual of freedom of choice" (p. 17).

The second position respecting the enforcement of morality, the "necessitarian thesis," Hart identifies with Stephen. This "strong" version maintains that, while one may accept that an individual action may be condemned as destructive of the shared social morality, independently of whether it actually causes harm to any member of the society, it is not necessary to do so in order to declare an action immoral and hence violative of public law. Here, "the enforcement of morality is regarded as a thing of value" in and of itself, independently of its actual effects (Hart 1963, p. 49).

In Stephen's view, there are three general categories respecting the legitimate use of coercion: in the establishment of and the maintenance of religion; in the establishment and the maintenance of morality; and in the alteration of existing institutional forms (Stephen 1874, p. 61). Moral and religious coercion Stephen conceives as absolutely essential as socializing influences; they are so completely intertwined that, while for taxonomic reasons he accounts them distinct, for all intents and purposes they may be viewed as inseparable. Religion is a most powerful motive to virtue. Morality and our sense of duty in the end depend upon religion, not upon the nature of man; more so, they depend upon the *right* religion, so that "morality is good if it is founded on a true estimate of the consequences of human actions" (Stephen 1874, p. 333). These two forms of coercion – morals and religion – are so overwhelmingly important that they serve as the basis for the formation of social customs, and even become ingrained in the individual and social consciences. While he later amended his views on the significance of religious belief to the functioning of society, he nonetheless continued to assign it an important role as an instrument in the formation of the social consciousness; its validity is not at issue, only the fact of its influence in promoting the virtues of benevolence and justice, virtues essential to the good society.[5] The mere fact that someone may refrain from conduct held to be immoral or licentious by others in the society is evidence of the force of this custom in forming social behaviors.

The question then becomes one of the *source* of this custom. For Stephen, the answer is clear: the source rests with a dominant minority which imposes its will on the majority. The fear of disapprobation evident in the appeal to conscience "could never have become customary unless it had been imposed upon mankind at large by persons who themselves felt it with exceptional energy, and who were in a position which enabled them to make other people adopt their principles and even their tastes and feelings" (Stephen 1874, p. 63). All religion and morality developed in this manner, through some form of force, "until the new creed has become sufficiently influential and sufficiently well organised to exercise power both over its own members and beyond its own sphere" (p. 63). The customs associated with religion and with systems of morality that have come to be accepted as regulators of conduct are all "restraints imposed by the will of an exceedingly small numerical minority and contentedly accepted by a majority to which they have become so natural that they do not recognise them as restraints" (p. 64).

In like measure, all political and social change has been the result of force and compulsion, not the outcome of a popular movement or a mass urge to cooperate to effect some common end. To argue otherwise is to ignore the historical record. Even parliamentary democracy, typically regarded as the most highly developed form of governance, "is simply a mild and disguised form of compulsion," for although there is a general agreement "to try strength by counting heads instead of breaking heads," in the end "the principle is exactly the same" (Stephen 1874, p. 70). Coercion is thus justifiable to an extent that even Mill would have to accept. Yet Mill's system of liberty affords little place for coercion and force beyond the limited area of self-preservation and this, suggests Stephen, represents a fatal flaw. To attempt to extend the principle without radical alteration presents insurmountable difficulties. To argue, for instance, that revolutionary action which results in a demonstrably superior state of affairs can be characterized as a form of self-protection, and so justified within Mill's system as a valid form of coercion, "reduces the principle to an absurdity," as then it could justify force and violence as a remedy to *any* state of affairs with which someone had become disenchanted (p. 66). This suggests that Mill's principle respecting the legitimacy of interference with individual conduct cannot be granted the level of generality he pretends, for, by distinguishing between self-regarding and other-regarding acts, it ignores or minimizes the importance of acts that are *both* self- and other-regarding, In so doing, it "cannot be applied to the very cases in which it is most needed," i.e., it cannot explain the phenomenon of socially efficacious revolutionary change. Instead, as the principle "assumes the existence of an ideal state of things in which everyone has precisely the position which, with a view to the general happiness of the world, he ought to hold," it is only within this ideal state that it has any validity (p. 66).

As the efficacy of coercion is indisputable, Stephen advocates a form of liberalism consistent with this truth. An appeal to popular sentiment, whatever that sentiment may be, is an insufficient and even dangerous foundation upon which to rest liberal democracy; such an appeal represents only half of the liberal project, that of giving voice to the masses. Those most deeply concerned with the continued existence of such systems of governance must beware of basing their standards on an appeal to "casual public opinions and slight and ineffectual public sentiments" (Stephen 1862, p. 80). They need also concern themselves with the flourishing of the citizenry itself, "raising thereby the general tone of public life," and as a result "causing it to be pervaded by a higher conception of the objects of national existence" (p. 73). The true mark of the liberal is one "who recognize[s] the claims of thought and learning, and of those enlarged views of men and institutions which are derived from them, to a permanent preponderating influence in all the great affairs of life" (p. 80). If he is to be true to the creed, the liberal must acknowledge and accept that

> [t]he highest function which the great mass of mankind could ever be fitted to perform, if the highest dreams of the most enlightened philanthropists were fully realized, would be that of recognizing the moral and intellectual superiority of the few who, in virtue of a happy combination of personal gifts with accidental advantages, ought to be regarded as their natural leaders, and of following their guidance, not slavishly but willingly, and with an intelligent co-operation.
>
> (Stephen 1862, p. 80)

The conclusion is evident, that the true liberal must realize that "the wise minority are the rightful masters of the foolish majority," and they, as the leaders of this minority, should willingly accept this role (Stephen 1874, p. 32).[6]

Coercion and civil law

For Stephen, the civil law has a valid role to play in the promotion of morality and virtue. There are certain acts that are of their very nature inherently immoral, irrespective of whether the consequences of such acts are confined to the actor. As morality is manifest in the rules of the society, it is incumbent upon society to employ the law as a means to the enforcement of morality, with the aim of deterring those acts deemed offensive to the community's notions of decency and right. It is in fact "easy to show that nearly every branch of civil law assumes the existence of a standard of moral good and evil which the public at large have an interest in maintaining, and in many cases enforcing," a position, he quickly adds, "which is diametrically opposed to Mr Mill's fundamental principles" (Stephen 1874, p. 155).

In support of his contention, Stephen maintains as a predicate that, while rights and duties fall chiefly within the province of the law, implicit in the definitions of these rights and duties is a theory of morals. One cannot begin to comprehend any system of law absent a consideration of the moral code which must antedate and inform it, and which thus serves as the foundation upon which the edifice is erected. To make his point Stephen offers the cases of contract, marriage and inheritance, and education. It seems rather obvious that no society would seek to enforce a contract that required the performance of an immoral act, or one that was predicated on an immoral stand; in favoring the institution of marriage, "the foundation of civilized society," laws governing the legal status, in terms of inheritance, of bastard children, while harsh, are nonetheless morally legitimate and right; in education, moral principles are essential – they represent "a standard by which the conduct of individuals may be tried, and to which they are in a variety of ways, direct and indirect, compelled to conform" – and so the State has an ethical duty to inculcate in the youth of society these standards of conduct and behavior (Stephen 1874, pp. 156–7).

As morality informs the civil law, and the law then tends to its enforcement, so should the weight of public opinion be called into service to the same end. It is in this context that Stephen takes up the issue of respectability. Public approval is essential to the continuation of society; to gain such approval, i.e., to be socially respectable, means

> to come up to that most real, though very indefinite standard of goodness, the attainment of which is exacted of every one as a condition of being allowed to associate upon terms of ostensible equality with the rest of the human race.
> (Stephen 1863b, p. 282)

Stephen is not willing to accept Mill's charge "that the coercive influence of public opinion ought to be exercised only for self-protective purposes." Such a position ignores the inherent social nature of public opinion, and is analogous to "telling a rose that it ought to smell sweet only for the purpose of affording pleasure to the owner of the ground in which it grows" (Stephen 1874, p. 158). Public opinion is of its very nature a powerful and potentially coercive influence on individual conduct. In Stephen's estimation, the *source* of this opinion is quite irrelevant, so long as one recognizes it as a legitimate and at times an overwhelming force for acceptance or for condemnation.

Opinion can indeed be capricious, and as a means of restraint it is certainly open to abuse. Acknowledging the potential for abuse, Stephen – always suspicious of the potential excesses of majoritarianism – places limits on the degree to which both the law and public opinion may legitimately interfere with individual conduct. Briefly, the law and public opinion: (1) must not interfere with those acts which are of no serious consequence, i.e., acts for which the consequences to the society as a whole are of no great import; (2) must proceed in any efforts on the basis of clear and demonstrable evidence, not on suspicion or surmise; (3) must correspond to the existing social, cultural, and moral climates, i.e., the law must not be employed in the service of a morality which does not at the time exist or for which there is no public acceptance; and (4) must at all turns seek to protect privacy, i.e., to allow that there is in fact a sphere surrounding each person within which the law and public opinion must not intrude (Stephen 1874, pp. 159–62).

One may note in this last restriction a similarity to the position of Mill. This is not insignificant. Stephen is perfectly willing to accept what appear to be limits Mill himself places on the degree to which the law and public opinion may interfere with individual, self-regarding conduct; he even warns of the dangers inherent in such attempts:

> To try to regulate the internal affairs of a family, the relations of love or friendship, or many other things of the same sort, by law or by the coercion of public opinion, is like trying to pull an eyelash out of a man's eye with a pair of tongs. They may put out the eye, but they will never get hold of the eyelash.
>
> (Stephen 1874, p. 162)

But there is a difference between the sphere established by Stephen and that established by Mill. Mill's principle, if taken at face value, would appear to leave little if any role for legitimate interference or the coercion of public opinion in conduct offensive to the standards of the community, so long as that conduct can be construed as self-regarding. To Stephen, this is an unacceptable standard which, if followed, would coarsen the society. Granted, the role of public opinion may be capricious. Nonetheless, its employment as a tool of moral enforcement is essential to the maintenance of a good society:

> If people neither formed nor expressed any opinions on their neighbours' conduct except in so far as that conduct affected them personally, one of the principal motives to do well and one of the principal restraints from doing ill would be withdrawn from the world.
>
> (Stephen 1874, pp. 162–3)

Assignability and punishment

In opposition to Mill's rejection of the doctrine of "social rights," Stephen affirms a decidedly conservative and even communitarian position, maintaining as an indisputable fact "that every human creature is deeply interested not only in the conduct, but in the thoughts, feelings, and opinions of millions of persons who stand in no other assignable relation to him than that of being his fellow-creatures" (Stephen 1874, p. 139). Mill does of course allow that, in those instances in which an act that had been classed as self-regarding can be shown to have violated another's protected sphere, the person committing the act may be subjected to sanctions. Yet he maintains that an act which causes "contingent, or … constructive injury," so long as the conduct "neither violates any specific duty to the public, nor occasions perceptible hurt to any assignable individual except himself," should not be the subject of disapprobation (p. 140).

Mill's argument seems to imply that assignability is a criterion in motivating the legitimate use of punishment: an act may be subject to sanction only if it can be demonstrated to have inflicted injury or harm to another. Stephen does of course accept that, especially in respect of the criminal law, this is a valid point: before a person can be called to account for a criminal act, there must be evidence that indeed such an act has occurred. Stephen finds it extraordinary, however, that Mill would apply this as the *sole* criterion. Absent a finding of constructive injury and assignable blame, Mill rejects the invocation of any legal sanction. More importantly, he rejects the invocation of any *moral* sanction as well. To attempt to apply moral coercion to a person who has committed acts that clearly are an affront to common decency, but that have otherwise no demonstrable or assignable effects (i.e., the action cannot be said to have caused any *particular* person to have suffered any *particular* loss), is to Mill an affront to liberty. While it may be appropriate to cajole, to condemn in forceful terms, to make it clear to others that certain conduct is unacceptable in a civil society, it can never to a true Millian be acceptable to invoke the force of moral sanction against such conduct (Stephen 1874, p. 141).

Stephen especially takes issue with the position of Mill that, if some in the society undertake to commit grossly reprehensible acts, it must be in some measure the fault of society as a whole for not inculcating in them a sufficient respect for social values, and with failing to instruct them in rational deliberation, and so to effect a punishment would be a violation of simple justice. It simply does not follow that, because society has failed in its educative function, those who commit offenses should be excused from suffering the consequences of their actions. "It is illogical, for it does not follow that because society caused a fault it is not to punish it" (Stephen 1874, p. 142). To insist as does Mill that through education alone society might continually advance, making each generation morally better than the last, is to exaggerate its power and its effectiveness. There are and always will be some incorrigible elements in every society, and no amount of education or moral training will serve to alter their constitutions. "Society cannot make silk purses out of sows' ears, and there are plenty of ears in the world which no tanning can turn even into serviceable pigskin" (p. 142).

A chief difficulty with Mill's moral philosophy, notes Stephen, involves a tension between his conclusions in *On Liberty* respecting interference with the personal sphere, and certain passages in *Utilitarianism* suggesting a role for moral sanction. Mill's statements in *Utilitarianism* regarding inappropriate or wrong conduct

> We do not call anything wrong, unless we mean to imply that a person ought to be punished in some way or other for doing it: if not by law, by the

opinion of his fellow creatures; if not by opinion, by the reproaches of his own conscience.

(Mill 1861, p. 663; quoted in Stephen 1874, p. 143)

and the nature of justice

> The sentiment of justice ... is ... the natural feeling of retaliation or vengeance, rendered by intellect and sympathy applicable to those injuries ... which wound us through, or in common with, society at large. This sentiment, in itself, has nothing moral in it; what is moral is, the exclusive subordination of it to the social sympathies, so as to wait on and obey their call.

(Mill 1861, p. 665; quoted in Stephen 1874, p. 143)

seem to be in conflict with his professed position in *On Liberty* that punishment and coercion be limited to circumstances of self-protection, that we ought not to interfere with conduct productive of no external consequence.

Stephen himself expresses a qualified agreement with the Mill of *Utilitarianism*, with the position that the moral sanction is an appropriate restraint on actions deemed detrimental to the common good. Yet to inject these passages into the message of *On Liberty* would be to dilute its message, to convert it into an essay on the efficacy of the criminal law. Instead of concluding "that nothing but self-defence can justify the imposition of restraint by public opinion on a man's self-regarding vices" (Stephen 1874, p. 145), the message would become

> [m]en are not justified in imposing *the restraint of criminal law* on each other's conduct except for the purpose of self-protection, but they are justified in restraining each other's conduct by the action of public opinion, not only for the purpose of self-protection, but for the common good, including the good of the persons so restrained.

(p. 144; emphasis in original)

Only the former is consistent with the philosophy of *On Liberty*, to wit, that all interference with the personal sphere is illegitimate when there are no external consequences. While one may wish to believe that Mill, for the sake of consistency alone, would grant legitimacy to moral persuasion, to do so in Stephen's opinion would be to accept that man can indeed distinguish between conduct punishable by criminal sanction and that punishable by moral sanction (p. 145).

Stephen's utilitarianism

The received doctrine

As mentioned above, Stephen embraces the chief tenets of Utilitarianism as a principle by which morality may be tested. A system of morality, the avowed purpose of which is to secure the greatest happiness of the greatest number, has an appeal if only because it seems to provide a scientific basis for the study of human action. Happiness as the test of morality has an intuitive appeal for, after all, it is quite obvious that the pursuit of happiness is the end to which all rational men must strive. With this end affirmed, it is equally obvious that

> some external standard must always be supplied by which moral rules may be tested; and happiness is the most significant and least misleading word that can be employed for that purpose.... A moral system which avowedly had no relation to happiness in any sense of the word would be a mere exercise of ingenuity for which no one would care. I know not on what other footing than that of expediency, generally in a wider or narrower sense, it would be possible to discuss the value of a moral rule or the provisions of a law.
>
> (Stephen 1874, p. 227)

Stephen thus must be held a true believer in the moral philosophy of Utilitarianism. His objection lies with the manner of its elucidation. We have already seen that, while disturbed with what he perceives to be Mill's debasement of certain elements of the doctrine as handed down by Bentham, Stephen is not *completely* dismissive of Mill's interpretation. As Leslie Stephen notes, Fitzjames Stephen esteems Mill, "in his sentimental mood," to have been "a deserter from the proper principles of rigidity and ferocity in which he was brought up," and regards himself as "writing as an orthodox adherent of the earlier school [of Utilitarianism]. He had sat at the feet of Bentham and Austin, and had found the most congenial philosophy in Hobbes" (L. Stephen 1895, p. 308). Stephen is the true disciple of these philosophical giants, the one principled adherent of the true moral doctrine. In Leslie Stephen's view, Fitzjames Stephen, while unabashedly Puritan, nonetheless embodies all the elements of this old school:[7]

> Respect for hard fact, contempt for the mystical and the dreamy; resolute defiance of the *à priori* school who propose to override experience by calling their prejudices intuitions, were the qualities of mind which led him to sympathise so unreservedly with Bentham's legislative theories and with Mill's "Logic." Let us, before all things, be sure that our feet are planted on the solid earth and our reason guided by verifiable experience.
>
> (L. Stephen 1895, p. 309)

Fitzjames Stephen is so enamored of Bentham that he comes to defend him from the ruthless attacks launched by Thomas Carlyle, who, while a personal friend, nonetheless expounds views repugnant to Stephen.[8] In this defense not only of Benthamism but also of democracy, which he sees as twin pillars of a just and moral society, Stephen demonstrates his appreciation of Bentham's portrayal of the "greatest happiness" formula. Specifically, he argues that Bentham's provision of a "pocket definition" of justice predicated on the greatest happiness principle is "the best ... yet propounded," producing results at least as good as those which may have been imposed on an unwilling citizenry by any of Carlyle's "heroes" (Stephen 1865, pp. 790–1). In fact, notes Stephen, in many cases of social reform it has been "the pig philosophers [Carlyle's term for economists and utilitarians], with their dismal science," who have "contributed more to the result than any other body of men in England" (p. 792).[9]

Stephen's ultimately negative position on Bentham's "greatest happiness" formula, and even Mill's proposed alternative, are motivated not by errors of design but, rather, by his contention that they have taken inadequate account of the *reality* of political society. To Stephen, laws and moral rules pertain to act-types, not to specific acts themselves, and so each "must thus, of necessity, be a general proposition, and as such must affect indiscriminately rather than equally the interests of as many persons as are subject to its influence" (Stephen 1874, p. 227). Rules reflect the desire of the legislator to "impose" certain conditions on the governed "either by political power or by the force of argument" (pp. 227–8). It is clear that the rationale behind such enactments is not the promotion of the greatest happiness of the greatest number but is, rather, an effort to impose an ideal structure upon social interactions. In utilitarian parlance, "the happiness which the lawgiver regards as the test of his laws is that which he, after attaching to their wishes whatever weight he thinks proper, wishes his subjects to have, not that which his subjects wish to have" (p. 228). Stephen's view may therefore be termed a utilitarian Hobbesianism, whereby the State exists as a mechanism for the furtherance of a moral political and social order.[10]

Stephen's own redefinition of Mill's standard is thus:

1   The utilitarian standard is not the greatest amount of happiness altogether, … but the widest possible extension of the ideal of life formed *by the person who sets up the standard.* (Stephen 1874, p. 228; emphasis added)
2   [L]aws and moral rules must from the nature of the case be indiscriminate, and must in that sense treat those who are subject to them as equals, but in no other sense than this is it the case that every one's happiness either is or ought to be regarded either by moralists or legislators or by any one else as of equal importance. (p. 231)

It is to an examination of Stephen's redefined standards of Utilitarianism that we now turn.

The nature of the ideal

To motivate the first emendation, Stephen offers that one cannot construct the edifice of morality on such insecure a foundation as happiness, if only because there does not exist one universal *standard* of happiness. As different standards of happiness co-exist, with each person insisting that his personal standard must be the one to which all should adhere, it is not possible to arrive at a universal code of morality upon which all would agree, nor is it acceptable to suggest that those who object to a standard simply do not have the proper understanding to allow them to make the necessary judgment.

The legislator may, in enacting rules governing behavior, consider in his deliberations the wants and desires of the members of the society; Stephen in fact holds that he is obligated to do so, being all the while free "to oppose, counteract, and sometimes even to change them" (Stephen 1874, p. 228). (Moral philosophers, whom Stephen frequently links to legislators, are less bound by a need to consider conceptions of happiness and the good different from their own, and so may rightly erect moral systems on their own personal designs.) As weakness makes possible the erection of a *legal* code, so ignorance can be employed as justification for the authority vested in the *moral* order (p. 228). Both sources coincide, to the extent that, being "conscious of their own weakness and ignorance," men come to "feel that to live without any sort of principle or rule of conduct, to be guided as we suppose animals to be, merely by the impulse of the moment, is morally impossible," leading them "to accept what is prescribed to them by persons who claim authority" (p. 228).

This alternative removes the problem as perceived by Stephen, for it does not rely on the assumption that there exists a single accepted form of happiness, nor does it lead to the contradiction inherent in Bentham that, while each is to count for one, and none for more than one, nevertheless some one conception of happiness ultimately wins out. A concern with the promotion of the greatest happiness of the greatest number, or the egalitarian principle of Bentham, is no longer relevant, since the basis for the moral system lies with the perception of happiness of the legislator as moral philosopher.

Stephen does not, then, object to Utilitarianism as the foundation of an ethical theory, and in fact agrees with Mill on certain very important tenets. Both argue, for instance, that right acts are those which tend to promote the general happiness, and wrong acts are those which tend to diminish it. (See especially Stephen 1874, p. 274.) In terms of the *knowledge* of right and wrong, Stephen in fact accepts – as he suggests nearly all utilitarian writers have – the existence of a conscience, for it is undoubted "that men do pass moral judgments on their own acts and those of other people, that these moral judgments are involuntary when the moral character is once formed" (p. 275). Utilitarian and intuitionist ethical theories are thus not in conflict on the point, the conscience being a device to recognize the tendency of an action to produce happiness (and so promote right) or diminish it (and so promote wrong).

The difference between the utilitarian and the intuitionist (as Mill himself holds) is that the intuitionist sees in the conscience "the ultimate test of right and wrong in the sense of being able to tell us with unerring certainty whether a given action is or is not in accordance with a rule calculated to promote the general happiness of mankind" (Stephen 1874, p. 275). To Stephen this is inadequate, as it cannot provide a means to compute "the balance of motives" (p. 279). It relies on a sense of duty which, while important to utilitarians as "one of the chief sanctions … of morality," is in itself insufficient to the promotion of right conduct; because the force of duty varies with circumstance, "it often is too weak to restrain men from every sort of iniquity, even when it is backed by all the sanctions of religion, conscience, law, and public opinion" (p. 280).

The standard of morality

To motivate the second emendation, Stephen notes the impossibility of the impartial spectator which Mill requires as a "first truth." Self-love is far too important a sympathy in motivating *individual* action to suggest it could ever be "sublimated into a general love for the human race," a position Stephen suggests represents a fundamental point of disagreement between himself and Mill (Stephen 1874, p. 232). By contrast, Stephen relies on obligation and duty to take the place of Mill's (and Bentham's) principle of promoting the general happiness.

It is in this context that Stephen offers his quite interesting rendering of utilitarian morality. Virtue Stephen defines as "the habit of acting upon principles fitted to promote the happiness of men in general, and especially those forms of happiness which have reference to the permanent element in men." This sentiment "is connected with, and will, in the long run, contribute to the individual happiness of those who practise it, and especially to that part of their happiness which is connected with the permanent elements of their nature" (Stephen 1874, pp. 250–1). Virtue is in essence then a "law" imposed on man, and as such implies the existence of certain social relations, to wit, that all members of the society see one another as equals and treat one another as brothers (p. 251); in this sense, "to be virtuous is man's duty" (p. 252). In short, there is then really no distinction between the public interest and the private interest, if only because there is no such thing as a "public interest" to be advanced "as an end in itself." Rather, it is evident that what is typically identified as the public interest – the furtherance of some notion of the social welfare – coincides with the private interest – the pursuit of personal desires – to the extent that the former is internalized in the latter (Stephen 1867, p. 501).

But virtue is only of this nature so long as it is understood and accepted that there exists a future state toward which man is destined and a superior being from whom such law derives, for only then can the law serve as the requisite moral sanction. Without a belief in such transcendence, one no longer has any place for God or Providence as the author of the moral code, and happiness then becomes egoistic fulfillment with morality defined with respect to personal desire. Should this be the case, then in promulgating the laws of society the legislator need seek only to promote his own conception of happiness, not the *general* happiness or the general morality of society, for this is the most that can be forthcoming. It is simply an undeniable fact that "men are so constituted that personal and social motives cannot be distinguished and so do not exist apart" (Stephen 1874, p. 232), and so despite Mill's admonition that justice demands strict impartiality, any ethical theory which does not accept a supreme being as the author of the moral code is lacking in this necessary prerequisite to order. With a belief in Providence and a future state, however, morality takes the form of an inviolable law – religion and morals "having been established ... by word of command" (p. 63) – and this law is virtue, which becomes the duty of man to obey.

Duty then "refers not to the rules of conduct which abnormal individuals may recognize, but to those which are generally recognized by mankind"

(Stephen 1874, p. 279), and it is these rules of social conduct which bind mankind together. The form of this duty must be understood. Stephen does not go so far as to maintain that the individual must succumb to the coercive power of the State or to any other superior, for to do so is *blind submission* to force, not *obedience* to a higher authority. What he does argue is that, following Mill, it is impossible for the individual to function in society without some reference to principles. Rules serve "to prevent certain evils, which always will exist, from rising to a height which would make it impossible for human beings to associate together at all" (Stephen 1863b, pp. 287–8). They do not exist to maintain any given structure of social relations or social classes, nor do they exist for the benefit of any economic order. The rules serve the function of conserving social relations, but are not to be seen as affirming any particular arrangements.

Stephen allows that, as each person in the society "lives to develope [sic] his own faculties, or to benefit his race or nation," he of necessity "subordinates his temporary inclinations to those ends, and raises and purifies his character by doing so" (Stephen 1859, p. 214). Of the utmost importance in this regard is self-control, "the highest and most distinctly human function of life," the mechanism by which each individual accepts his social duty but which "differs as widely as possible from a slavish mechanical submission to superior force." In fact, notes Stephen,

> [w]illing obedience enforced on oneself at all risks, and in the face of any amount of dislike, is the greatest of all agents in ennobling and developing the character, whether it is rendered to a principle or to a person; for it implies action, and action of the most unremitting and various kinds.
>
> (p. 214)

In the same paragraph, just prior to this general statement regarding the efficacy of obedience as a stabilizing influence, Stephen is more specific, as he propounds that it is obedience to *God's will* that is "the highest aim of human existence," which "far from being a slavish one, is the noblest conception of life that any mortal creature can form" (p. 214).[11] Thus is Stephen led to his conclusion that "morality depends upon religion – that is to say, upon the opinions which men entertain as to matters of fact, and particularly as to God and a future state of existence" (Stephen 1874, p. 232).

Justice and the law

Finally, we will briefly review Stephen's position on justice and the law. Justice derives from the impartial application of "benevolent" rules (Stephen 1874, p. 183). It is here that Stephen engages what appears to be a semantic distinction between justice and expediency. While the *misapplication* of a law may be termed unjust, the law itself cannot be so designated, as the law can only in such circumstance be termed inexpedient. The popular designation of a law as just or unjust thus means simply "that it does or does not in fact promote the interests of those whom it affects" (p. 181). Justice then "means the impartial administration of rules (legal or moral) founded on expediency" (p. 182), a concept advanced by Mill and with which Stephen readily concurs.

One cannot then speak of the justness or unjustness of a law or rule absent some consideration of expediency, as it is the impartial *application* of the law or rule which promotes justice. With this Stephen broaches the subject of the "rights of man." Proponents of natural rights argue that, while in ordinary circumstances laws cannot be unjust, only inexpedient, this assertion cannot be made without qualification. Specifically, the rights of man are a special category of rights, existing independently of law, and on this account a law may be termed unjust to the extent that it violates any of these antecedent rights, and inexpedient if it, "without violating them, does more harm that good" (Stephen 1874, p. 183). But if one accepts this doctrine, which Stephen does not, one must also accept that justice and expediency have no necessary connection, and further that law and justice have no necessary relation to utility, an admission Stephen is unwilling to make. All law resolves ultimately into a question of expediency, and the elements of the natural rights school are no exception. For, as Stephen notes, whether God or nature is the "ultimate legislator," the criterion of which we seek and which we label as such is (in the case of God) "the tendency of a rule or law to promote the welfare of men in general" or (in the case of nature) "simply to know how far and on what terms we ... can get what we want." In either case, "each resolves right into general utility" (p. 184).

Thus is Stephen in league on this issue with Bentham. Bentham is emphatic in his condemnation of the very concept of natural rights: "*Natural rights* is simple nonsense: natural and imprescriptible rights, rhetorical nonsense, – nonsense upon stilts" (Bentham 1843, p. 501). Rights cannot exist prior to the existence of government, and so "rights" can only have any meaning as "legal rights." It is in this context that Bentham makes his case for the resolution of rights into utility:

> That in proportion as it is *right* or *proper*, i.e. advantageous to the society in question, that this or that right – a right to this or that effect – should be established and maintained, in that same proportion it is *wrong* that it should be abrogated: but that as there is no *right*, which ought not to be maintained so long as it is upon the whole advantageous to the society that it should be maintained, so there is no right which, when the abolition of it is advantageous to society, should not be abolished. To know whether it would be more for the advantage of society that this or that right should be maintained or abolished, the time at which the question about maintaining or abolishing is proposed, must be given, and the circumstances under which it is proposed to maintain or abolish it; the right itself must be specifically described, not jumbled with an undistinguishable heap of others, under any such vague general terms as property, liberty, and the like.
>
> (Bentham 1843, p. 501; emphasis in original)

Remarks

Mill and Stephen are employed here as faithful representatives of two strains of the liberal philosophy. Mill's "libertarian" liberalism is clearly established, and has been the subject of countless debates since the publication of *On Liberty*. (Can one even begin to address the issues involved in the liberal philosophy without confronting this essay?) As for Stephen, it should be evident from the above why his brand of liberalism deserves the appendage of the adjective "conservative." Russell Kirk assesses *Liberty, Equality and Fraternity* as "the most penetrating defense of conservative values written in Victorian times" (Kirk 1952, p. 564). Consider the following assessment by Richard Posner:

> We modern Millians are apt to be classified as conservatives rather than as liberals because we are not strongly egalitarian ... and oppose various features of the welfare state.... The real conservatives are not the Millians; they are social and religious conservatives and neoconservatives.... They believe with Plato and with Leo Strauss that the state should not be content with protecting property and personal rights and access to education and civic participation all to the end of fostering material prosperity and a climate of free inquiry and debate, of diversity and experimentation (including experiments in living), and a mild benevolence. The state should inculcate virtue, promote piety, punish immorality, discourage hedonism. It is among believers that the state has a moral mission – that the state must know right from wrong and impose its view of the right – that we find the Stephen of *Liberty, Equality, Fraternity*.
>
> (Posner 1995, p. 264)

As Posner sees it, Stephen replaces the three tenets of the French Revolution – Liberty, Equality, Fraternity – with his own "challenge": Power and Restraint, Natural Inequality, Enmity. These are the true bases of the social compact, the true motivations behind social intercourse (Posner 1995, pp. 264–5). Power and Restraint promote virtue and morality, both of which are essential to the maintenance of the good society, while an unfettered Liberty has the potential for debasing the culture, as it inevitably fosters an ever-growing inequality and ultimately reduces the standards of the society to the lowest common denominator; Natural Inequality conduces not only to the stability of the society, but to economic prosperity as well, while concerted attempts at fostering Equality are little better than contrivances masking inherent distinctions among individuals, distinctions which themselves actually serve to the overall betterment of the community; Enmity accepts that not everyone is deserving of respect and affection, and compels all to virtue and self-control as it compels each to make moral demands on others which cannot be sustained by an unconstrained Fraternity, an erroneous understanding that all men are brothers who strive for a virtuous life and the pursuit of the common good.[12]

Posner, rightly or wrongly, esteems Stephen a neoconservative, a term that was originally coined to apply to a group of dispossessed American political and social thinkers (primarily Marxists and Trotskyites) who had become disillusioned with the excesses of the welfare state and the preachings of the American left, but which seems to have taken on a prominence all its own. Yet, in applying the term to Stephen, there is a danger of minimizing the importance in Stephen's own mind of the individual and his place in society. Stephen does, after all, propound an *individualist* ontology, not a *social* one, and so would seem out of place in the conservative ranks (as defined in Chapter I).

Stephen of course does hold to the view which Posner assigns to him. We have only to note Stephen's "emphasis on force rather than on consent, tradition, inertia, or mutual advantage as the cement of society implied to him a natural and radical inequality among persons." The sentiment that there *must*, in any society, "be an elite to wield the lash, and hence a division between masters and slaves," gives Stephen's outlook a Marxist and even Weberian tint, with shades of Carlyle, as it emphasizes the contention "that Mill-style bourgeois liberty amplifies rather than mitigates the consequences of inequality" (Posner 1995, p. 267). Yet we should not take the comparisons too far. Stephen is neither Marx nor Veblen (as to Carlyle, we shall withhold judgment). While there are some points of similarity, the differences are much more significant. An important distinction centers on the appropriate ontology: as Marxism demands a *social* and not an *individual* perspective, class relations for Marx are *real* and not *nominal*, and class is reified. Stephen's position is quite different. For Stephen, his professed liberalism recognizes the individual as the basic unit of account, as his professed Hobbesianism supports the understanding that man is not an inherently social creature, but rather one capable of *being* socialized. It is for society and the institutional arrangements therein to see to this socialization.

But this must not be construed as suggestive of the reification of society. As does Mill, Stephen interprets society as merely a term applying to the relations of individuals to one another, and thus socialization means simply the promotion of an attitude or demeanor in harmony with the interests of the whole. "Society" or "community" has no demands on the individual independent of or superior to the identified interests of those comprising the collective. This understanding of society, however, represents but one of the ways in which liberalism deals with the concept. In an effort to elucidate an alternative meaning, we must next turn to an appreciation of the important work of Herbert Spencer.

Notes

1   As a biographical curiosity, note that Sir James Fitzjames Stephen was the son of Sir James Stephen (1789–1859), barrister, historian, and under-secretary for the colonies. He in turn was the son of James Stephen (1758–1832), who was the son of James Stephen (?1733–?). His family tree also includes such notable families as Arnold, Macaulay, Strachey, and Thackeray. On Stephen's lineage, see Leslie Stephen (1895) and K. J. M. Smith (1988).

2   The distinction between positive and negative liberty is perhaps most clearly expressed by Isaiah Berlin. See especially *Four Essays on Liberty* (New York: Oxford University Press, 1969).

3   It should be noted that, even in his *Principles of Political Economy*, Mill presents a case for liberty and the liberal ethic not distinct from that in *On Liberty*.

4   "Men whose passions are so regulated and proportioned as habitually to cause them to observe or break the rules of morality are virtuous or vicious men respectively" (Stephen 1867, p. 502).

5   Stephen's limited recantation of the significance of religious belief can be found in "The Unknowable and the Unknown" (1884).
6   Stephen proposes that the true liberal politician would exhort the population to engage in political activity in the manner of a lord grooming a potential heir.

> [H]e would teach those whom he addressed to see in the institutions of their native land neither a prison to escape from nor a fortress to storm, but a stately and venerable mansion which for eight centuries had been the home of their ancestors, and in which they were now to take their place and play their part. He would try to fix their attention, not on the petty side of institutions, which little men can always think of in a petty spirit, but on their dignified aspects; and he would show them how that dignity was, in a vitally important sense, their own.
>
> (Stephen 1862, p. 75).

7   Leslie Stephen observes that the marriage of Puritanism and Utilitarianism was not at the time "strange or unusual." Both "were allied in the attack upon slavery, in the advocacy of educational reforms, and in many philanthropic movements ..." In addition, "[a] common antipathy to sacerdotalism brought the two parties together in some directions, and the Protestant theory of the right of private judgment was in substance a narrower version of the rationalist demand for freedom of thought" (L. Stephen 1895, p. 309).
8   "Carlyle's teachings were connected with erroneous theories indeed, and too little guided by practical experience. But the general temper which they showed, the contempt for slovenly, haphazard, hand-to-mouth modes of legislation, the love of vigorous administration on broad, intelligible principles, entirely expressed his own feeling" (L. Stephen 1895, p. 315).
9   Carlyle had coined the term "dismal science" to apply to those political economists such as Mill who had sided with the abolitionists and the evangelists in the debate on black emancipation. See especially the excellent book by David Levy (2001). Carlyle and Stephen had been on opposite sides in the Governor Eyre controversy, with Carlyle supporting the actions of Eyre in ruthlessly suppressing the revolt, and Stephen, who is said to have been sympathetic to Eyre, serving as the legal representative of the Jamaica Committee seeking his prosecution.
10   One biographer, James Colaiaco, refers to Stephen as "a Hobbes of the nineteenth century" (Colaiaco 1983, p. 27).
11   The reader may note that Stephen commends that "the highest function which the great mass of mankind could ever be fitted to perform" is the recognition of "the moral and intellectual superiority of the few" (Stephen 1862, p. 80), while "the highest aim of human existence" is the obedience to God's will (1859, p. 214).
12   On this aspect of Stephen's thought, see John Roach (1957), especially pp. 66–9, and Benjamin Lippincott (1938), especially pp. 144–55.

4 Spencer and the evolution of moral society

Herbert Spencer (1820–1903) is one of the more interesting characters in our story, as he is one of the more improbable figures with whom we shall deal. William James appraises him as "the philosopher of vastness," and "the philosopher whom those who have no other philosopher can appreciate" (James 1904, p. 104).[1] One of the most prolific of nineteenth-century writers on nearly all matters of scientific and social scientific interest, he is perhaps best known as the expositor of a theory of evolution rivaling that of his contemporary Charles Darwin; in terms of priority, Spencer actually published his essay "Development Hypothesis" seven years *before* Darwin published *Origin of Species*. Spencer's influence was in fact so great and his stature so immense that through the latter half of the nineteenth century he actually eclipsed Darwin; after considerable review, Darwin (at the behest of Alfred Russel Wallace) eventually incorporated Spencer's phrase "survival of the fittest" in the second edition of *Origin of Species*, and his use of the term "evolution" in the sixth.[2]

For Spencer, evolution becomes *the* essential organizing principle, and the accompanying terminology plays a significant role in his extrascientific work. Yet, while "survival of the fittest" may have some relevance to a theory of *biological* evolution,[3] it was Spencer's use of the phrase in respect of *social* evolutionary development that was to cause alarm. For using it in such a context he has even to the present been (rightly or wrongly) branded a Social Darwinist,[4] a pejorative label that is so telling and has had such staying power that many find it unnecessary any longer to read Spencer's works in order to pretend to "know" his social philosophy.

It will be argued here that the popular apprehension of Spencer is actually a caricature, based on selective citation with little if any appreciation of his larger work. Where his work is actually cited, the citations rarely move beyond the popular *The Man Versus the State*, a polemic written as a libertarian manifesto. The problem is that even this popular work assumes some appreciation of Spencer's *oeuvre*, specifically *Principles of Psychology*, *Principles of Sociology*, and *Principles of Ethics*, each an exhaustive survey of the field, composed around Spencer's peculiar understanding of the theory of evolution.

The ethical realm

Conduct defined

The Principles of Ethics represents Spencer's most complete statement of the conditions underlying the moral social order; James attests to the importance of this work in his observation that here "in general breathes the purest English spirit of liberty" (James 1904, p. 107). For Spencer, conduct "is an organic whole – an aggregate of interdependent actions performed by an organism." Yet a significant qualification is in order: conduct is not to be generalized to apply to *all* actions, but rather is confined to "acts adjusted to ends," and so excludes actions to which a purpose cannot be ascribed (Spencer 1897, §2).

Just as not all actions are identified with conduct, so not all conduct is to be subsumed under the heading of ethics. The everyday actions we undertake are typically associated with means or ends that are "ethically indifferent," i.e., one cannot ascribe to them any quality of good or bad. The desires to read a book, to eat dinner, to go to work, to vacation at the beach, are all associated with ends that have no ethical content; the decision to walk instead of ride, to drive to a destination instead of fly, are associated with means that are likewise ethically neutral. Yet it is just as obvious that the transition from ethically neutral conduct to ethically imbued conduct is gradual and imperceptible (Spencer 1897, §2). If an act is associated with more than a single end or means, to which may be made a comparison in terms of better and worse according as they succeed or fail in fulfilling their prescribed role, then the ethical component becomes clear. For the sake of one's health, it may, from an ethical standpoint, be better to walk than to ride; if one needs to keep an appointment in another town, flying may provide an ethically better means. The terms good and bad then may be applied to objects and actions in respect of their efficiency, i.e., "according as they are well or ill adapted to achieve prescribed ends" (§8). As flying achieves the end more efficiently than driving, the former may be termed good, the latter bad.

From this depiction of good and bad we may assess conduct. Immoral conduct is characterized by excess and a lack of restraint, a quality suggesting "extreme divergences of actions from some medium," subject to "great and incalculable oscillations." Such conduct is abnormal and socially deviant, diverging considerably from the mean of conduct deemed acceptable in the society; this anti-social behavior is ethically bad in that it threatens to interfere with the smooth functioning of the society as a whole. Moral conduct, by contrast, is characterized by "maintenance of the medium," such that "the oscillations fall within narrower limits"; it is conduct consistent with the values and the temperament of the community, conduct that promotes social stability and social cohesion. Moral conduct implies conscientiousness, and equitability and judiciousness in dealings; the moral agent in his relations with others "adjusts his acts to their deserts" and "portions out his aid with discrimination instead of distributing it indiscriminately to good and bad, as do those who have no adequate sense of their social responsibilities" (Spencer 1897, §26).

Moral conduct conduces to the advancement of civilization; it is descriptive of the behavior and the attitudes of man in society. One may envision Spencer accepting Émile Durkheim's observation that man's morality is a consequence of his being in society, "since morality consists in solidarity with the group, and varies according to that solidarity. Cause all social life to vanish, and moral life would vanish at the same time, having no object to cling to" (Durkheim 1893, p. 331).[5] This is not to imply that as a species man tends to become more homogeneous with respect to moral development as civilization progresses. In fact, and as the ethical counterpart to his theory of evolutionary development, Spencer regards it as a necessary attribute of the moral agent that, with the advancement of civilization, the activities of the individual become *more* varied, *more* heterogeneous – "increasing diversity in the sets of external motions and combined sets of such motions."[6] This is especially evident in respect of social intercourse. As social relations become more complex, so the social processes underlying these relations become more "multiform," and the duties and obligations of each individual become more complex and heterogeneous (Spencer 1897, §27).

Significantly, Spencer sees in the process of the evolution of conduct a movement toward equilibrium; as is his theory of *biological* evolution, Spencer's theory of *social* evolution is progressionist.[7] He "who thus reaches the limit of evolution, exists in a society congruous with his nature," i.e., he is "a man among men similarly constituted, who are severally in harmony with that social environment which they have formed." The conduct of individuals in the "complete society" is such that each complements the others, so that each can undertake actions secure in the knowledge that others will not act to his detriment. One sees, then, that good conduct is that which is more fully evolved, as it tends to the preservation of the individual and the preservation of the species, in serving to promote the completeness of life. Thus, "[c]omplete life in a complete society is but another name for complete equilibrium between the coordinated activities of each social unit and those of the aggregate of units" (Spencer 1897, §28).

Moral obligation and moral sentiment

Spencer's treatment of moral obligation may best be seen as an extension of Adam Smith's presentation in *Theory of Moral Sentiments* as interpreted through the prism of the method of the physical sciences. In Spencer's terms, moral obligation "is an abstract sentiment generated in a manner analogous to that in which abstract ideas are generated" (Spencer 1897, §46). As in the case of our perception of colors, e.g., what is initially perceived as the property of a specific object – an orange is said to be orange, a violet is said to be violet, because the attribute of color is associated with the object we apprehend as possessing this attribute – becomes "dissociated" from that object as it is apprehended that other objects share the "common attribute": orange and violet become identified not with the objects designated by those names, but with an abstract quality.[8]

What is true with respect to physical phenomena is true also of the emotions and other subjective states of consciousness. Abstract feeling emerges as we perceive common attributes among those states; then, "by the consequent mutual canceling of their diverse components," once again dissociating the trait from the object of introspection, "this common component is made relatively appreciable, and becomes an abstract feeling" (Spencer 1897, §46).

In terms of moral obligation or moral duty, the genesis follows the same course. As man evolves, he develops "more compound and more representative feelings," which serve "to adjust the conduct to more distant and general needs" (Spencer 1897, §46). These feelings become themselves recognized, with the advent of civilization and the concomitant development of the mental faculties, as being authoritative as guides to conduct. The feelings that motivated early man were base, generally conducive to the satisfaction of the most immediate desires; as he evolved, man began to be guided by those more complex feelings – including "honesty, truthfulness, diligence, providence" – which are associated with the cultivation of future satisfaction. As they correspond with future rather than immediate gratification, these "higher self-regarding feelings" are imbued with a moral authority absent from the more instinctual feelings of early, pre-civilized man, and it is this "authoritativeness" which is essential to the formation of "the abstract consciousness of duty" (§46).

But while perhaps sufficient as an explanation of the *origin* of abstract rules of moral obligation, this rationale is not sufficient as an explanation for the *continued existence* of such rules. A second element to be considered is coerciveness. It is certainly conceivable that some abstract feelings may have developed and persisted, and even become authoritative, that come to be seen as ultimately destructive of community; taken individually they may appear to be consistent with social duty and obligation, but together and unchecked may actually promote asocial attitudes. Is there then a mechanism that might ensure that those abstract feelings conducive to social cohesion and social stability will flourish, while those destructive of community will not? For Spencer, the answer is in the affirmative, and the necessary element in achieving this is coercion. While the understanding that certain complex feelings should be granted a position of moral authority over the simpler, more basic feelings may have been responsible for the *genesis* of obligation, Spencer acknowledges the position of Alexander Bain that the fear of political, social, and religious penalties was at least indirectly responsible for the recognition of certain feelings as moral. Fears excited by the "political, religious, and social restraining motives" in compelling action, the benefits of which can only be realized at some future time, became conjoined with the "moral restraining motive" which serves to inculcate feelings of moral duty (Spencer 1897, §46). The abstract feelings associated with duty and obligation may have evolved spontaneously, but the continued adherence to those most essential to social solidarity is the result of a conscious effort at ensuring the continuance of society.

Yet this is not the complete story. The "moral motive" may be imputed through its connection with the coerciveness of the political, religious, and social motives, but eventually "it becomes distinct and predominant" and so ceases to be so associated (Spencer 1897, §46). In effect, "the sense of duty or moral obligation is transitory, and will diminish as fast as moralization increases" (§46). As one continually performs an act because it is demanded, eventually the performance will be seen not as coerced or compulsory but as pleasurable. At this stage, when the coercive element is perceived as being no longer the basis for the action, the action itself loses the component of obligation: it has become so much a part of our nature that we become unconscious of the reasons for performing the act. From that point on, the individual "does the right thing with a simple feeling of satisfaction in doing it; and is, indeed, impatient if anything prevents him from having the satisfaction of doing it" (§46). This "adaptation to the social state," in which one is motivated to "higher actions" not by obligation but by the same unconscious desires as prompted the "lower actions" of pre-civilized man, is nothing but an explanation of the evolution of the "moral sentiments" or the "moral sense" (§46); in fact, Spencer defines the moral sense as that "special agent by which the distinction between right and wrong exercise of faculties is recognized and responded to" (Spencer 1954, p. 84), and so it appears as though Spencer should be classed as an ethical internalist.

Mill's attempt, then, to elaborate on the nature of moral obligation, especially his effort to distinguish the concept from the notion of the moral sense, seems from the perspective of Spencer to have been misguided, as it considers only one side of the question. While Adam Smith (rightly, in Spencer's opinion) demonstrates the significance for the stability of the society of the moral sense, and understands the important regulatory function of the sentiment of sympathy, Mill, in eschewing any such devices, is compelled to offer a more instrumental approach, one in which punishment is essential to the institution of moral conduct. In reflecting on the idea of obligation from the utilitarian perspective of the calculus of pleasure and pain, even with his refinements over the approach of Bentham, Mill could not have envisioned a moral sentiment divorced from the need for compulsion in its performance.

Absolute and relative ethics

Spencer is not prepared to accept that an action which "ought" to be taken is necessarily equivalent to a "right" action, for this assumes that the right is knowable and realizable, and even desirable in itself. He in fact holds that the very division of acts into right and wrong is invalid, as "it may be contended that in multitudinous cases no right, properly so-called, can be alleged, but only a least wrong," and that even here it is not always possible to distinguish the "least wrong," or, as Spencer prefers, the "relatively right" (Spencer 1897, §100).

The understanding of these notions follows from an application of the utilitarian calculus. Notions of right and wrong are only conceivable "in relation to the actions of creatures capable of pleasures and pains" (Spencer 1897, §99). Conduct identified as "good" is associated with "a surplus of pleasure," while conduct identified as "bad" is associated with "a surplus of either positive or negative pain" (§101). In addition, good and bad are to be understood as utilitarian concepts. A "good life" is that which, on the whole, will produce "a surplus of agreeable feeling." Good conduct is then that "which subserves life" and bad conduct that "which hinders or destroys it," so that in all "conduct is good or bad according as its total effects are pleasurable or painful" (§10). This is a standard of perfection recognized as basic to all moral systems and ethical theories (§§11–12). With this premise in mind, "absolute good" or "absolute right" will equate with conduct productive of "pure pleasure," i.e., "pleasure unalloyed with pain anywhere." Any conduct associated with the least amount of evil, then, i.e., conduct "which has any concomitant of pain, or any painful consequence" (wherein evil and pain are correlative), is termed "partially wrong." Conduct which is "the least wrong" in the given situation is then termed "relatively right" (§101). In general, "conduct which achieves each kind of end [affecting the individual, the family, and the society] is regarded as relatively good; and is regarded as relatively bad if it fails to achieve it" (§8). That conduct is "best" which succeeds in all three areas at once (§8).

Included in those "absolutely right" actions are actions derived from pre-social sentiments. The mother–child relation and the father–son relation are both of this type, each member of the pair receiving an absolute gain from the relationship, while suffering pain at its suspension. In the evolved community, artistic output and acts of benevolence (strictly defined) fall also within this category, as well as, in the advanced stage of evolutionary development, those "industrial activities carried on through voluntary cooperation" (Spencer 1897, §102).

Included in those "relatively right" actions are "productive labor" (which to the extent it is "wearisome" is a "wrong," while failure to so provide would lead to deprivation and suffering, and an even greater wrong), child care (which produces hardships on the mother or the care provider, and yet failure to perform would lead to far greater misery and so would produce a greater wrong), the termination of an incompetent employee (while his discharge may be to him painful, to others who must suffer his incompetence his continued employment would produce a greater wrong) (Spencer 1897, §102).

Now, Spencer continues, it may not be possible even to identify among possible relative wrongs that action which is *least* wrong. In the above-mentioned case of child care, is it not possible that, at some point, "self-sacrifice" for the sake of the family unit may itself lead to greater "evils"? In the case of the incompetent employee, at what point should the employer intervene: after the first offense or the tenth? In general, it is not, in the usual scheme of things, possible to "sum up either the amount of positive and negative pain which tolerating them involves, or the amount of positive and negative pain involved by not tolerating them; and in medium cases no one can say where the one exceeds the other" (Spencer 1897, §103). In like measure, one may be so uncertain as to the consequences (near and remote) of an action as to become nearly paralyzed into inaction, incapable of arriving at a "correct" or "right" judgment. Each potential choice of action will entail pleasures (benefits) and pains (costs), but the arrival at a relative measure may be impossible due to the problem of incommensurability (e.g., in questions involving social vs. family duties, which obligation is to be granted preference?). Here there simply may be no principle of conduct to which we may appeal for guidance in determining the greater net good or the least wrong (§103).

Be that as it may, Spencer is convinced that, as in physical science, once absolute or ideal truths are discerned they may be applied as bases of comparison to specific empirical instances, so in ethics we must endeavor to adduce absolute right before we are in a position to determine instances of relative right (Spencer 1897, §104). Absolute ethics thus must begin with a postulate of the "ideal social being," "so constituted that his spontaneous activities are congruous with the conditions imposed by the social environment formed by other such beings." Further, it must be postulated "that there exists an ideal code of conduct formulating the behavior of the completely adapted man in the completely evolved society," this code being the code of absolute ethics (§105). This code of *ideal* conduct must be apprehended before it can be applied to *actual* conduct, if only because there must be pre-existing an external ideal standard by which such conduct may be assessed (§105a). It is not sufficient to adjudge the ideal man on the basis of the prevailing morality, for the result would be a mere re-affirmation of current conduct. Rather, we must inquire into the nature of man, respecting "those objective requirements which must be met before conduct can be right," in other words, with ideal man as he would be in the ideal state (§106). Relative ethics then follows as derivative from this perfection standard.

Self- and other-regarding actions

Ethics has as its subject only a part of the wider notion of conduct, *viz.*, "all conduct which furthers or hinders, in either direct or indirect ways, the welfare of self or others" (Spencer 1897, §107). So, at the outset, ethics may be categorized as dealing with personal well-being on the one hand, and social well-being on the other. To the former belongs that "class of actions directed to personal ends," self-regarding actions "classed as intrinsically right or wrong according to their beneficial or detrimental effects" on the actor (§107). (Whether these actions are truly self-regarding is an open question, as Spencer notes that they may in fact have secondary, external consequences.) In Spencer's estimation, the self-regarding desires that motivate these actions are such that to be realized they do not require much "prompting," and so the actions themselves are typically beyond the bounds of "moral enforcement." For the most part, we tend to perceive these actions as affecting only the individual concerned, and so regard him as responsible for the consequences appertaining (§8). This explains the reticence in applying the terms "good" and "bad" in their ethical meaning to actions having only external consequences.

To the extent that ethics relates to matters affecting social well-being, it must attend to that class of actions "which affect fellow men immediately and remotely," i.e., those other-regarding actions the effects of which "must be judged as good or bad mainly by their results to others" (Spencer 1897, §107). These other-regarding actions may be classified according as they "do or do not unduly interfere with the pursuit of ends by others," a category in which may be found notions of unjust and just conduct, respectively; and according as they "influence the states of others without directly interfering with the relations between their labors and the results," a category that includes beneficence and maleficence (§107). The other-regarding desires that motivate these actions are typically such that "prompting" is necessary in facilitation, and so "moral enforcement" is essential to their fulfillment. Here,

> adjustments of acts to ends are so apt to hinder the kindred adjustments of other men, that insistence on the needful limitations has to be perpetual; and the mischiefs caused by men's interferences with one another's life-subserving actions are so great, that the interdicts have to be peremptory.
>
> (§8)

It is these other-regarding actions which give rise to the popular interpretations of good and bad in respect of conduct, as appertaining to "acts which further the complete living of others and acts which obstruct their complete living" (§8).

Sociality and sympathy

In *The Principles of Psychology* (1905), Spencer treats in some detail of the mechanism producing the sentiments of sociality and sympathy. Studies of animal behavior (at the time Spencer is writing) show that predatory animals tend to lead solitary lives, while herbivorous animals tend to gregariousness and hence cooperation: the predatory animal, being in search of widely scattered prey, sees little advantage in cooperative arrangements, each additional member of the group diminishing the amount available to each; the herbivorous animal, tending to graze in open areas and so prone to attack from predators, finds such arrangements beneficial in minimizing the probability that any particular member of the herd would fall prey. In addition, as the cooperative sentiment increases the chances of survival of the group, the traits that correspond to this sentiment are reproduced in the population and the sentiment is enhanced. Thus the tendency to sociality emerges in cases in which "there is less tendency than usual for the individuals to disperse widely," and is "strengthened by the inherited effects of habit." The strength of this sentiment becomes such "a predominant part of consciousness … that absence of it will inevitably cause discomfort." The very thought of being in the company of others similar in nature and circumstance is seen as pleasurable (Spencer 1905, §504).

In a similar manner, the sentiment of sympathy is cultivated. The condition of living in a society tends to the production of associative actions on the part of the members: in a society under constant threat of attack, for example, there will develop "an association between the consciousness of fear and the consciousness of these signs of fear in others," a sympathetic, habitual reaction to the actions of those in similar circumstances (Spencer 1905, §505). Sympathetic pleasures may be excited as well, in response to the perceived pleasures of others in similar circumstances (§§505–6). One need not himself directly experience the incident, so long as the actions of others in the group are seen as corresponding with its occurrence.

Spencer then defines "sympathetic feeling" as "one that is not immediately excited by the natural cause of such a feeling, but one that is mediately excited by the presentation of signs habitually associated with such a feeling." The extent to which the sympathetic feeling is manifest depends on "ability to perceive and combine these signs, as well as ability to represent their implications, external or internal, or both" (Spencer 1905, §507). Where fear is most easily aroused, fear becomes the manifest sympathy, and the common experience elicits from the group similar responses to actions associated with it. Where the experience is lacking, there cannot develop the representations necessary to elicit sympathy.

In general, "the capacity for being sympathetically affected, implies the capacity for having an ideal feeling of some kind aroused by perception of the sounds and notions implying a real feeling of the same kind in another" (Spencer 1905, §508). While sympathy may be manifest in the lower animals, this capacity is most complete in man. Here the three primary causes of sympathy, as they pertain to the relations of parent and child, male and female, and members of the group (species), combine with a fourth condition – "elevated intelligence" – in producing the most evolved form of social cohesion (§509). In this, the highest state of development, there emerges the "social instinct."

Cooperation and political power

Society is said by Spencer to exist only when the object of combination is co-operation. Cooperation "is at once that which can not exist without a society, and that for which a society exists" (Spencer 1886, §440).

Cooperation is of two forms. The first is the result of spontaneous order, "which grows up without thought during the pursuit of private ends," while the second is the result of deliberate design, which "implies distinct recognition of public ends" (Spencer 1886, §441).[9] The first form of cooperation includes the relations of exchange, division of labor, specialization of industry, and even the regulation of economic action; each of these relations, "spontaneously formed in aid of private ends and continued only at will, is not formed with conscious reference to achievement of public ends" (§441).[10] The second form of cooperation includes the provision of public accommodation, comprising provision for the common defense (and, while Spencer is not specific on this point, presumably any essential public end to which legislation may be directed); here "social cooperation is a conscious cooperation, and a cooperation which is not wholly a matter of choice," one which may in fact be "at variance with private wishes" (§441). Spontaneous concerted action "directly seeks and subserves the welfare of individuals, and indirectly subserves the welfare of society as a whole by preserving individuals," while directed concerted action "directly seeks and subserves the welfare of the society as a whole, and indirectly subserves the welfares of individuals by protecting the society" (§441). The former is liberty-enhancing, while the latter has a tendency to become coercive.

With this preface in mind, we are then led to consider the import of the two forms of cooperation to the realm of the political. Political power, as seen by Spencer, "is the feeling of the community, acting through an agency which it has either informally or formally established" (Spencer 1886, §466). It is a feeling both "spontaneously formed" and "imposed" or "prescribed": it is passed on through custom and habit, as it is inculcated through education and indoctrination. This "sentiment" through which government is made possible "is, in short, mainly the accumulated and organized sentiment of the past" (§467). Thus the prevailing political will is in large measure dependent upon inherited opinions and conduct, the wisdom of the past, as evidenced by the ultimate codification of social custom into formal rules of law (§468). Such is the power exercised by the working of the "dead hand," that "accumulated and organized sentiment felt towards inherited institutions made sacred by tradition," which "produces the obedience making political action possible" (§469).

Justice

Justice defined

Justice falls within the domain of that branch of ethics "which, considering exclusively the effects of conduct on others, treats of the right regulation of it with a view to such effects." As it "formulates the range of conduct and limitations to conduct," justice "is at once the most important division of ethics and the division which admits of the greatest definiteness" (Spencer 1897, §109). The scientific nature of justice is evident once it is understood that there is underlying it a fundamental principle, the principle of equivalence, which gives rise in social relations to the idea of equity, or "equalness" in respect of social relations. As it is focused on "*quantity* under *stated conditions*" (§60; emphasis in original), this Spencer takes as indicative of the scientific status of justice: as each member of the community is to be granted equal status "in virtue of their common human nature," it is then possible in dealing with questions of equity to "reach conclusions of a sufficiently definite kind" (§109).

Justice has both a positive and a negative element. The positive element is manifest in "each man's recognition of his claims to unimpeded activities and the benefits they bring"; the negative element is manifest in "the consciousness of limits which the presence of other men having like claims necessitates" (Spencer 1897, §267). The positive element "expresses a prerequisite to life in general," while the negative element "qualifies this prerequisite" to man as a social creature (§272). The positive element has the potential for producing inequality: as each is to enjoy the benefits of his actions, then, to the extent that men differ in their constitutions and abilities, these differences must produce unequal outcomes. The negative element, by contrast, has the potential for producing equality: a recognition by each of the limits of action implies an awareness of competing claims and so a recognition of the need to act with due regard for others and their claims (§267).

A "true" theory of justice must provide for both the positive and the negative elements, and so incorporate the conflicting notions of equality and inequality. Equality redounds to those limitations conducive to cooperation; inequality redounds to the free actions of individuals within prescribed limits. It must then be the case that justice demands "the liberty of each limited only by the like liberties of all" (Spencer 1897, §272). As equality provides the boundary condition, inequality provides the rationale for desert. Thus the tension is removed: to facilitate the idea of equality means fashioning bounds to individual conduct, within which each is free to pursue his own course of action, gathering benefits which, because of differing individual constitutions and endowments, generate, at least in one sense of the term, inequalities (§270). From whence derives the Law of Equal Freedom: "Every man is free to do that which he wills, provided he infringes not the equal freedom of any other man" (§272).[11]

Spencer expresses his disagreement with Plato, Aristotle, and Hobbes in their collective designation of notions of right and wrong conduct as originating in the law. On this interpretation, rights and duties derive solely from "convention." Such a disposition, notes Spencer, is tantamount to arguing "that moral obligation originates with acts of Parliament, and can be changed this way or that way by majorities" (Spencer 1897, §19). The absurdity of such a belief is evident. It is not from a prescribed set of generally agreed-upon moral codes that rights and duties gain their currency. It is the moral sense which impels us, through an implicit understanding that right conduct will promote the general happiness, to just behavior. If indeed justice is merely "fulfillment of covenant," as Hobbes believes and, further, this fulfillment "implies a power enforcing it," then justice must derive from compulsion, and *only* from compulsion: there is no place here for voluntary just acts, as they are expressly denied in the premise (§19).

For his part, Spencer insists that rights, far from being conferred by law, are in fact "corollaries from the law of equal freedom," which "one and all coincide with ordinary ethical conceptions," and "one and all correspond with legal enactments" (Spencer 1897, §283). The ideal of equal freedom is readily seen to be a part of the essential nature of man. Man is endowed with an "instinct of personal rights" through which he is impelled "to repel anything like an encroachment upon what he thinks is his sphere of original freedom" (Spencer 1954, p. 86). It is through this "instinct" that individuals, "as units of the social mass," form social bonds, finding the essential balance between "repulsion" and "attraction" upon which the cohesiveness of the community must ultimately depend (p. 86). The very idea of rights thus antedates any attempt at codification of laws, and consequently rights do not derive from the law, but rather laws derive their justification from rights (Spencer 1897, §283).

In respect of the governing authority, the sovereign retains legitimacy only so long as the purpose for which it was instituted remains, and its actions must then be constrained to the discharge of that purpose. As any actions of the sovereign that "do not respond to the necessities ... are unwarranted," so law "can never transcend the authority of that from which it is derived." Laws have the claim to authority and legitimacy only to the extent that they conduce to the attainment of the "general good" or some other such "supreme end." In like measure, conduct is designated good or bad not because of grant of the sovereign, but because it either does or does not serve to further the welfare of those in the society (Spencer 1897, §19).

Justice and the need for restraint

The primary "law of relation between conduct and consequence" as it relates to the individual in isolation from society is "that each individual ought to receive the good and the evil which arises from its own nature" (Spencer 1897, §256). By contrast, the actions of man in society are subject to a second law, *viz.*, "that those actions through which, in fulfillment of its nature, the individual achieves benefits and avoids evils, shall be restrained by the need for noninterference with the like actions of associated individuals" (§256). This second law is an essential condition for the maintenance of a society, as social organization is impossible in its violation. But, notes Spencer, this second law is nothing more than an extension of the first to "the conditions of gregarious life." As in respect of the first law, each individual is alone responsible for the consequences attending his actions, so in society each is liable to others for the external consequences of his actions (§256). As society continues its advance, there comes into play a third law respecting conduct. The continued prosperity and even the very survival of the group may demand "occasional sacrifices" of certain of its members, a "qualification" being "that each individual shall receive the benefits and evils of its own nature." This third law is motivated by the need of society as a whole to exist in the face of external threats; the continued existence of the group is of greater import than the protection of the rights or even the security of the lives of any one of its members (§256).

For Spencer, the first law is "absolute for animals in general," while the second is "absolute for gregarious animals," and so is essential to the existence of society. The third, however, is necessary only while the conditions of external threat remain: once the threat is removed, the third law ceases to have any rationale (Spencer 1897, §256).

It is in the context of the first and second laws that justice derives its significance. More importantly, these laws are essential not merely to the preservation of the *society* but also to the preservation of the *species*, as they ensure that, in each individual reaping the rewards and suffering the evils of his actions, without interference and with due concern for any external consequences, only the "fittest" will survive and therethrough the species and hence the society will be strengthened (Spencer 1897, §257). The survival of the group, then, is furthered by any condition which maintains the necessary connection between action and consequence, and which provides sanctions should that connection be severed. This is a primary demand, and in fact a constituent part, of justice.

Justice, then, establishes itself the more organized the society. As society progresses from the primitive communal form, variety and complexity necessarily increase. This variety and complexity compels cooperation. But, notes

Spencer, cooperation is impossible unless it conforms to certain formal (and informal) requirements respecting the maintenance of social interactions. Important in this regard is the need for restraint. Unchecked aggression, even when advancing the utility of the actor, nevertheless is injurious to society as a whole, while placing limits on acceptable conduct generally conduces to the advantage of all (Spencer 1897, §262). The need for the social restraint of individual conduct in the maintenance of order compels the use of punishment for violations of public decorum, for conduct deleterious to the social order. The laws restricting conduct and instituting punishment for violations of that conduct, as a means to securing order, represent "a natural product of human life carried on under social conditions" (§259). Justice follows in allowing

> that each individual carrying on the actions which subserve his life, and not prevented from receiving their normal results, good and bad, shall carry on these actions under such restraints as are imposed by the carrying on of kindred actions by other individuals, who have similarly to receive such normal results, good and bad.
>
> (Spencer 1897, §259)

Egoism, altruism, ego-altruism

Justice as primary among the social sentiments has, in Spencer's portrayal, both an egoistic and an altruistic component. The egoistic sentiment "is a subjective attribute which answers to that objective requirement constituting justice – the requirement that each adult shall receive the results of his own nature and consequent actions" (Spencer 1897, §263). Just as in nature one sees resistance to restraint and a "love of unfettered movement," so in human society anything which acts to interfere with or to prevent the attainment of a goal is seen as burdensome and unduly restrictive to personal choice (§263). Any action that tends to restrict freedom of movement (in the large sense of the term) calls forth feelings of agitation, "a multitudinous re-representation of denials of all kinds"; any action that is apprehended as liberating calls forth feelings of exaltation, a re-representation of past gratifications (Spencer 1905, §516). The evolution of society, specifically the evolution of *political* society, strengthens the re-representations and hence the sentiments.[12] The increasing awareness on the part of the citizenry that their actions are restricted to a greater extent than those of their leaders, or on the part of members of a lower socioeconomic class that their lot is the result of actions of a higher class, excites feelings of repression and even envy, "ending in a more decided repugnance to those social relations whence they are seen to grow" (§516). These re-representative sentiments thus produced then serve to shape political arrangements by fashioning systems of ideal social and political relations "under which no citizen shall have privileges that trench upon the claims of others." It is here "that all ideas of concrete advantages are merged in the abstract satisfaction derived from securities against every possible interference with the pursuit of his ends by each citizen" (§516).

The altruistic sentiment, by contrast, is more complex. A hallmark of a civilized society is the mutual dependence of its members; as the welfare of each becomes tied to the welfare of all, "it results that the growth of feelings which find satisfaction in the well-being of all, is the growth of feelings adjusted to a fundamental unchanging condition to social welfare" (Spencer 1905, §525). Social collectives develop practices that tend to promote common feelings in the members. Each begins to see in the others sentiments consistent with his own, as he perceives his own pleasure and pain in the pleasures and pains of those in similar circumstance; it is this connection which defines the community relation, each member of the society being cognizant of and sympathetic to the welfare of the others. As each understands that his conduct necessarily corresponds to the welfare and happiness of others in the group, *individuals* are impelled to such conduct as benefits the *society as a whole*, as promotes the good and the right. This Spencer identifies with the Moral Sense.[13] The very condition of social life, the proximity of which exposes all "to like causes of pleasure and pain," arouses within each individual sympathetic sentiments, "capacities for participating in one another's pleasures and pains" (§526). The altruistic sentiments, then, "are all sympathetic excitements of egoistic feelings," which feelings "vary in their characters according to the characters of the egoistic feelings sympathetically excited" (§527).

It is important to understand that the altruistic sentiments do not include all sympathetic feelings. To qualify as an altruistic sentiment, the feeling must be re-representative and not merely representative, i.e., it must impel action not merely on the basis of *feelings*, but also on the basis of *ideas* corresponding to these feelings; it must call forth past emotional remembrances, not merely elicit sympathetic feelings, for else the feelings elicited are little more than egoistic reactions to an event and do not qualify as sentiments (Spencer 1905, §527). In addition, certain sentiments typically regarded as altruistic may actually be seen as egoistic. An act of beneficence may be egoistic to the extent that the act affords pleasure to the actor, directly and in the response of the recipient, while an act of "generosity proper" is altruistic "in those cases where the benefaction is anonymous: provided, also, that there is no contemplation of a reward to be reaped hereafter" (§528). There is thus seen a necessary component of unselfishness in an altruistic act.

While the altruistic sentiment develops as a *consequence* of social intercourse, it is equally true that this sentiment is essential *both to the emergence and to the continuance* of the social sentiments; it derives from the conditions of social life and is essential to the maintenance of equitable social relations (Spencer 1897, §264). Yet to say that the conditions of social life both compel and are compelled by the altruistic sentiment of justice is to engage in circular logic. One must temporally precede the other. Spencer avoids this circularity by arguing that initially the egoistic sentiment is restrained by a "proaltruistic" or "ego-altruistic" sentiment, "sentiments which, while implying self-gratification, also imply gratification in others: the representation of this gratification in others being a source of pleasure not intrinsically, but because of ulterior benefits to self which experience associates with it"

(Spencer 1905, §519). As for the individual, experience results in the connection of certain actions with feelings of pleasure or approbation, and others with feelings of pain or reprobation, so these same sentiments are extended to social actions, "actions that are beneficial to the tribe, and actions that are detrimental to the tribe" (§520). The self-same feelings that arouse pleasure in the *individual* are found to be instrumental in furthering the welfare of the *community*. The difference lies in the basis of their re-representation. While the egoistic sentiments are formed largely through personal experience, the ego-altruistic (proaltruistic) sentiments are inculcated through an association of symbols and even institutional forms with social utility or social disutility. The personal need for approbation translates into social cooperation. Actions and even demeanors are viewed favorably or unfavorably as they tend to promote or to hinder the social welfare.

In pre-modern societies, restraints on aggression include fear of retaliation, fear of reprobation (the reproach of public opinion), fear of transgression against authority, and fear of transgression against the supreme authority, the combination of which serve to check the anti-social tendencies inherent in primitive egoism as they act "temporarily to cause respect for one another's claims, and so to make social cooperation possible" (Spencer 1897, §264). Religious sentiments, then, as well as ethical notions of right conduct, are but types of the ego-altruistic sentiments. The feelings giving rise to both derive from latent feelings of personal gratification to which belief may be associated. The positive feelings that derive from a belief in a supreme being or in the pursuit of the good are themselves the result of a felt connection between the belief or action and a perceived positive consequence. Yet in neither case "is there involved a consciousness, pleasurable or painful, caused by contemplation of acts considered in their intrinsic natures, apart from any consequences to self, immediate or remote" (Spencer 1905, §521).

With the conditions so laid, the altruistic sentiment can then develop. It is important to note here that the altruistic sentiment cannot materialize unless and until it is preceded by a corresponding egoistic sentiment. The altruistic sentiment may in fact be defined as the egoistic sentiment "sympathetically excited" (Spencer 1905, §529). Where the egoistic sentiment is lacking, the altruistic sentiment must be retarded. Thus the very conditions that serve to advance the egoistic sentiment also serve to advance the altruistic. As egoism is furthered by the unfettered pursuit of personal desires, so altruism is furthered as a social sentiment by the maintenance of conditions conducive to the pursuit of such desires. The personal desire for property, e.g., will generalize into the development of an institutional framework – a framework of laws – supportive of that desire, strengthened by a social sentiment that both acknowledges and pledges to its preservation (Spencer 1897, §265).

Altruism, justice, and the moral sentiments

Spencer identifies justice with the most complex form of altruistic sentiment (Spencer 1905, §530). As we have seen, justice, itself a form of sentiment, "consists of representations of those emotions which others feel, when actually or prospectively allowed or forbidden the activities by which pleasures are to be gained or pains escaped." Justice "is thus constituted by representation of a feeling that is itself highly re-representative," this feeling being "love of personal freedom" (§530). As a desire to be free of restraint, to have the ability to pursue personal ends unfettered by external agency, is a sentiment conducive to the sentiment of justice, justice must then have as a principle aim "to maintain intact the sphere required by the individual for the due exercise of his powers and fulfillment of his desires." As it is an altruistic sentiment, justice also "serves, when sympathetically excited, to cause respect for the like spheres of other individuals" and by so doing "prompt[s] defence of others when their spheres of action are invaded" (§530). So while stimulated initially by egoistic feelings connected to fear of restraint, justice ultimately "becomes more highly re-representative" and, as a result, evolves into a sympathetic sentiment by which each realizes in an attack on the liberty of others a personal disgust (§530).[14]

With this we return to a consideration of the significance of the moral sentiments and their role in forming moral principles. Egoistic sentiments are those subjective feelings at play in the individual; ego-altruistic sentiments, as derivative from the egoistic, are likewise unique to the specific culture and the specific time in which they are manifest. Altruistic sentiments, by contrast, are those which are so highly developed as to be of near-universal design. In the manner of their evolution – "conforming to the conditions needful for the highest welfare of individuals in the associated state" – these sentiments "adjust themselves to the modes of conduct that are permanently beneficial" (Spencer 1905, §531).

Here we see the connection to Spencer's "Evolution-theory of moral feelings" and Utilitarianism. For Spencer, utility is a concept encompassing more than merely a consideration of acts, or of connections between acts and the pleasures or pains resulting as consequences. In the common use of the term, it "ignores the multitudinous cases in which actions are determined and made habitual by experiences of pleasurable or painful results, without any conscious generalizing of these experiences," i.e., it fails to account for representations and re-representations of feelings (Spencer 1905, §531). Once these representations and re-representations are accounted for, i.e., once Utilitarianism "recognizes the accumulated effects of inherited experiences," it can then be seen to be consistent with the evolutionary theory. With this recognition comes the understanding that "even sympathy, and the sentiments resulting from sympathy, may be interpreted as caused by experiences of utility" (§531).

With this in mind, it is evident that moral sentiments do not *follow from*, but rather *cause us to recognize* the utility of our actions. This is clear from the need for representation and re-representation of sentiments. Actions become associated with pleasures and pains *before* they are perceived as good or bad. A sympathetic act produces in the actor a pleasurable feeling to which the act is then associated (an egoistic sentiment). This pleasurable feeling and its allied action then become represented in the perception of pleasure in others (an ego-altruistic sentiment), and eventually becomes re-represented through repeated experiences of others in the group to form a more universal sentiment (an altruistic sentiment). It is at this last stage, in which "the ultimate effects, personal and social, have gained general recognition, are expressed on current maxims, and lead to injunctions having the religious sanction," that we see the strengthening of the sentiments that elicit sympathetic action (Spencer 1905, §531). Moral feelings become associated with these actions, sympathetic actions garnering acceptance, unsympathetic actions fostering disgust. Further, as the actions, having gained the approval of the society at large, "bring a sympathetic consciousness of pleasure given or of pain prevented," they as well "bring a sympathetic consciousness of human welfare at large" (§531). At this stage we see emerge the altruistic sentiments, paramount over any vestige of the egoistic, and with their ascendence the recognition by the members of the group of the primacy of those ethical and moral ideals, the fulfillment of which marks the ultimate state of mankind.[15]

The individual and the group

In the above, allusion has been made to Spencer's theory of the evolution of social arrangements. Specifically, it has been suggested that collective society is fostered as a means by which the members derive mutual benefit, all the while being cognizant of the fact that they must conform to the strictures of the corporation. In terms of his Utilitarianism, Spencer sees in the evolution of society a demand that "[t]he mutual hindrances liable to arise during the pursuit of their ends by individuals living in proximity, must be kept within such limits as to leave a surplus of advantage obtained by associated life" (Spencer 1897, §259).

In this section, we will examine the process of the evolution of such collective arrangements, as they pass through what Spencer describes as the militant and industrial stages.

Militant society

The state of pre-modern man is best described as a Hobbesian state of constant conflict. It is this state of conflict which is responsible for the development of social and political structures essential to the common protection, as it becomes evident that the preservation of the society "is the more probable in proportion as its corporate action is the more complete" (Spencer 1886, §548). The need for social preservation compels an organization of society "such as will bring into play the effectually combined forces of its units at specific times and places" (Spencer 1897, §349). The mechanism underlying this *social* organization is not in any important respect different from that underlying *biological* evolution: as in the evolution of species "the regulatory and expending systems ... are developed into fitness for dealing with surrounding organisms," so too in the evolution of human society, "that organization which fits the aggregate for acting as a whole in conflict with other aggregates, indirectly results from the carrying on of conflicts with other aggregates" (Spencer 1885, §249). Society is merely an adaptation to circumstance.

The institutional structures within which individuals function originate through instrumental needs in the conflicts among groups. In diffuse societies (in Spencer's reading of the anthropological record), intergroup conflict is virtually unknown, as there is little contact among disparate groups and so little competition for resources, and so there is no need to forge arrangements for the provision of the common defense. As social groups become larger and more complex, with definite territorial boundaries and even group (tribal) loyalties, there quickly emerges a need to institute defensive measures against incursion by hostile forces. This necessity to provide a defensive force impels a complementary need to provide the wherewithal to sustain that force. Here we see develop a division of responsibility similar to the development of specialized structures in the organism, each member compelled to do his part in the service of the whole.

The hallmark of the militant society then is that each member must contribute to the good of the whole, the good being in this instance survival; only when each member of the collective is performing his given function will the whole be able to achieve its corporate end. Yet it is obvious that not all members of the society are capable of performing directly in the service of the common defense, i.e., acting in the role of soldier; even if they were so capable, it would not necessarily be in the corporate interest that they do so. There must be in any such society a "permanent commissariat," the function of which is to contribute to the maintenance of the armed force. Should each soldier be compelled to maintain himself, while at the same time prepare for combat, his efficiency in the latter role would be greatly compromised. There is therefore a need for a support staff, the function of which is to tend to the needs of the protective forces and at the same time to the non-military needs of the general society. The commissariat fulfils this support role, allowing those in the military to concern themselves with the more important matter of preparing for the common defense.

Thus develops a division of the society into two orders: those assigned the task of mutual defense (or offense), and those assigned the task of support and maintenance. As success (defined not exclusively as survival, but including military supremacy as well) depends on the most efficient combination of the efforts of each group, it must be the case that the supporting group becomes intimately tied to, even subservient to, the military group: the commissariat cannot be independent, for then its product may become inefficiently distributed, leaving the military inadequately provisioned; and, since the ultimate end is protection from outside forces, the commissariat cannot be of equal status with the military, but rather must be seen as an appendage. This suggests that the superior society – that which is most efficiently organized to the task of securing its military aims (defensive or offensive) – is that which succeeds most effectively in forging a "solid phalanx," in the "binding of the society into a whole" (Spencer 1886, §550), all the while aware of the priorities involved.

Individuality, then, in this earliest of communal arrangements is submerged by the need for collective action, the life of the individual citizen placed "at the disposal of his society," his own will subservient to the public will, with any pursuit of personal desire allowed "only when the tribe or nation has no need of him." This applies to *all* aspects of life, and especially in regard to the question of property. In the militant society, the very idea of private ownership is anathema to the stability of the social order. Property is either a community resource or, if private, held "by permission only," liable to expropriation as those in control see fit (Spencer 1886, §551). To countenance individual control over resources would be tantamount to admitting an *individual* interest, and so would create the conditions for a potential conflict with the *social* interest, a conflict that could only be to the detriment of the welfare of the collective.

In terms of governance, the need for action to be directed, arising from the potential for annihilation faced by these early militarist societies, compels their constitution around a central governing authority. The mere fact that the society is under external threat is sufficient to justify such centralized control, not simply of the military as the protective organ, but of the society as a whole. A centralized command authority offers the most efficient means by which action can be taken and resources marshaled to the (very limited) ends to which the society is directed. The militant State must, in seeking self-protection, stress the collective will over any individual will, allowing individual rights "only on sufferance" (Spencer 1897, §349).

Critical to the achievement of such a unified corporate State, wherein each order fulfils its duty and each member subordinates "life, liberty, and property" to the advancement of the corporate end, is a "coercive instrumentality," a "controlling agency" the function of which is to regulate the society so as to guarantee the most efficient use of resources. As the military order vests ultimate control in a supreme military commander, so the commissariat, the supporting order, must be similarly regimented to ensure it performs its functions with equal dispatch. Typically, the choice of civilian leader is the supreme military authority. His abilities in marshaling forces against hostile incursions (or in the quest for domination of neighboring states) proves invaluable in marshaling the economic forces to the production of socially necessary output. With the military leader in control of the society, the resulting "militant form of government" takes on the characteristics of the military. Civilian life becomes severely regimented, both negatively and positively: not only is each member of the society limited in his actions, restrained from engaging in certain practices, but he is also compelled to engage in other actions with the express aim of fashioning an efficient social organism (Spencer 1886, §554). The "militarist" society in fact is defined as "one in which the army is the nation mobilized while the nation is the quiescent army," an organization which "acquires a structure common to army and nation" (Spencer 1885, §259).

In closing this brief overview, two further points should be emphasized. First, to Spencer, such an arrangement of society, to the extent that it is necessitated by the need to defend against the possibility of external aggression, is granted a "quasi-ethical warrant" for the subjugation of the rights of individuals to the survival of the State (Spencer 1897, §349). But this warrant is only valid so long as the efforts of the State are defensive in nature (although Spencer explicitly recognizes that among the actions of the collective will be offensive pursuits to the end of expanding dominance as well as securing the survival of the society). Any State which engages in offensive actions against a rival no longer has any ethical claim to its actions (§349). Second, Spencer is not willing to grant Hobbes's contention that the individuals in the group relinquish authority "with a view to the promised increase of satisfactions," but instead argues that the satisfaction realized through gradual subordination gives rise to more concentrated forms of authority, a manifestly utilitarian consideration (§19).

Industrial society

Once we pass to the industrial State, the relations are inverted. While in the militant State the preservation of the society takes precedence over the rights of individuals, in the industrial State the individual is granted primacy while the social interest is fulfilled in consequence. Protection in this instance is to be directed internally, to the preservation of the laws and the administration of justice. This requires a wholly different type of administrative order. There is no longer a need for the single directing political authority, as there is no need for the direction of activity to meet in an efficient manner a common threat; the need for coercion and autocratic rule disappears with the ending of the external state of emergency. What is required in the new circumstances is "a rule adapted for maintaining the rights of each citizen against others," a rule under which the State "is also regardful of those rights in its own dealings with citizens," in other words, the rule of law (Spencer 1897, §350). This new form of State administration, then, must be constituted so as to secure equal rights and protections and an equal share in the governance of the society. (Spencer leaves it to speculation whether such an arrangement will, through "the development of cooperative organizations," eventually "obliterate the distinction between employer and employed" and so eradicate class conflict (§352).)

What characterizes industrial society is the "form of cooperation," the "mode of organization of the labourers" in the community (Spencer 1886, §562). While in the militant society, as well as communist and socialist communities, life is regimented and labor commanded to perform in the interest of the whole, in the industrial state no such interference with the "natural system" is contemplated. The industrial organization, in a nutshell, "is exclusively fitted for maintaining the life of the society by subserving the lives of its units" (§562), but this is true only to the extent that man has achieved that level of fitness necessary to the fulfillment of the conditions of the absolute ethics. To the extent that man has evolved the requisite sentiments, essential to the maintenance of the Law of Equal Freedom, i.e., to the extent that he internalizes the moral virtues, the standard of good to which the industrial State is to lead will be achieved.

The militant society is structured in response to external threats to the existence of the community. This form of social organization is successful to the extent that external threats are extinguished. Once this has been accomplished, once enemies are vanquished and the threat of annihilation is no longer manifest, the rationale for the militant structure no longer exists. With the first impediment to the existence of the community – external aggression – removed, there remains the need to guard against an equally destructive force, *viz.*, "failure of its [the society's] members to support and propagate themselves" (Spencer 1886, §563). Whereas social welfare in the militant State is defined in terms of the survival of the whole, requiring that the parts work in concert to the attainment of the single good, in the industrial State the welfare of the whole is actualized only through the advancement of the individual welfare of each member of the society. At this stage, collective action is not advanced by direction or coercion. The sole "end to be achieved by public action is to keep private actions within due bounds" (§563). The industrial state, then, represents the most evolved social form, "because it is the one which most subserves that happiness of the units which is to be achieved by social organization, as distinguished from that happiness of the aggregate which is to be achieved by individual organization with its centralized structures" (Spencer 1885, Postscript to Part II, p. 588).

In addition, as the militant State is organized through coercion, the conditions are lacking within which the egoistic sentiment of justice may form. The evolution of voluntary cooperative arrangements in the industrial State, replacing the compulsory arrangement in the militant State, leads, *pari passu* with the emergence of contract relations, to a flourishing of the sentiments associated with and conducive to justice. The lessening of restraints on individuals thus provides conditions under which the egoistic and ultimately the altruistic sentiments of justice may develop (Spencer 1897, §265).

The dawn of the industrial State, then, signals the demise of directed corporate action. The militant State demands subordination to the corporate end; the industrial state, by contrast, defends individuality as a social duty. "Life, liberty, and property," subordinated in the militant State, must be secured in the industrial. The reason for this change in perspective reflects the order of things. Whereas competition among militant societies takes the form of wars of conquest, competition among industrial States is centered on relative prosperity. To this end, the "new" State which emerges is one "in which individual claims, considered as sacred, are trenched on by the State no further than is requisite to pay the cost of maintaining them, or rather, of arbitrating among them," and so the new "corporate function becomes that of deciding between those conflicting claims, the equitable adjustment of which is not obvious to the persons concerned" (Spencer 1886, §564). Thus it follows that "the cardinal function of the State" becomes the protection of individual interests, to ensure "that the individuality of each man shall have the fullest play compatible with the like play of other men's individualities" (§§564–5).

Having thus identified the constitution of the industrial State, Spencer moves to the conditions necessary to the encouragement of individuality, conditions generally subsumed in the category of the administration of justice (Spencer 1886, §567). As Spencer defines it, in respect of industrial society, justice "means preservation of the normal connexions between acts and results – the obtainment by each of as much benefit as his efforts are equivalent to – no more and no less." Each must accept the consequences of his actions. In Spencer's colorful terminology, "[t]he superior shall have the good of his superiority; and the inferior the evil of his inferiority" (§567). The State is not to interfere in redistributing advantages from those who earn to those who do not; any such interference is disruptive of the natural evolutionary progress of the social order, and can lead only to a retardation of the moral and ethical development essential to an advanced state of civilization. Industrial society, then, is inimical to "all forms of communistic distribution," if only because these policies tend to pervert the relations among those in the society, as "they tend to equalize the lives of good and bad, idle and indigent" and so give currency to the very traits which must be extinguished (§567).

Once again Spencer's argument takes the form of the biological analogy: in competition among other industrial societies, survival and ultimately dominance will depend on the ability to "produce the largest number of the best individuals," those "best adapted for life in the industrial state." To the extent that each retains the proceeds of his labor, the "superior" individuals, by definition more productive, will thrive, while those less capable will not, and so the superior element will eventually become the more numerous. Should the State intervene, taking some of the produce from the "superior" ranks for redistribution to the "inferior," the natural order of the society is upset, the result being moral retrogression (Spencer 1886, §567). (Although this is not to imply that those "superior" elements should not endeavor to assist the "inferior," and in fact this action from sympathy will be on the whole "beneficial" to society. It is when such aid is compelled that the negative consequences for the society as a whole are felt.)

Being of such a constitution, then, industrial society brings about its desired end through the use of the instrument of contract. Lacking the formal distributive mechanisms of the militant society, industrial society relies on the contract to perform the functions previously left to a command authority. But the difference is more pronounced: whereas in the militant society there need be no relation between individual output and individual apportionment of the product, under the system of contract, equitable distribution, defined in this instance as "correct apportioning of reward to merit," is guaranteed (Spencer 1886, §568).

In like measure, as the State has the limited function of providing the means for the flourishing of individual initiative (of which the contract is merely the instrument), the regulative function of the State evolves from positive and negative to strictly negative. The ultimate end of the State is the promotion of a protective sphere around each individual, within which each may pursue his own desires without interfering with others or being interfered with.

As suggested at the beginning of this section, the functions of the industrial State are minimal. As administration becomes decentralized, "[n]early all public organizations save that for administering justice, necessarily disappear; since they have the common character that they either aggress on the citizen by dictating his actions, or by taking from him more property than is needful for protecting him, or by both" (Spencer 1886, §569). With the diminution of the role of the

State, there is afforded a greater role to private organizations in dispensing these functions. It is here that we see the workings of the spontaneous order. From individual free exchange, and voluntary cooperative arrangements, we see develop a "multiplicity and heterogeneity of associations, political, religious, commercial, professional, philanthropic, and social, of all sizes" (§570).

The "ultimate man" in this ideal state "will be one whose private requirements coincide with public ones," such that "in spontaneously fulfilling his own nature" he "incidentally performs the functions of a social unit" (Spencer 1954, p. 397). The virtues associated with the ideal state are those, as noted above, implied in the Law of Equal Freedom, "the law under which individuation becomes perfect." The recognition of this moral law "is the final endowment of humanity" (p. 395). That this must be the case is beyond question, as it is evident that only "when each possesses an active instinct of freedom, together with an active sympathy," will restrictions to individuality be removed. There will simply be no further need for the restrictions on individuals demanded by government, for it will then be second nature that, "while everyone maintains his own claims, he will respect the like claims of others." In this ideal state of being, "perfect morality, perfect individuation, and perfect life will be simultaneously realized" (pp. 395–6).

Yet it is significant that this attainment of perfect individuation is not at the cost of a loss of sociality. In fact, the attainment of perfect individuation is to coincide with the greatest degree of mutual dependence: "complete separateness" is in harmony with "complete union" (Spencer 1954, p. 366). The maintenance of the "greatest happiness" demands both "the most elaborate subdivision of labor," suggesting "the extremest mutual dependence," and the freedom to pursue individual desires. This is possible to the extent that society continues to evolve, such that "all desires inconsistent with the most perfect social organization are dying out and other desires corresponding to such an organization are being developed." In effect, perfect altruism or the perfected social consciousness becomes manifest as perfect individuation. The form of individuality necessary to the realization of the ideal state is then that which recognizes "in the most highly organized community the fittest sphere for its manifestation, which finds in each social arrangement a condition answering to some faculty in itself" (pp. 396–7).

Interestingly, as David Wiltshire (a recent biographer of Spencer) has noted, Spencer's theory of the evolution of society toward a more perfect individualism appears inconsistent with his understanding of the evolution of biological organisms.[16] Biological evolution (as portrayed by Spencer) tends to the formation of integrative structures under the control of a coordinating central "organ of cerebration" (Wiltshire 1978, p. 239). Extended to the social order, this would imply that the more complex the society, the greater would be the need for a central controlling authority, as it must be the case by analogy with the biological realm that the most perfect *social* organism would be one through which decisions were directed by a single central organ. Yet Spencer's theory of social evolution proceeds in just the opposite manner: as society evolves, the functions of the

State gradually diminish, with individual morality and a more acutely developed sympathetic sense taking on those coordinating functions which would have been consigned to a directing organ. Spencer could only maintain his allegiance to individualism, then, by limiting the extent of the analogy of the biological to the social. But then Spencer explicitly maintains just this position:

> The social organism, discrete instead of concrete, asymmetrical instead of symmetrical, sensitive in all its units instead of having a single sensitive centre, is not comparable to any particular type of individual organism, animal or vegetal.
>
> (Spencer 1885, §269)

The social order is subject to the same laws directing biological evolution, but this is the extent of the application of the biological metaphor. As with respect to the evolution of biological species, society is continually progressing to a more complex, or to a more perfect, form (and so Spencer's evolutionary theory is teleological). However, the concept in respect of society is entirely rhetorical, for Spencer seeks to draw attention to the *process* of societal change, and does not seek to describe the *internal structure* of the social organism. (This will be discussed again in this chapter, in the section entitled "The social organism.")

The moral constitution: a paradox

We can derive from this sequence of events, in conjunction with the earlier remarks on sociality and sympathy, some formal conclusions. Spencer asserts that the "ultimate end" must be the advancement of individual welfare, the "furtherance of individual lives." Yet the advancement of individual welfare can only be actualized under the aegis of a stable and secure society. Social arrangements emerge primarily as a result of the need for individual protection and self-preservation among an otherwise heterogeneous set of individuals with no predisposition for social interaction. Groups simply afford a means by which individuals may be unburdened of the need to undertake for themselves those tasks essential for survival. Thus the rationale behind the emergence of early communities was very utilitarian: the net advantages of concentration in a social union outweighed any net advantage that could be derived from solitary existence (Spencer 1897, §49).[17]

With the instrumental benefits of communal life demonstrated, it soon became canon that "[t]he life of the social organism must, as an end, rank above the lives of its units" (Spencer 1897, §49). As individuals organized communities for their own preservation, it must then follow that maintenance of the *community* is indispensable to the preservation of *individual* lives. Consequently, *individual* welfare must be seen as subordinate to the *social* welfare, and so it seems a contradiction to suggest that the "ultimate end" is the development of individual welfare. Spencer avoids this contradiction by arguing that in fact social preservation is merely a *proximate* end, instrumental to the attainment of the *ultimate* end of individual welfare, made necessary by the existence of rival communities which pose a potential external danger. So long as this potential remains, it must be accepted "that the interests of individuals must be sacrificed to the interests of the community, as far as is needful for the community's salvation" (§49). In the event that such intergroup rivalries surcease, the need for the sacrifice of individual to social interests will no longer have any rationale, and so "there cease to be any public claims at variance with private claims." At this point, the pursuit of individual welfare as the ultimate end can proceed unabated (§49).

It is in this context that Spencer offers an explanation for what seems to be a paradox, an inconsistency in the "moral constitution" of man. With those within his own society, the individual expresses feelings of comity and fraternity; with those outside his society, he expresses feelings of antipathy and even deep-seated hatred. Conduct condemned as morally wrong when directed to one's own may be condoned and even morally justified when directed to outsiders. Certain "destructive activities" directed at outsiders are deemed necessary to the survival of the group, and so these activities become represented as pleasurable actions; infliction of pain generates no feelings of sympathy to the affected party as he has no status within the community. At the same time, the need for cohesion in the group calls forth cooperation and trust among the members, feelings which become represented as pleasurable actions (Spencer 1905, §510). That these sensibilities exist simultaneously suggests a moral gulf, "a kindred irreconcilability between the sentiments answering to the forms of cooperation required for militancy and industrialism," a disconnection induced by the need to subsume individual welfare and hence individual moral reason to the greater interests of the collective (Spencer 1897, §50). The imperative of the continuation of the society effectuates the need for the development of two inconsistent moral codes, each relevant to conduct relative to a given set of interactions, *viz.*, to internal and to external relations (§50).

With the evolution of social conduct, the chasm between these two distinct codes of morality is lessened. The existence of two incongruous moral codes is indicative of "incomplete conduct," conduct not "fully evolved" (Spencer 1897, §50). It is this lack of a fully evolved moral code which is at the heart of the various intergroup disputes, and so its completeness advances the means to the quelling of tensions. The cessation of mutual conflict between societies sanctions the realization of the ultimate end: the cessation of conflict allows for the unification of the moral code, *consistent with* an ethic conducive to the furtherance of individual welfare.

"Completely evolved" conduct will then be seen as requiring as a first step the elimination of "all acts of aggression," major and minor (Spencer 1897, §51). This is fundamental to the achievement of a "complete life," the harmonic existence characteristic of industrial society, yet it is not sufficient. What is required beyond the security resulting from the general acceptance of the "primary moral laws" is an understanding of the importance of "cooperation for satisfying wants" (§51). Cooperation demands facilitation, as it provides the necessary motive. Should the outcome of cooperation not be to mutual advantage (some subjective measure of equivalence, including the possibility of reciprocation in the future), then cooperation itself is nonsensical (§§52–3). Thus Spencer concludes that "the universal basis of cooperation is the proportioning of bene-fits received to services rendered," a conclusion which is significant in explaining the emergence of the division of labor as well as the contract (§53).

Yet Spencer is not willing to end at this point. Equitability in exchange and the pursuit of the ultimate aim of individual welfare are essential to the moral society. "Industrialism" does not require that members of the society receive more than "the benefits given and received by exchange of services" (Spencer 1897, §54). Still, it must be acknowledged that some in the society, while adhering to its norms, nonetheless "fall short of that highest degree of life which the gratuitous rendering of services makes possible." Amelioration of this condi-tion Spencer believes essential, if only because failure to do so would adversely affect "private interests" and by extension the social welfare (§54). Failure to act in accordance with the dictates of beneficence and self-sacrifice is evidence of the fact that "social man has not reached that harmonization of constitution with conditions forming the limit of evolution" (§54). Indeed, the "moral modifi-cation" brought about through the evolution of society is the very thing responsible for philanthropic efforts and other altruistic endeavors; the altruistic feeling is a result of "that same growth of sympathy which checks cruelty and extends justice," providing "positive exertions for the benefit alike of individual and the community at large" (Appendix, p. 324). The full realization of the "industrial state" then simply cannot be manifest absent the affirmation that "sympathy is the root of both justice and beneficence," a motive conducive to the ideal society (§54).[18]

The utilitarian dimension

Despite his apparent sympathy for Utilitarianism, Spencer takes issue with certain aspects of the doctrine as advanced by Bentham. Spencer's chief problem with the ethical philosophy of Utilitarianism is that it seeks to establish moral rules by reference to inductive inferences. Right and wrong are appended to behavior that is seen to produce, respectively, good and evil and, further, this connection is assumed (by virtue of the workings of the inductive hypothesis) to continue to hold in respect of future acts. The problem, of course, is that, absent the expression of a law or the identification of a causative mechanism, one simply cannot assert such generalizations; a "scientific" ethics cannot be fash-ioned along merely inductive lines, which recognize "only *some* relation between cause and effect, ... and not *the* relation" (Spencer 1897, §21; emphasis in orig-inal).

This Spencer perceives as a fatal flaw in intuitionist ethics as well, with its understanding of "moral perceptions" as innate. The moral sense is here *assumed*, as a "supernaturally given conscience," to be capable of distinguishing of itself right from wrong actions, and this is the *sole* mechanism for such knowl-edge. But acceptance of this position implies rejection of "any natural relations between acts and results" and so limits if not destroys the ability to apprehend these relations. Since the relations cannot be known, it cannot be known what conduct is productive of happiness (and so deserving of praise) and what conduct is productive of misery (and so deserving of condemnation), other than by intuition. As intuition produces right actions, (immediate) consequences are irrelevant (although perhaps not *all* consequences) (Spencer 1897, §20). Utilitarian ethics, as it depends solely on "observation of results," also provides "no possibility of knowing by deduction from fundamental principles, what conduct *must* be detrimental and what conduct *must* be beneficial" (§21; emphasis in original). As Spencer notes in a letter to Mill regarding the latter's appraisal of him as "anti-utilitarian," the results of conduct "must be necessary consequences of the constitution of things." This demands that action conducive to happiness be deduced "from the laws of life and the conditions of existence," these deductions "recognized as laws of conduct ... to be conformed to irrespective of a direct estimation of happiness or misery" (§21).

Consider now the position of G. E. Moore, who is adamant is his depiction of Spencer as a hedonist. To Moore, Spencer's statement, to wit, "that conduct gains ethical sanction in proportion as the activities ... are such as do not necessitate mutual injury or hindrance, but consist with, and are furthered by, cooperation and mutual aid" (Spencer 1897, §7; quoted in Moore 1903, p. 100), is evidence of his commission of the "naturalistic fallacy": while the "Evolution-Hypothesis" states merely that certain conduct associated with industrial society is more highly evolved than conduct encountered in militant societies, Spencer contends that this fact alone is sufficient to endow it with *ethical* sanction (Moore 1903, p. 100). Yet Moore accepts that Spencer does not always hold to this principle, and indeed requires for his ethics a second principle, this equating the good life (or good conduct) with pleasurable feelings, along the lines of Bentham and Mill. The textual evidence surely gives reason for such an appraisal. So, argues Moore, Spencer actually rejects an equation of ethically better conduct with more highly evolved conduct, and offers instead a "naturalistic" equation of goodness with pleasurable or agreeable feeling, thus making him a "naturalistic Hedonist" (p. 102).

Yet Moore ignores the fact that Spencer explicitly and emphatically rejects hedonism, as he contrasts empirical or hedonistic Utilitarianism with rational Utilitarianism. Empirical Utilitarianism takes happiness (or some such measure of personal and social welfare) as the "intelligible end," that end toward which, it is abundantly obvious, all should strive. Rational Utilitarianism, by contrast, "does not take welfare for its immediate object of pursuit, but takes for its immediate object of pursuit conformity to certain principles which, in the nature of things, causally determine welfare" (Spencer 1897, §60).

To clarify the distinction, Spencer fixes on the relative places of happiness and justice. To Bentham, happiness is the *summum bonum*, obviously true since everyone agrees as to the constitution of happiness; justice, less readily acceded to, and so "unintelligible as an end," can be no more than a *means* to the promotion of happiness. To Spencer, the reality is the reverse. There can be no general agreement as to the constitution of happiness, as each individual identifies for himself aspects of a pleasurable existence; even Plato and Aristotle could not define, for any other than the Philosopher class, the constituents of happiness. Justice, on the other hand, is easily conceptualized, and in fact there is a remarkable "coincidence of view" among both pre-modern and modern peoples as to its "cardinal principles" (Spencer 1897, §60). The reason is obvious: whereas justice "is concerned exclusively with *quantity* under *stated conditions*," happiness is more elusive, "concerned with both *quantity* and *quality* under *conditions not stated*" (§60; emphasis in original). Justice succeeds in large measure because its fundamental principles specify conditions in respect of reciprocity; happiness fails because no such definite initial conditions can be established. Empirical Utilitarianism expressly rejects the need for initial conditions, for then the "fulfillment" of these conditions would be seen as the immediate end. This cannot be allowed, as happiness would then be contingent on some other end, contrary to the premises of the theory. The difficulty is that, if happiness is unconditional – meaning its attainment does not require the prior fulfillment of conditions necessary to its "compass" – then it cannot suffice as the basis of an ethical theory: without a standard of comparison, any action is as good as any other.[19] This suggests that indeed such conditions "controlling conduct" are necessary to the *promotion* of happiness. In addition, notes Spencer, these conditions "have already been partially, if not wholly, ascertained," and so "our rational course is to bring existing intelligence to bear on these products of past intelligence, with the expectation that it will verify the substance of them while possibly correcting the form" (§60).

As if it were not enough to demonstrate the inadequacy in general of hedonistic Utilitarianism, Spencer also confronts the "greatest happiness" principle as introduced by Bentham. To motivate his presentation, Spencer confronts the principle of altruism, or "pure unselfishness," as it relates to the impersonal "others" of the social community. The principle of maximizing the greatest happiness of the greatest number can only be understood in the sense of each individual member of the society regarding his personal needs and wants as but a mere part of the whole. Since any individual share is "infinitesimal in comparison with the aggregate," any individual action "if directed exclusively to achievement of general happiness, is, if not absolutely altruistic, as nearly so as may be" (Spencer 1897, §83).

As justification for the conclusion, Spencer quotes Mill to the effect that Bentham's principle gains "signification" only if one allows that each person's happiness counts as much as every other (Spencer 1897, §83). The question as Spencer sees it, then, is whether the principle is "a principle of guidance for the community in its corporate capacity" or "a principle of guidance for its members separately considered," or perhaps some combination of the two (§83). If the first, if the principle is to guide the *community* (i.e., if one accepts a role for governmental action), then another ethical principle must be proposed for the regulation of *individual* conduct; if the second, if the *individual* takes as his aim the pursuit of the happiness of the *community*, and acts in a political capacity to effectuate that aim, then some additional principle must be proposed for the regulation of his private conduct.

The question then redounds to the justification of altruism as a rule governing both individual and social conduct. Here Spencer considers altruism as it relates to Bentham's maxim in respect of both public policy and private action. In respect of public policy, meaning as a principle of distribution, the greatest happiness principle fails. In apportioning the product in accordance with the principle, the society must do so with respect to desert, as otherwise vice is placed on the same level as virtue and society can no longer be in accord with the dictates of the principle. In apportioning the product so as to effectuate equal degrees of happiness, the principle also fails, because (1) happiness cannot be measured and so cannot be divided, and (2) each person in the society differs in his capacity for happiness and so in the type and quality of goods conducive to this happiness. As the principle fails as a guide to the division of the product, it may yet still find utility as a principle of justice, a principle of equity. But then the altruistic motive disappears, as does the rationale for the principle (Spencer 1897, §84).

In respect of private action, Spencer dissects Mill's statement that Utilitarianism demands that each behave towards others as though an impartial spectator, practicing the art of Christian charity. The question here is, What would the impartial spectator do in respect of securing the greatest happiness? To Spencer the answer is straightforward. The impartial spectator can only succeed in distributing happiness equally if that happiness appears as manna from heaven. Should "the quantum of happiness" be the result solely of the efforts of one member of the group (to take a simplistic example), then any attempt to distribute it equally to all will lead ultimately to nothing being produced; in addition, each recognizes the *unequal* treatment generated by a principle of alleged *equal* benefit (those who do not contribute realize they are receiving favorable treatment, and also realize that the sole provider is being exploited for their benefit). This leaves the possibility that the spectator will actually choose to distribute according to desert, the claim to the output resting with he who produced or otherwise secured it. This suggests that the greatest happiness principle is merely a means to the maintenance of "equitable relations among individuals," and so "utilitarian altruism becomes a duly qualified egoism" (Spencer 1897, §85).

While altruism is then shown to be an absurd basis for action, egoism fares no better for what Spencer stipulates are obvious reasons. His solution is that both are necessary to the constitution of a moral society. The individual in pursuing his own happiness brings about the general happiness, while at the same time bringing about his own happiness by pursuing the general happiness (Spencer 1897, §91).[20]

The social organism

As Wiltshire notes, for Spencer "society was a real entity, existing independently of the perception of its constituent members." The rationale for such a conclusion is that it is the only explanation consistent with Spencer's teleology

(Wiltshire 1978, p. 234).[21] Spencer himself seems to concede as much: it is a "primary truth that no idea of a whole can be framed without a nascent idea of parts constituting it, and that no idea of a part can be framed without a nascent idea of some whole to which it belongs" (Spencer 1897, §1). It is to a review of Spencer's presentation in respect of this contention that we shall now turn.

In *Principles of Sociology* (1885), Spencer holds society to be more than a mere collection of individuals, rejecting nominalist conceptions. Society is indeed an entity unto itself, with a real existence, "implied by the general persistence of the arrangements among them [the individual discrete units] throughout the area occupied" (Spencer 1885, §212). It is this persistence, "the permanence of the relations among component parts which constitutes the individuality of a whole as distinguished from the individualities of its parts" (§212).[22]

From this concession – that society has a real existence independent of its parts – Spencer moves to consider the manner in which we may apprehend its existence. Society, though real, cannot be directly observed; it does not lend itself to sensory apprehension. To form an understanding of society, its structures, functioning, growth, and development, it is necessary to proceed through analogy, to identify a "parallelism of principle in the arrangement of components" (Spencer 1885, §213). The best way in which to demonstrate the attributes of society is to treat it as analogous to a biological organism.[23]

Societies and organisms have much in common. Both "exhibit augmentation of mass," and both are subject to processes of growth and evolution (Spencer 1885, §214). As they evolve, both exhibit an increasing complexity, forming differentiated structures (§215), which are "accompanied by progressive differentiation of functions" (§216); we see a consistent movement "from the homogeneous to the heterogeneous ... from the indefinite to the definite" (Spencer 1860, p. 106). In addition, we may note that, in both cases, though *individual* units (cells in organisms, citizens in societies) may expire or otherwise vacate their positions, the *structures* (organs, unions, guilds, manufacturers, religious associations, governmental entities, etc.) of which they are part nonetheless continue to function (Spencer 1885, §219). Thus, in biological organisms as in social systems, "the units as well as the larger agencies composed of them, are in the main stationary as respects the places where they discharge their duties and obtain their sustenance" (Spencer 1860, p. 98).

Significantly, both the organism and the society are dependent for their existence and development on the division of labor. While in primitive organisms, as in primitive societies, the parts (meaning the *structures*, not the *individuals*) may appear to be independent, they "gradually acquire a mutual dependence, which becomes at last so great, that the activity and life of each part is made possible only by the activity and life of the rest" (Spencer 1860, p. 95). Interdependence of the parts is as essential in the formation of society as it is in the formation of complex organisms; Spencer even argues that the very idea of specialization in *biological* organisms – the "physiological division of labour" – actually developed through analogy with the division of labor in *political economy*, in which the notion of interdependence is of the utmost importance to economic and social development (Spencer 1885, §217).

Despite these obvious similarities, Spencer also notes some fundamental differences between organisms and societies. The components of an organism "are bound together in close contact," while the components of a society are "more or less widely dispersed." The organism is *concrete*, while the society is *discrete* (Spencer 1885, §220). What is missing in society, the element that serves to distinguish it from an organism, is some form of propagation mechanism, by which we may apprehend the manner of cooperation which is essential to the unity of the structure. The social propagation mechanism Spencer proposes is language, the ability to communicate thoughts, feelings, motivations, desires. It is language, maintaining "the inter-nuncial function, not achievable by stimuli physically transferred," which provides the critical element to social cohesion (§221).[24]

There is, of course, a telling difference between an organism and a society. In the former, the division of labor is so complete that the sub-divisions are rigidly defined. As "the whole has a corporate consciousness capable of happiness or misery," the obvious implication is that each part "should be merged in the life of the whole," that each unit must work to the common welfare (Spencer 1860, p. 98). In the latter, the relationship is reversed. In human society (and, by extension, *all* societies), there is no rigid definition of roles, no social function to which any given order must be held to perform. The individual members of the society retain their individual consciousnesses; there being no "social sensorium," the welfare of the whole cannot be said to be the primary goal of the parts. Now we may inquire as to whether Spencer is involved in a contradiction, i.e., has he in one instance (in respect of the evolution of the social order) advocated holism, while in another become the champion of individualism? The conclusion drawn here is that he has not, as the first instance must not be taken as anything more than an effort at clarifying the anthropological record. We have already seen that, at least in respect of militarist society, the welfare of the whole must take precedence over the welfare of the individual in instances in which the two conflict. But this is true only to the extent that each member of the society finds his personal interests, and indeed survival, inextricably linked to the survival of the whole, and this becomes less of a consideration the more advanced the society. The *ontology* Spencer offers is individualist, not social or organicist, and in this regard he is consistent.[25] In general, then, one must conclude with Spencer himself that "society exists for the benefit of its members; not its members for the benefit of the society." To the extent that the society as a whole has any "claim," as would be necessary for an organicist interpretation to hold, these claims are valid "only in so far as they embody the claims of its component individuals" (Spencer 1885, §222). That no corporate consciousness exists is reason enough to conclude that the society as a whole – the political State – has no independent end and so is not justified in demanding from its members a sacrifice to the greater benefit (Spencer 1860, p. 99).

T. S. Gray observes that Spencer's individualism is entirely compatible with social organicism because of the way in which Spencer *defines* these concepts. For Spencer, the individual is not to be seen as isolated or separate, but is rather socially situated, recognizable only through his connections to others in the society. Spencer's man is not Hobbes's man, nor is Spencer's individualism Hobbes's individualism, for Spencer is resolute in his rejection of the atomic postulate.

This is made clear in Spencer's distinction between militant and industrial societies. As Gray notes (and as we have seen above), industrial society is both more individualistic *and* more organic than militant society, and it is here that organicism and individualism are "reconciled." Industrial society is individualist to the extent that the members of the society are free to act in pursuit of their personal interests within the confines of the social structure; industrial society is organicist in that the component parts are interrelated and interdependent, with the regulative mechanism – the "moral code" – being a spontaneously generated order and not a coercive imposition. Militant society, by contrast, is obviously not individualist, but it is also not organic: the fact of a central legislative and executive authority consciously directing all activity – positive regulation – is inconsistent with the organic model by which the governing mechanism would be positively regulative with respect to "outer organs," but negatively regulative with respect to "inner organs" (T. S. Gray 1985, pp. 250–2).

Remarks

Spencer's influence in the sciences, sociology, and social theory of the period was quite profound. While his contributions may not have had the impact he desired – he is today regarded as an apologist for, and even the philosopher of, *laissez-faire* and the staunchest of critics of government – one may with little exaggeration suggest that the works of many of those considered as the great expositors of late nineteenth- and early twentieth-century liberalism and even social organicism would not have been as pronounced had Spencer not taken the initiative. Alfred Marshall's letter to *The Daily Chronicle* (published 23 November 1904) on the possibility of raising a national memorial to Spencer sums up quite nicely his place in nineteenth-century social and scientific thought:[26]

I have no hesitation in giving an appreciative answer to your question whether a national memorial should be raised to Herbert Spencer. His attempt to lay down the outlines of a unified sociology was, in my opinion, premature by at least 100 years. He spread his strength over too wide an area; and his fame has suffered from many attacks, not always based on a generous interpretation of his words, by specialists, each of whom was more at home in his chosen ground than Spencer could be. And, again, his fame has suffered because his general remarks as to the principles of evolution dealt with conceptions which were themselves in process of rapid evolution; and the younger students of today are often inclined to find little that is both new and true in a saying of him which had sent the blood rushing through the veins of those who a generation ago looked eagerly for each volume of his as it issued from the press. There is probably no one who gave as strong a stimulus to the thoughts of the younger Cambridge graduates thirty years or forty years ago as he. He opened out a new world of promise; he set men on high enterprise in many diverse directions; and though he may have regulated English intellectual work less than Mill did, I believe he did much more towards increasing its vitality. He has, perhaps, been more largely read and exercised a greater influence on the Continent than any other recent English thinker except Darwin.

The industrialist Andrew Carnegie was a devout follower of Spencer; his *Gospel of Wealth* is a testament to the ideas of the great man. The sociologist Ferdinand Tönnies incorporated Spencer's ideas on evolution and society in his 1887 *Gemeinschaft und Gesellschaft* (*Community and Civil Society*). The sociologist Thorstein Veblen, whose works have of late been given a Marxian flavor, also credits Spencer with having been a critical influence in his own intellectual development.[27] As William Miller has shown, even the sociologist/economist Vilfredo Pareto can be seen to have borrowed heavily from Spencer,[28] especially with respect to his identification of the social optimum, although Spencer would never have thought it proper to limit its application merely to *economic* welfare (Miller 1972, pp. 230–1).

To these testaments of the positive influence of Spencer must be counterpoised the opinion of Émile de Laveleye. Responding to what he regards as Spencer's Darwinian account of social development, Laveleye warns of the coarsening effects on individuals and thus society were the laws of natural selection allowed to play out in the social arena. Were this to occur,

the utility of history, considered as a moral lesson for both kings and people, would be destroyed. The history of man might then be looked upon as a mere zoological strife between nations, and a simple lengthening out of natural history. What moral instruction can possibly be drawn from the study of the animal world, where the strong devour or destroy the weak? No spectacle could be more odious or more demoralizing!

(Laveleye 1885, p. 506)

So far as Laveleye is concerned, in applying naturalistic theories to the social realm, i.e., in suggesting that "natural laws" underlie the transformation of society in the same way as they apply to the evolution of biological organisms, we diminish and ultimately destroy those human sentiments that are responsible for the formation and the maintenance of human social arrangements. Yet Spencer's moral theory is not as Laveleye suggests. Far from providing a justification for the elimination of the unfit – Spencer cannot be classed with such eugenicists as Francis Galton, Sidney Webb, Irving Fisher, and Margaret Sanger – Spencer stresses the cooperative aspects of man's nature and the positive elements of natural selection: it is not so much that the weak lose as it is that the strong survive and prosper. It is this element of Spencer's thought which is important for our purposes here, and is the reason for his inclusion.

Perhaps the most consistent adherent of Spencer's philosophy was the American sociologist and economist William Graham Sumner, credited with having established sociology as an academic subject in the United States. His effort to have Spencer's *Study of Sociology* included in the curriculum at Yale ignited a debate over academic freedom that was to have profound consequences. It is to a review of the works of Sumner that we turn in the next chapter.

Notes

1 James further observes: "Rarely has Nature performed an odder or more Dickens-like feat than when she deliberately designed, or accidently stumbled into, the personality of Herbert Spencer. Greatness and smallness surely never lived so closely in one skin together" (James 1904, p. 99).

2 Darwin, in his autobiography, is actually dismissive of Spencer:

> Herbert Spencer's conversation seemed to me very interesting, but I did not like him particularly, and did not feel that I could easily have become intimate with him. I think that he was extremely egotistical. After reading any of his books, I generally feel enthusiastic admiration for his transcendent talents, and have often wondered whether in the distant future he would rank with such great men as Descartes, Leibnitz, etc., about whom, however, I know very little. Nevertheless I am not conscious of having profited in my own work by Spencer's writings. His deductive manner of treating every subject is wholly opposed to my frame of mind. His conclusions never convince me: and over and over again I have said to myself, after reading one of his discussions, – "Here would be a fine subject for half-a-dozen years' work." His fundamental generalisations (which have been compared in importance by some persons with Newton's laws!) – which I daresay may be very valuable under a philosophical point of view, are of such a nature that they do not seem to me to be of any strictly scientific use. They partake more of the nature of definitions than of laws of nature. They do not aid one in predicting what will happen in any particular case. Anyhow they have not been of any use to me.
>
> (Darwin 1969, pp. 108–9)

However, in correspondence with Spencer (25 November 1858), Darwin seems far more charitable: "[I]n my opinion, your argument [in 'Development Hypothesis'] could not have been improved on & might have been quoted by me with great advantage" (Darwin 1991, p. 210).

3 It must be clarified at the outset that Spencer's understanding of the concept is Lamarckian, not Darwinian, i.e., for Spencer, an organism adapts to environmental changes, which adaptations are then transmitted so as to achieve an equilibrium. This contrasts with Darwin's theory of accidental variations, which become ultimately "selected" as a result of their survival value.

4 Although Jonathan Turner argues that one could more accurately claim Darwin as a biological Spencerian. See Turner 1985, p. 11.

5 Durkheim further notes that "[m]orality, at all levels, is never met with save in the state of society and has never varied save as a function of social conditions" (Durkheim 1893, p. 332).

6 The philosopher Michael Ruse (1986) notes that natural selection is actually "opportunistic," and so, in general, change is from the heterogeneous to the homogeneous. However, it is Spencer's Lamarckian focus which allows him to extend his biological theories to the study of social development.

7 As Ruse (1995) demonstrates, this places Spencer in the company of the paleontologist Stephen Jay Gould (although Gould rejects the application to himself of the term, given

its distasteful connotations), and the biologist Edward O. Wilson (a Spencer admirer) (see especially Ruse 1995, ch. 8). That Gould is a progressionist is evident in his elucidation of the concept of punctuated equilibrium (just to take one example). Thus one can only express wonder at the unsubstantiated conclusion that Gould is "[a] leading figure in the revival and renaissance of biological evolution freed from reactionary notions from the nineteenth century and freed from absolutist belief in inevitable progress" (Dugger and Sherman 2000, p. 6). Such a conclusion is ideological, not scientific.

8 Whether this is in fact a true statement of the derivation of the ideas of orange and violet is another topic. For Spencer, it makes for a good story.

9 The notion of spontaneous order is found in Ferguson's *Essay on the History of Civil Society*, where he defines it as "the result of human action, but not the execution of any human design" (Ferguson 1767, p. 119). This idea will be seen to have great importance throughout this work.

10 "[T]hat societies are not artificially put together, is truth so manifest, that it seems wonderful men should have ever overlooked it.... You need but to look at the changes going on around, or observe social organization in its leading peculiarities, to see that these are neither supernatural, nor are determined by the wills of individual men ... but are consequent on general natural causes" (Spencer 1860, p. 91).

11 Note here the similarity to Mill's principle of liberty. Mario Rizzo allows that the Law of Equal Freedom applies "only to the perfect man in the perfect society," so that adherence to ethical injunctions is "spontaneous" (Rizzo 1999, p. 119).

12 Sentiments are "those highest orders of feelings which are entirely re-representative" (Spencer 1905, §513).

13 This is stated explicitly in *Social Statics* (Spencer 1954, p. 20).

14 In *Social Statics*, Spencer defines justice as "nothing but a sympathetic affection of the instinct of personal rights – a sort of reflex function of it" (Spencer 1954, p. 90).

15 This interpretation of social evolution has been taken as evidence of Spencer's social fatalism. See Ralph Eaton (1921, p. 389).

16 One finds similar interpretations in Richard Hiskes (1983) and T. S. Gray (1985). While both are charitable toward Spencer, Gray argues that Spencer's approach is not internally inconsistent or contradictory, a position argued here.

17 Durkheim takes issue with Spencer on this point. Following Auguste Comte, Durkheim concludes that men are drawn to society by

> mechanical forces and instinctive forces such as the affinity of blood, attachment to the same soil, the cult of their ancestors, a commonality of habits, etc. It is only when the group has been formed on these bases that co-operation becomes organised.
>
> (Durkheim 1893, p. 219)

However, on the similarities between Spencer and Durkheim, see Robert Perrin (1995). For an attempt at reconciliation, see Lorenzo Infantino (1998), especially pp. 90–5.

18 Note the following interpretation of Spencer's classification from Gaetano Mosca:

> If we follow not so much Spencer's criteria of classification as the mass of his incidental assertions, and especially the spirit that animates his work as a whole, we cannot fail to see that by a 'militant state' he means a state in which juridical defense has made little progress and by an 'industrial state' another type of society in which justice and social morality are much better safeguarded.
>
> (Mosca 1939, p. 100)

19 "It is sufficient for present purposes to remark that were it [the greatest happiness principle] true it would be utterly useless as a first principle; both from the impossibility of determining specifically what happiness is, and from the want of a measure by which equitably to mete it out, could we define it" (Spencer 1954, p. 87n.).

20 Francis Edgeworth agrees with Spencer on the inadequacy of the utilitarian calculus to handle such things as self-indulgence. But he observes that the philosophy of utilitarianism was never meant to apply so rigidly as to compel the actor to "wrap himself up in his utilitarian virtue so as to become a wet blanket to his friends." One should not view utilitarianism as demanding that he "should have an eye to the general good while kissing his wife." Edgeworth goes on to consider that Spencer's marriage of egoism and altruism could be seen as "the transformation of mixed into pure utilitarianism, the psychical side of the physical change in what may be dimly discerned as a sort of hedonico-magnetic field" (Edgeworth 1881, p. 82).

21 Although Geoffrey Hodgson (1993) argues against such a reading, describing Spencer as an unabashed atomist for whom society is little more than a set of relations holding between individual, independent parts. Such an interpretation, however, cannot be sustained, except through a very select and thus incomplete reading of Spencer's works.

22 Spencer's position is thus at odds with the modal individualism adumbrated by Unger:

> Individualism recognizes the reality of the social bond, but it treats that bond as both precarious and threatening to individuality. It is precarious because of the fragility of every sharing of values and the impossibility of administering a system of rules in the absence of shared ends. It is threatening because the greater the sharing of ends the more is the substance of individuality eviscerated.
>
> (Unger 1975, p. 155)

But then Unger provides no source for this interpretation.

23 Ferdinand Tönnies employs Spencer in his own analysis of the formation of society:

> The human *self* or the "subject" of human natural will is, like the system of natural will itself, a *unity*. That is to say it is a unit within a larger unit, as well as containing other lesser units within itself. Like an organism and its component parts, however, it is a unity because of its inner self-sufficiency, *unum per se*, and because its parts are all related to it as a living entity. It maintains itself by changing these parts, discarding old parts (robbing them of *their* life and their particular unity), and creating new parts or assimilating them from inorganic matter. Thus nothing is a unified system that is merely a 'part', and everything that is a 'whole' forms some kind of unified system
>
> (Tönnies 1935, p. 179; emphasis in original)

24 In "The Social Organism" (1860) Spencer handles the question of continuity versus dispersion by expanding the domain. Specifically, if one considers, not simply separate societies, but the entire surface of the planet, the entire food chain, if you will, one sees not merely "dead space," but rather connections between human life and "lower-order" life. Vegetation and lower forms of animal life are essential to the maintenance of human life, and so must be included within the scope of the analogy of societies to organisms. "And when we do this, we see that the citizens who make up a community, may be considered as highly vitalized units surrounded by substances of lower vitality, from which they draw their nutriment" (Spencer 1860, p. 97). Taking the whole into consideration thus removes the objection that society is not comprehensible as a continuous mass.

25 Thus the conclusion of Ellen Frankel Paul (1983), to the effect that Spencer "evolved" into a "full-blown holist" (albeit of a different stripe than Hegel), cannot be sustained, not even when confined to the character of the militant society.

26 Reprinted in John K. Whitaker (1996, vol. III, pp. 97–8).

27 On Spencer's influence on Veblen, see Joseph Dorfman, 1935, 1959.

28 Turner (1985) arrives at a similar conclusion, especially with respect to Pareto's *The Rise and Fall of Elites*.

5 Sumner: tradition and custom in the social order

William Graham Sumner (1840–1910), Yale economist and sociologist, is generally regarded as having been the leading American disciple of Herbert Spencer,[1] and the figure who more than anyone else is (perhaps erroneously) credited with, or blamed for, the flourishing of the Social Darwinist movement in the United States.[2] Yet his writings encompass a wide range of topics and disciplines, making it difficult to assign him to any one category. An Episcopalian minister, his early published writings on political and social issues seem in the nature of sermons, confronting issues of individual freedom and responsibility, always with the aim of promoting social solidarity and social welfare. As a polemicist – what in an earlier time would have been termed a pamphleteer and later a political pundit – he addressed issues of election reform, bimetallism, labor reform, and even social relations. As an historian, he authored biographies of Robert Morris, Alexander Hamilton, and Andrew Jackson. As an economist, his advocacy of *laissez-faire* and private property rights commended him to the business classes even as he championed the plight of the "forgotten man," while his commitment to free trade at a time when the orthodoxy demanded protective tariffs shows in him a need for consistency over pragmatic politics. As a sociologist, he was to produce one of the more important tracts of the early twentieth century, *Folkways*, and even became president of the American Sociological Society.

For the present, it is Sumner the sociologist with whom we shall deal. It is in his sociological writings, including in this category some of his more popular-press pieces, that his view of man and society are the most clearly and succinctly stated.

The advance of the social order

Society defined

Society is a living organism. While it is possible to dissemble it and seek to analyze it with reference to its constituent parts, in so doing one is engaged in little more than an idle exercise from which no substantive claims can be had. Society cannot be apprehended as a mere collection of otherwise independent individuals or as a set of autonomous institutions, for it is the interrelatedness among the constituent parts which gives it its essence.

Sumner's most expressive depiction of the organization of society is presented in the 1927 *The Science of Society*, published posthumously and written with the assistance of his erstwhile student and principal disciple, Albert Galloway Keller (Sumner and Keller 1927). While there is some apprehension in utilizing this work in support of Sumner's positions on the questions before us here – there is much evidence that *The Science of Society* is more the product of Keller than of Sumner, and so reflects the former's social Darwinist frame of reference[3] – it nonetheless serves the purpose of placing in context some of the concepts addressed by Sumner in his earlier writings. Specifically, it is useful in setting before the reader some important definitions. To begin, the authors define society as "[a] group of human beings living in a coöperative effort to win subsistence and to perpetuate the species" (Sumner and Keller 1927, pp. 6–7). Notwithstanding the inclusion of the word "human," the authors insist that this is a *general* definition of society, descriptive of the social organization of *all* species; it has an "objective quality ... which locks immediately with facts observable in nature" (p. 7). Further, while the family, the nation, and even the race fit squarely within this definition of society, it is not to be taken to apply to just any form of association: it specifically excludes those collective groupings, such as unions, schools, benevolent associations, cooperatives, etc., which, while important in maintaining social ties among the members, nonetheless do not fulfill the "self-maintenance and self-perpetuation" functions essential to society.

Society requires for its very existence that individuals engage in those cooperative activities that redound to the cohesiveness of the whole; society, in other words, is a collection of disparate individual elements organized to the end of communal self-maintenance and self-perpetuation. In Sumner and Keller's estimation, it is the "differentiation of function, invention of appropriate new structure, adaptation, perfection, coöperation, and rhythmic effort under command and discipline," the hallmarks of organization, which have been critical to the advance of civilization (Sumner and Keller 1927, p. 9). In the absence of such an organization – a means to structure – the individual and parochial interests would take precedence over the social, and would seek to influence the direction of the whole. Pluralism is indeed disruptive and destructive, as unfettered individuals coalescing into disparate groups represent the antithesis of society. Recognizing the difficulties inherent in a liberal social order, specifically the problem of compelling individuals to accept that there is a *community* purpose which supercedes any *personal* interest, they seek to provide a rationale for the formation and perpetuation of institutional structures the function of which is to create the conditions through which such interpersonal bonds may be formed. Organization as structuration serves to promote the cohesion essential to society, even as it provides the means for the restriction of individuality and unencumbered action essential to the social order; it "restrains and constrains the individuals to a common purpose and, while hostile to liberty, gives aid and protection and is the sustaining structure within which individual life goes on in security" (p. 9).

The notion of organization as hostile to liberty and individuality, while at the same time supportive of both, requires some elaboration. The fact of living in society demands restrictions on individual action, where these actions are seen as having a disruptive and even anti-social influence, and as society progresses these demands become more significant; even Mill recognizes this to be true. Yet, paradoxically, it is the advance of civilization which, while *restraining* action, actually *expands* the domain of individuality: as civilization evolves, its hold on individuals becomes more complete while, at the same time, institutions develop which, in their effect, endow "each member of society with a sphere of individual activity so widened that his experience of individuality, liberty, and independence far surpasses anything which men on lower civilization can know" (Sumner and Keller 1927, p. 9).

Man as social being

As with Spencer, Sumner and Keller agree that society, "in the abstract," can only be understood as a whole (Sumner and Keller 1927, p. 9); we study *social* structures, *social* outcomes, *social* constructs. Unlike Spencer, they do not hold that man is *naturally* a social being; they reject not only the notion of man as *zoon koinonikon*, but also of man as *zoon politikon*, noting that the latter has been incorporated into the sociological and philosophical lexicon without realizing that it represents a category mistake – it is no more valid now than it was when Aristotle mistakenly advanced it as descriptive of all men, based as it was on a depiction of idealized Greek urban life.

On this reading of the anthropological record, man formed social bonds solely from necessity, not as a result of a social nature, and so any attempt to portray man as a "social animal" is misguided. There is simply no basis upon which one can conclude "that man was outfitted with any innate quality of sociability implanted in his germ-plasm." On the contrary, "the tendency to associate is acquired rather than inherited," and so we must conclude "that man's association with his kind is a product of societal rather than of organic evolution" (Sumner and Keller 1927, p. 11). This is the man of Hobbes, not the man of Locke.

Some clarification of this contention may be in order. For man to be, in the nature of things, a social being, it would have to be the case that there is in his constitution an inclination to group activity; a predilection to sociality – a social sense – would be a necessary constituent of human nature. Alternatively, were it the case that man apprehends society as the most rational means to the advancement of ends, society (or rather the inducement to social order) could be justified on instrumentalist grounds. One then would need no coercion to social integration, no instruction in the advantages to be gained through social interaction, for cooperation would appear as the obvious means to the advancement of the interests of the individual. But, Sumner and Keller argue, what we observe is that "all those qualities which are indispensable to membership in society have to be learned, like language, by each generation anew." Man is not by nature associationist, nor is he a hedonic rationalist. The "capacity to live in society" is not an innate trait, nor is it "the result of rational choice and resolution," by which we may surmise on the basis of self-interest alone that social cooperation will result in greater personal benefits than living in isolation. Social life is rather "traditional in custom," the result of habit, and became dominant solely as a result of an acknowledgment of "its high survival-value in the evolution of civilization" (Sumner and Keller 1927, p. 13). The impetus to society is nonetheless utilitarian: as (1) man seeks pleasure over pain, (2) pleasure is manifest in those acts "which bring adaptation to life conditions," and (3) association with others has proven to be highly effective as a survival mechanism, one must conclude that the formation of individuals into society is a reasoned response to a given set of circumstances and not the result of either an innate individual need for social contact or a conscious and deliberate decision to enact a social compact (p. 32).

Individual freedom

Important here is the notion of individual freedom. The isolated individual is, virtually by definition, completely free to do as he wishes, with no concern for the feelings or the interests of others, and no concern that others may infringe upon his domain. When removed from that environment and placed in the company of others, the formerly isolated individual no longer has the freedom he once experienced. As he must now interact with others whose personal interests may not coincide with his own, he finds himself compelled to conform to the rules of the society, to subject himself to limitations on conduct and behavior heretofore not contemplated. To do so, to function within society, requires a discipline brought about by training. The social life is not one which comes naturally: one does not instinctively feel a compulsion to limit one's personal freedom of action in deference to the interests of others, but rather does so "because he is compelled by circumstances" (Sumner and Keller 1927, p. 14). This compulsive aspect is essential to the maintenance of society, and is evident in the very earliest civilizations: "association was a species of insurance which one could not afford to be without" (p. 14). Man did not simply reason that, since social life would grant him greater benefits and rewards than the solitary life, he would gather with others into groups so as to appreciate this benefit; societies evolved, and those who accepted the strictures of social life thrived, while those who opted for the alternative perished.

Sumner and Keller's answer to their own question:

> whether society is a great club, enjoying privileges and advantages by nature, with free membership for everybody; or whether it is a gild of workers, with high admission fees and strict rules of general welfare, which imposes heavy penalties on dissenters, and confers no privileges except a costly insurance against certain massive ills

is then most assuredly the latter. It is through a combination of social conditioning through education and "labor and sacrifice" in maturity that man actually *becomes* a social being, not through a rational assessment of alternatives culminating in the forging of a social consensus or social compact. Reflection may allow one to ascertain that indeed "the benefits of association are worth the cost," and so to conclude (erroneously) that society is the result of deliberative action. However, in truth, the vast majority have become so habituated to the social life as to know no other means of existence (Sumner and Keller 1927, p. 12).

Social norms

One of Sumner's most important works, and the one that most clearly and succinctly presents his view of the nature of the social order, is his 1906 *Folkways: A Study of the Sociological Importance of Usages, Manners, Customs, Mores, and Morals*. It is in this monumental work that we find his best-known and most enduring contribution to sociology and to our understanding of the processes of social evolution.

Folkways

Folkways are those habits, routines, and skills that have been proven effective or "expedient" as means to the achievement of desired ends. They are in the nature of "mass phenomena," "uniform, universal in the group, imperative, and invariable" (Sumner 1906, p. 2). Folkways represent that "great mass of usages, of all degrees of importance, covering all the interests of life, constituting an outfit of instruction for the young, embodying a life policy, forming character, containing a world philosophy, albeit most vague and unformulated, and sanctioned by ghost fear so that variation is impossible" (p. 67). More generally, they "are the widest, most fundamental, and most important operation by which the interests of men in groups are served," and the process behind their creation "is the chief one to which elementary societal or group phenomena are due" (p. 34).

Folkways develop through "the frequent repetition of petty acts, often by great numbers acting in concert or, at least, acting in the same way when face to face with the same need" (Sumner 1906, p. 3). In this way they become ingrained as individual habit or social custom. What begin as individual acts dedicated to the satisfaction of certain desires, gradually, as their efficacy in achieving ends is realized, take on the role of devices essential to social intercourse. Individual acts build upon one another to produce institutional structures and social customs such that define a community; the interests of the group derive from the purpose of the group, and these group interests supersede any individual interest (p. 63). Yet the manner of this evolution is entirely haphazard. Each action "fixes an atom in a structure, both fulfilling a duty derived from what preceded and conditioning what is to come afterwards by the authority of traditional custom," which then reacts and "produces continuity, coherence, and consistency" on the structure as a whole (p. 35). The initial habits may have their genesis in the most basic desire to produce pleasure and to avoid pain. Those actions that serve the purpose are repeated, adopted by others who seek similar outcomes. As they continue to produce the desired effects, the actions become habits and ultimately social customs. The important conclusion to be drawn is that these habits do not come about because of some rational, deliberative process tying means to ends. Instead, they emerge spontaneously as the seemingly random outcome of a developmental process, akin to Ferguson's spontaneous order and Spencer's spontaneous concerted action. Folkways, "one of the chief forces by which a society is made to be what it is" (p. 3), are by and large little more than derived customs, i.e.,

> consequences which were never conscious, and never foreseen or intended. They are not noticed until they have long existed, and it is still longer before they are appreciated.... They are like products of natural forces which men unconsciously set in operation, or they are like the instinctive ways of animals, which are developed out of experience, which reach a final form of maximum adaptation to an interest, which are handed down by tradition and admit of no exception or variation, yet change to meet new conditions, still within the same limited methods, and without rational reflection or purpose.
>
> (Sumner 1906, p. 4)

Folkways are "true" or "right" in the sense that they are proven ways of achieving ends. They persist because they work and so, as utilitarians (as early man must surely have been), we view this as sufficient motive to continue employing them, to treat them as "traditions." As these habits take on the label of tradition or custom, significantly they move from being "right" as efficacious to "right" as "authoritative" or "correct." The might of tradition is sufficient "warrant" for a mode of action to be considered socially correct and even beyond question; no independent test of their right is possible, nor is rightness itself a test. "The notion of right is in the folkways.... In the folkways, whatever is, is right" (Sumner 1906, p. 28).

As folkways are the embodiment of cultural tradition, as they are granted "the authority of the ancestral ghosts," they are testaments to right conduct and so guides to what is acceptable; in the folkways, "right and ought" coincide (Sumner 1906, p. 28). Here we see the mechanism behind the development of morality and social welfare. Morality "is the sum of the taboos and prescriptions in the folkways by which right conduct is defined" (p. 29). Sumner denies the existence of natural rights and intuitive morality, as did Mill, arguing instead that morals "are historical, institutional, and empirical," in sum, "products of the folkways," and so indirectly (or directly at one remove) "reflections on, and generalizations from, the experience of pleasure and pain which is won in efforts to carry on the struggle for existence under actual life conditions" (p. 29).

Mores

Mores are folkways to which have been appended concerns for moral judgment and social welfare; they are folkways "raised to another plane" (Sumner 1906, p. 30). The term itself Sumner appropriates from the Latin, where it is identified with "customs in the broadest and richest sense of the word, including the notion that customs served welfare, and had traditional and mystic sanction, so that they were properly authoritative and sacred" (p. 37). Mores may be usefully differentiated from usages, "folkways which contain no principle of welfare, but serve convenience so long as all know what they are expected to do." Also excluded are rational social orders (whether or not they are predicated on any welfare basis) not derivative from custom or habit, i.e., those "[p]roducts of intentional investigation or of rational and conscious reflection, projects formally adopted by voluntary associations, rational methods consciously selected, injunctions and prohibitions by authority, and all specific conventional arrangements." In short, the mores exclude any arrangement that may be the result of reasoned, deliberative motive. Yet the mores *do* include such vagaries as "[f]ashions, fads, affectations, poses, ideals, manias, popular delusions, follies, and vices," as these are social habits that "have characteral qualities and characteral effect," i.e., "they have the form of attempts to live well, to satisfy some interest, or to win some good" (p. 57); even though ephemeral, not completely amenable to understanding, and not designed to any definite end, they may be seen to function in the furtherance of a social prospect. Mores are "the underlying facts in regard to the faiths, notions, tastes, desires, etc., of that society at that time" (pp. 57–8). As such, they are the facts of our existence, typically beyond reflection, the norms into which we are born and within which we function. They are truth, commandments directing conduct to a moral end, "final and unchangeable," complete within themselves (p. 79).

As rightness inheres in the folkways, goodness and rightness inhere in the mores. They serve to delimit those customs and traditions that are associated with just, right, and proper conduct, as they provide the justification and the rationalization for the institutional arrangements themselves; they represent, in effect, conduct sanctioned by society. The mores are important precisely because of their ability to dominate the individuals, presumably to the greater benefit of the whole. They coerce, demand and enforce submission, as they do not merely express the "underlying facts" of the society, but inculcate in each member "his outfit of ideas, faiths, and tastes, and lead him into prescribed mental processes" (Sumner 1906, p. 174). They are the means of acculturation and assimilation. But, cautions Sumner, one must be aware that the goodness and rightness of the mores are context-dependent and situational, i.e., mores can be justified only in respect of a given time and place, and then only so long as they serve the interests of those in the community (p. 58). The mores of the time are so because they serve to the promotion of the social welfare *of the time*; the mores of any given period then are "good" to the extent that they "are well adapted to the situation."[4] They are *not* categorical imperatives, but "are forever moving towards more complete adaptation to conditions and interests, and also towards more complete adjustment to each other" (p. 58).

With this understanding, we are led to the third and most complete of Sumner's definitions of the mores: mores "are the ways of doing things which are current in a society to satisfy human needs and desires, together with the faiths, notions, codes, and standards of well living which inhere in those ways, having a genetic connection with them" (Sumner 1906, p. 59). In a sense, mores are a ritualization of folkways, an informal social codification of customs and traditions as expressions of the culture of the community. This "social ritual in which we all participate unconsciously" includes (as a partial list) "current habits as to hours of labor, meal hours, family life, the social intercourse of the sexes, propriety, amusements, travel, holidays, education, the use of periodicals and libraries, and innumerable other details of life" (p. 62). The mores *define* the culture; they are not mere appurtenances to the social order. The pervasiveness of the mores is sufficient evidence of their "wisdom and utility." They allow us to judge situations without having to rely on reason in every step of the process.

It is of profound significance for Sumner that the modern (early twentieth-century) usage of the term is so divorced from its roots. Morality has become a separate area of consideration, no longer connected to custom, religion, politics, philosophy, or civil discourse. Modern concerns with "ethics" (as distinct from "the ethos of a people," from which derive the mores) are little more than "attempt[s] to systematize the current notions of right and wrong upon some basic principle, generally with the purpose of establishing morals on an absolute doctrine, so that it shall be universal, absolute and everlasting" (Sumner 1906, p. 37). In so doing, the "ethical generalities" so derived are deemed authoritative on that ground alone, and so become disconnected from concerns for the furtherance of social welfare.[5]

In a large sense, mores are "causative." The very "sentiments" deemed essential for the continuance of modern societal development – including justice, fairness, humanitarianism, altruism, sympathy – are not merely abstract principles one may come to view as generalizations of the underlying bases of action, but are derivative from the mores themselves: "they came out of the mores into which they return again as a principle of consistency" (Sumner 1906, p. 39). It is in the evolution of human society that one sees the manifestation of the folkways, and it is the folkways which have been largely responsible for transformations in the constitution of man, including concern with the welfare of the whole. Sumner thus breaks with the classical liberal philosophers on this issue, principally those Scottish philosophers, Ferguson, Hutcheson, Hume, and Smith, as he denies the importance in the development of sociality of the sympathies. Sympathy is not the guide in these matters; sympathy is but one of the *consequences* of the mores (p. 39).

Class structure

For Sumner, the mores of any society are held most strongly by the masses. Here one must distinguish between "masses" and "classes." A class is merely a subgroup within a society, identified by certain common and definable traits. Using Francis Galton's notion of "natural gifts," and accepting its extension by Friedrich Ammon, Sumner identifies class with "societal value," a rather imprecise and amorphous concept that is eminently useful as a means of categorization (Sumner 1906, pp. 40–2). Classes are merely "clusters" of otherwise different (in terms of social value) individuals who, for the sake of classification, are seen as possessing certain common features.

While the *classes* have, for the most part, been the driving force behind historical change, and have developed conventions (group mores) which have served as regulators of conduct within the group, it is the *masses* which have been responsible for holding fast to the moral and ethical soul of the society. The classes have introduced variety to the community, "luxury, frivolity, and vice," as well as "refinement, culture, and the art of living" (Sumner 1906, p. 45). They are the force of novelty and change. The masses, by contrast, are conservative. Not to be confused with the "large classes at the base of a social pyramid," they are rather better understood as being the "core" of the community. They are imitative, not innovative, tied to habit and tradition.[6] This basic conservatism is inertial, and not due to any felt need to hold on to the past to protect position and status. Change is "irksome," as it requires the acceptance of new and untried habits and traditions. When change does occur, it is gradual and is typically imitative of those ideas of the classes which are seen as potentially advantageous over the long term, while being minimally destructive of the old patterns of behavior. These ideas are then assimilated into the old traditions, which then in turn become standards rigorously defended (p. 46).

Notable here is the "great central section of the masses" otherwise known as the haven of the "common man" (Sumner 1906, p. 50). This all-important middle, identified as being "formed around the mathematical mean of the society, or around the mathematical mode, if the distribution of the subdivisions is not symmetrical," Sumner characterizes as bound "by routine and tradition," as "shallow, narrow-minded, and prejudiced," but otherwise as "harmless," and "neutral in all the policy of society." "It lacks initiative and cannot give an impulse for good or bad" (p. 50).

Yet, despite this character, it is this great middle which is the force for social stability. It is not a deadweight to society, nor is it the pool from which emerge the anti-social elements. On the contrary, it is the essential core responsible for the preservation and even the gradual alteration of the mores. Interestingly, the upper portion of this group is distinguished as highly disciplined, "with strong moral sense, public spirit, and sense of responsibility" (Sumner 1906, p. 53). The common man, as the representative of the group, holds to the traditions of the past, modifying them as need and circumstance arises. His importance is evident in the ways society caters to his desires: art, literature, theater, politics, commerce, all seek to satisfy his wants, as they seek also to "strengthen his prejudices." It is this common man and the great middle to which he belongs which are indispensable in determining the mores of the whole (p. 51).

At the same time, it is the constitution of the middle which prevents it from exerting a leadership role. It is of its nature quite incapable of being organized as an independent political force. Patriotism, symbolism, faith, morality, are emotions which can be ignited to impel it to action in support of specific causes or ends. The difficulty is in engaging this center with any consistency. Sumner sees in respect of this group that all impulses to action are "spasmodic and transitory," making it better subject to campaigns of agitation than to concerted efforts at education (Sumner 1906, p. 51). Education is time-consuming and may result only in reaffirming the popular sentiments; agitation, on the other hand, "appeals skillfully to pet emotions and to latent fanaticism," and so can more directly achieve the limited results desired. Still, even attempts at political agitation may fail to produce the desired results if they conflict with the underlying mores. It is the mores "which determine the degree of reserved common sense, and the habit of observing measure and method, to which the masses have been accustomed" (p. 52), and it is the mores which act as a bulwark against revolution.

Institutions

The very idea that early man lived in a state of equality represents for Sumner an erroneous reading of the anthropological record. Were it indeed the case that men in the "state of nature" enjoyed such a condition, there would be no society. It is only through concerted effort that society progresses. "Organization, leadership, and discipline are indispensable to any beneficial action by masses of men" (Sumner 1906, p. 48). If left to their own devices, the society of the "horde" would quickly become extinct, as it is directed to no purpose. However, when confronted with a rival, superior in skill and organization, and subjected to its dictates and discipline, the "horde" becomes an efficient and effective element of the new group; as the subject of a more dominant group, "it consists of workers to belabor the ground for others, or tax payers to fill a treasury from which others may spend, or food for gunpowder, or voting material for demagogues" (p. 48).

Thus emerge institutions, those arrangements "which will hold the activities of society in channels of order, deliberation, peace, regulated antagonism of interests, and justice, according to the mores of the time" (Sumner 1906, pp. 48–9). It is institutions which "put an end to exploitation and bring interests into harmony under civil liberty." The inequalities essential to social evolution are equally necessary to the development of institutions.

> They are produced out of the mores by the selection of the leading men and classes who get control of the collective power of the society and direct it to the activities which will (as they think) serve the interests which they regard as most important.
>
> (p. 49)

Institutions are not, then, the product of the "masses," but rather are products of the "classes," as their purpose is ultimately to "increase the economic power of the society and the force at the disposal of the state." Nor are they the outcomes of deliberate actions focused to the advancement of the social good. The classes are in constant competition, each vying for positions of power. In their struggle to achieve dominance, they unintentionally and even for very selfish reasons act to the good of the whole. Through this competition, institutions function as engines of social cohesion. "Compromise, adjustment on interests, antagonistic coöperation,

... harmony, are produced, and institutions are the regulative processes and apparatus by which warfare is replaced by system" (p. 49).

Institutions in general are comprised of two elements, a concept and a structure (Sumner 1906, p. 53). A concept is but "an idea, notion, doctrine, interest." A structure may be described as "a framework, or apparatus, or perhaps only a number of functionaries set to coöperate in prescribed ways at a certain conjuncture." Its significance arises from the reality that it "holds the concept and furnishes instrumentalities for bringing it into the world of facts and action in a way to serve the interests of men in society" (pp. 53–4). As mores began in custom and folkways, so institutions begin with the mores being refined and codified, with the creation of rules of conduct prescribing or proscribing action. With some institutions, such as private property, religion, and marriage, the connection with the mores is obvious and easily understood; with others, such as the banking, legislative, and judicial systems, institutions of deliberate design, the connection is far less easily ascertained. While it may appear, then, as though some of the institutions we can identify may have developed as the result of a deliberate intent, they all owe their formation to the mores (p. 54).

Laws

As in the case of institutions, laws – customary and legislated – develop from the mores, and in turn ratify and sanction them. In the earliest stages of civilization, conduct is regulated negatively by mores in the form of taboos – those acts expressly forbidden.[7] Unlike the "positive rules" governing the scope and limit of legitimate actions, taboos quite often are accompanied by an explicit rationale, as they "carry on the accumulated wisdom of generations, which has almost always been purchased by pain, loss, disease, and death" (Sumner 1906, p. 31). The seriousness of the offense to which the taboo is associated must be made abundantly clear, so that the proscription is accepted as legitimate. The seriousness of an infraction, of a violation of a taboo, may have important social consequences and, as they tend to reflect concerns for the welfare of the whole, they are generally associated with punishment for violation.

Taboos reflect the common law. Legislated law – positive law – is, by contrast, of a higher order. Customary law begins in the folkways as an expression of the cultural tradition of a people. While their origins are unknown – they appear to arise, as do the folkways, through the workings of Ferguson's spontaneous order – they embody the social customs of the group. While the customary law "may be codified and systematized with respect to some philosophical principles," it is nonetheless reflective of prevailing custom and tradition (Sumner 1906, p. 55). Positive law is altogether different, for, while the common law is the result of non-reflexive and spontaneous development, positive law in only possible once the individuals in the society develop a criterion of social welfare and are able rationally to appraise their circumstance. The distinction between the two – the customary and the positive – is significant. The mores upon which the common law rests are identified with "sentiment and faith," typically "unformulated and undefined"; the positive laws, by contrast, are "rational and practical," "more mechanical and utilitarian" (p. 56). Only when a "stage of verification, reflection, and criticism" has been attained, when "reverence for ancestors has been so much weakened that it is no longer thought wrong to interfere with traditional customs by positive enactment," when we have reached a period in "which traditional customs are extended by interpretation to cover new cases and to prevent evils," can we move beyond the strictures of custom and tradition, and only then can formal legislative codes be adopted (p. 55). This is essentially the interpretation of the development of the common law advanced by the American jurist Oliver Wendell Holmes, Jr. In Holmes's expression of the transformation from tradition to law:[8]

> [t]he customs, beliefs, or needs of a primitive time establish a rule or a formula. In the course of centuries the custom, belief, or necessity disappears, but the rule remains. The reason which gave rise to the rule has been forgotten, and ingenious minds set themselves to inquire how it is to be accounted for. Some ground of policy is thought of, which seems to explain it and to reconcile it with the present state of things; and then the rule adapts itself to the new reasons which have been found for it, and enters on a new career. The old form receives a new content, and in time even the form modifies itself to fit the meaning which it has received.
>
> (O. W. Holmes 1881, p. 5)

Despite the fact that it is the product of rational assessment, the positive law cannot, if its legitimacy is not to be called into question, be divorced from the customs and traditions that serve to ground the common law; those enacting such regulations cannot, in short, ignore the sentiments and even the peculiarities of the society to which the legislated acts are to apply. Attempts at legislating morality and regulating social conduct – enacting legislation with the purpose of altering widely accepted behavioral norms that appear to some to be inimical to social progress – quite often fail, for the simple reason that those responsible for the enactments refuse to acknowledge the conviction with which the mores are held and the command they have over social attitudes.[9] Legislation must, then, even though the result of a rational and deliberate process, derive force and legitimacy from the mores. Law codifies public expressions of moral and ethical conduct. In addition, argues Sumner, as different segments of the society abide by different sets of mores – the "classes" tend to have a different perspective on ethical conduct than do the "masses," which are more tradition-bound – the mores and hence the laws will indicate this difference. What is deemed appropriate or at least acceptable conduct in one setting may be deemed highly inappropriate and even reprehensible in another.[10] Thus we may conclude that "[i]t is always a question of expediency whether to leave a subject under the mores, or to make a police regulation for it, or to put it into the criminal law" (Sumner 1906, p. 56).[11]

A great difficulty, then, arises whenever conduct formerly under the control of the mores is brought within the confines of the positive law. Legislative enactment brings with it "a sacrifice of the elasticity and automatic self-adaptation of custom," replacing it with a rigid, formal system of sanctions (Sumner 1906, p. 56). The reason for this has to do with the nature of the advanced society. Mores and the taboos to which they are associated "are the customs which actually conduce to welfare under existing life conditions," and so are of value in that stage of society in which individuals are bound by ties of common values and common goals. The ends to which actions are directed are *individual*, not *social*, as the latter has no meaning as distinct from the former. In the more advanced societies, however, this relation no longer holds. As the society becomes more stratified, it becomes less cohesive, and there arises a need by those at the top of the hierarchy to impose some structure or purpose on the whole. Laws thus reflect this need, as they "come into use when conscious purposes are formed, and it is believed that specific devices can be framed by which to realize such purposes in the society" (p. 56).

Mores and social policy

The role of the mores in the emergence of social relations and their status as essential factors making for social cohesion make difficult efforts at social engineering. There is of course a need to collect social data, if only to provide to policymakers a picture of the state of the polity; the data provide evidence on social demographics and economic welfare, and so are useful in gauging conditions of change. Only after such conditions are are identified can policy-makers begin their efforts at "social amelioration and rectification" (Sumner 1906, p. 97).

A difficulty arises when the legislators attempt to go beyond the "amelioration and rectification" of social problems to force changes in the institutional relations themselves. Once

> the statesmen and social philosophers stand ready to undertake any manipulation of institutions and mores, and proceed on the assumption that they can obtain data upon which to proceed with confidence in that undertaking, as an architect or engineer would obtain data and apply his devices to a task in his art, a fallacy is included which is radical and mischievous beyond measure.
>
> (Sumner 1906, p. 97)

Here Sumner demonstrates a realization of the problems associated with social calculation. There is simply "no calculus for the variable elements which enter into social problems and no analysis which can unravel their complications." Basically, the mores shape the social fabric; they *are* "a societal equation" (p. 97). Thus one problem inherent in the *Sozialpolitik* is that of the participant-observer, whose own preferences, prejudices, and dispositions develop from the very environment he seeks to redefine. As he is constituted by the mores, it would be difficult to see how he might divest himself of their "prepossessions" so as to allow the neutrality necessary to such a task.

The mores themselves are by their very constitution not amenable to rational understanding or to social calculation. The mores are grounded upon "faiths," beliefs and constructs "not affected by scientific facts or demonstration." If one is prepared to accept the mores (and as each is the product of a specific set of mores, it is difficult to see how one could do otherwise), one must also be prepared to accept the "mythology" that develops around them (Sumner 1906, p. 98).[12] In Sumner's own time, the prevailing "philosophical drift in the mores" was "towards state regulation, militarism, imperialism, towards petting and flattering the poor and laboring classes, and in favor of whatever is altruistic and humanitarian." Those "ruling tendencies," which serve to fashion beliefs and convictions, "are only the present phases in the endless shifting of our philosophical generalizations." Any attempts at altering the social institutions and perforce the mores to which they are attendant is then nothing but a desire "to subject society to another set of arbitrary interferences, dictated by a new set of dogmatic prepossessions that would only be a continuation of old methods and errors" (p. 98).

The source of "moral power"

Social welfare proceeds alongside moral development. To understand the reasoning behind this conclusion, we must trace through the logical sequence. The well-being of those within a society is dependent upon economic growth outpacing population growth – the Malthusian argument again. Economic growth is a function of the growth of the stock of capital. Capital in turn "is the fruit of industry, temperance, prudence, frugality, and other industrial virtues," the "moral forces" of a society (Sumner 1887e, p. 1). If a society is efficient, to the extent that it "has developed all the social and economic welfare which its existing moral development will justify or support," social and economic welfare can be increased only by expanding moral development: "every increase of social well-being we must provide by ourselves becoming better men" (p. 1).

Sumner then proceeds to question the source of the additional "moral power." Specifically, can the State act as a font of moral development, adding to the total existing stock of "moral power" as a stimulant to economic growth and consequently social welfare? If so, society can make genuine progress by harnessing the moral forces of the State in "contributing the ethical energy" needed; if not, then there is no justification in asserting that the State is an "ethical person," no rationale for considering the State as anything beyond an association of individuals possessed of common attributes (Sumner 1887e, p. 1).

For Sumner, the State is *not* an "ethical person" in the sense of being a source of moral power. The true source of moral power, of "ethical energy," lies "in the hearts and minds of human beings and not anywhere else" (Sumner 1887e, p. 1). Institutions in general are not productive of moral energy; they serve merely as conduits, taking in the moral energies of individuals and redirecting them. Schools, for instance, take in the moral force of the parents and impart it to the child; they do not, and should not, impose a moral position that conflicts with that of the parents. Such an institution functions most effectively "when it allows this personal contact and relationship to be most direct and simple – that is, when the institution itself counts for the least possible" (p. 1).

The State, however, is an institution of a different sort. It is not a mere conduit, as is a church or a school. As an institution of "high and important" purpose, it must be a complete consumer of moral power. School, church, and even family are preparatory institutions, "preparing men and women of moral power for the service of the State," producing moral members of the community. The State is then able to draw upon this moral power to its own sustenance, actually depleting it in the process. Declaring the State to be an "ethical person," then, has no more validity than would declaring a corporation or a labor union as such (Sumner 1887e, p. 1).

Individualism

The incoherence of individualism

Sumner, contrary to the opinions of his detractors, and seemingly in contradiction with his own philosophy, actually holds that individualism can be a socially destructive force. Individualism is derivative of rationalism, as the rationalist is characterized as "one who tears off from himself the restraints of tradition and custom and asserts his absolute independence" (Sumner 1992, p. 5).[13] The rationalist, and by extension the individualist, "is destructive," as he "destroys all the faiths, customs, and institutions which we have received from the past" (p. 6). Rationalism proposes an individual who "is isolated and encouraged to selfish independence," "emancipated from his responsibility to God," "emancipated from his responsibility to the past or to history," "emancipated from his obligations to society," "emancipated from responsibility to himself," as he denies any responsibility to anything greater than himself, despises any appeal to tradition or convention, rejects any commitment to others, disavows the validity of any judgment other than his own, and foreswears any appeal to such a device as a personal code of honor (p. 7).

The individual in the rationalist conception is the supreme egoist. He is the man of Hobbes's primitive state, pursuing his own crass interests with not an iota of consideration to those around him for the consequences of his acts. This egoist has no community feeling, no attachment to society, and no interest beyond his own. The character of the rationalist individual, then, is such that his existence in any form other than the anomalous would lead not to the formation of a community but, rather, to social disintegration and anarchism. Individualism as a philosophy is inimical to the cohesiveness demanded of community. Society is based on considerations of "trust, faith, confidence, generosity, cordiality, good faith and charity." Individualism promotes the coarse traits of "suspicion, jealousy, envy, malice, selfishness" (Sumner 1992, p. 8). Society can exist only when these traits are arrested, i.e., only when individuals come to realize that they cannot demand an unfettered liberty, or pursue with abandon their personal interests; societies can only come into being once individuals become aware that such demands and pursuits have potentially socially-deleterious consequences. For a society to exist, individuals must accept the concept of responsibility as correlating with individual rights; they must acknowledge "the idea that each individual is under obligation to forgo something of his own rights, or interests, or pleasure for the common good" (p. 8).

For Sumner, individualism as a rationalist philosophy of egoism is incoherent, as it neglects the interconnectedness of men in society. To the individualist, personal happiness is the sole end to which actions are to be directed. The "law of life" to the individualist "is to struggle out of one situation into another in the pursuit of happiness" (Sumner 1992, p. 9), fulfilling the requirements of the hedonic calculus. The problem, of course, is that in a society in which each is dependent on others – and society cannot be understood in any other way – it must be the case that this continual shift from circumstance to circumstance in pursuit of personal fulfillment will affect others who are in similar straits, altering their circumstances in course and affecting their ability to achieve happiness: "it is impossible for one who considers himself unhappy under this set of circumstances to make a change without involving the happiness of all the others" (p. 9).

Thus individualism is an "absurd" philosophy in its very denial of those connections essential to society. One cannot base a political philosophy on the selfish pursuit of personal happiness, but instead must account for the obligations inherent in any social union. As justification for this conclusion, Sumner offers the following, rather communitarian, motto:

> We ought to consider the interests of others, or yield to them whenever they are important. In other words, we ought to live by duties, that is by our obligations to God and man; and not by rights alone, that is not by the claims which we may make on others. All rights and duties are reciprocal, and by the side of a right upon which we are ready to insist we shall always find a duty to modify it.
>
> (Sumner 1992, p. 9)

Obligations and duties

Social interconnectedness underlies the creation of obligations. Any attempt to assert a right or to justify an action taken under the pretense of personal satisfaction ignores the fact that, at any time and in any circumstance, there exists a set of obligations to others. As one finds oneself in a new set of circumstances, one must alter the existing set of obligations, and in so doing impose upon others changes which may be contrary to their wills, disruptive of their circumstances, and destructive of their happiness.

This is a theme found throughout Sumner's writings: there are no rights without corresponding duties. In his essay "Liberty and Responsibility," Sumner asserts that "[t]he worst modern political and social fallacies consist in holding out to the mass of mankind hopes and affirmations of right according to which they are entitled by prerogative to liberty without responsibility" (Sumner 1889a, p. 4). In his well-known and oft-cited "The Forgotten Man" (1883; reprinted in Sumner 1919), Sumner addresses these concerns within the frame of a physical-science analogy. Just as the law of conservation of energy applies to physical phenomena, so it equally applies to the moral realm, and its violation has dire consequences. The structures of the present are inheritances from the past, "paid for by the labor and sacrifice of preceding generations" (Sumner 1919, p. 472). So it is the *combination* of rights and duties which act to bind individuals in society. A liberty predicated on the unfettered pursuit of individual happiness and individual rights, lacking any notion of duty and obligation, would negate this law, and would reduce humanity "to everlasting anarchy and war as these erratic wills crossed and clashed against each other" (p. 473).

This notion must be replaced by a definition of liberty that accepts "the equilibrium of rights and duties, producing peace, order, and harmony" (Sumner 1919, p. 472).[14] It must acknowledge as a principle "a set of civil institutions and laws which are arranged to act as impersonally as possible." It is a manifestation of Mill's liberty principle: the institutions are such as to "leave each man to run his career in life in his own way, only guaranteeing to him that whatever he does in the way of industry, economy, prudence, sound judgment, etc., shall redound to his own welfare and shall not be diverted to some one else's benefit," with the proviso "that each man shall also bear the penalty of his own vices and his own mistakes" (p. 473). Liberty is not to be confused with the ability of members of a society each to do as he wishes, with no constraints regulating action. To define it as such would imply that each may elect to do nothing, and this would imply that as individuals we are endowed with inalienable rights to which are associated no corresponding duties or obligations.[15] With this Sumner profoundly disagrees: there is no society absent an acceptance that to each individual right is an equivalent social duty. This is the position of the classical liberal, not that of the libertarian advocate of a *laissez-faire* society. The result of advancing the libertarian program would be a society as a mere collection of individuals, with nothing holding them together; society would exist in name only, with each person being *in* society, but not *of* society. Man has rights, but these are meaningless if he does not respect the corresponding obligations. As T. H. Green defines it, "[a] right is a power (of acting for his own ends – for what he conceives to be his good) secured to an individual by the community, on the supposition that its exercise contributes to the good of the community" (Green 1879–80, p. 159). It is only in defining a series of rights and duties to which all are bound that society can be said to exist in any meaningful sense.

Sumner clarifies his understanding of duty in *What Social Classes Owe to Each Other* (1883), a book Alfred Marshall actually assigned to his students at Cambridge.[16] Here he offers that the "one big duty" each has as a member of society is to take care of himself. This is not an expression of egoism for, as Sumner sees it, the duty of caring for oneself is also a *social* duty. Self-interest and social-interest are inseparable: "the duty of making the best of one's self individually is not a separate thing from the duty of filling one's place in society," the social duty being seen as derivative from the individual duty (Sumner 1883, p. 98). This is significant, for it is diametrically opposed to the idea of a social duty independent of personal interest. In support of this contention, Sumner argues thus: A man who, after seeing to his personal wants and needs, and having still the capacity to provide for others, may consider starting a family. In his role as head of the family, he has a duty, which he willingly accepts, to provide for their welfare. In the process, he encounters others in an ever-widening circle who seek claims on his abilities. But to consider these additional claims as duties of equal merit is to suggest that he "must have a surplus of energy, wisdom, and moral virtue beyond what he needs for his own business," including in that business the interests of his own immediate family, a surplus which simply is not forthcoming (pp. 98–9).

There is then no social duty beyond that corresponding to the individual.[17] Liberty is in essence a means to the promotion of individual happiness. Any other aim – including pursuit of State or social aims – amounts only to the imposition of someone's personal desires at the expense of those of the rest of the community. To view the social interest as distinct from the individual interest is to engage in little more than an exercise in "minding other people's business" (Sumner 1883, p. 99). Sumner perceives two "dangers" in such an attitude. First, in attending to the affairs of others, one leaves his own affairs unattended. Second, the effort may be seen as unwarranted interference, an intrusion into matters with which he has no concern. This is not to suggest that one should not care for another, for clearly Sumner holds the opposite belief. He merely reiter-ates Mill's concern that the identification of a *social* interest by some may be taken as an indication that this interest *must* be held by all, if necessary by the force of law (p. 100).

Justice

As noted, Sumner perceives society as an organism, a whole with a unity of structure, and yet the structure itself is dependent upon individuals consciously deciding to enter into cooperative arrangements; society is not antecedent to the self, but is derivative, a position at odds with that of Spencer. It is in the forma-tion of the social union, in the realization by each that his interests are best served through collective action, that one's own interests and the interests of society become one and the same, and that one then appreciates that rights in a society cannot exist without a corresponding set of duties. This is especially important to an understanding of Sumner's depiction of justice.

The emergence of the idea of justice

Social institutions are the product of the mores, their purpose being the orderly direction of the activities of the individuals in the society. In Sumner's view, all societies are comprised of parts, each of which has "a legitimate share in the acts and sufferings of the society," as they together "contribute to the life and work of the society" (Sumner 1906, p. 49). In addition, the society – the social whole – must, in the interest of cohesion and stability, affirm an interest in the behavior of each member. The group is the important unit: the individual matters only to the extent that he is perceived as being part of the whole, and this extends to the definition and the delineation of rights. The mores, after all, serve the indispensable function of coercing the individual into internalizing the "correct" social behavior. To the extent that rights find their origins in the mores, and so their formulation seems independent of any authority (and in this sense rights appear "absolute"), the more basic of them appear as "natural" (Sumner 1913, p. 79). Yet rights are *not* natural, but "are a product of civilization, or of the art of living as men have practised it and experimented on it, through the whole course of history." They are "rules of the game of social competition which are current now and here" (p. 83). Social stability demands a guarantee of rights consistent with the maintenance of social welfare, with the understanding that the granting of a right or a privilege to any one person or group entails a restriction or a limitation of the rights or privileges of some other person or group.

On this argument, rights are defined negatively, "by the laying of restrictions upon all others" (Sumner and Keller 1927, p. 629). Justice involves little more than "an apportionment of rights and a guarantee of them at the hand of public opinion" (p. 629); it has "nothing to do with equality in apportionment but simply with the guarantee of the rights as they appear in the code" (p. 630).

Even in the earliest societies, there was a realization of the need to control and to discipline certain "instinctive impulses," to restrain individual actions which, while they may conduce to personal benefit, are nonetheless destructive of the social fabric (Sumner and Keller 1927, p. 635). The need to restrict aggressive behavior and to protect each against the encroachments of others, and specifically the need to prevent *individuals* from taking actions in retaliation against such transgressions, provided the impetus to *social* action. That transgressions against persons or property must be dealt with was never in dispute. "What society did was to define aggression by the apportionment of rights and then to utilize retaliation in modified form to sanction the rights." It is this "law of retaliation" which in fact is responsible for the notion of justice in modern societies, as society became the sole legitimate mechanism for the dispensing of retributive justice (p. 636). Justice, then, emerges with the monopolization of retribution by the State.

Finally, Sumner argues that law is essential to liberty – liberty cannot exist in the absence of legal codes regulating conduct and affairs. Contrary, for example, to the opinion of Bentham, Sumner holds that those restrictions inhering in the law – for law is, after all, proscriptive, not prescriptive – do not equate with demands upon liberty. Rather, law

> creates the only real liberty there is; for liberty in any real sense, belongs only to civilized life and to educated men.... It belongs to defined rights, regulated interests, specified duties, all determined in advance, before passions are excited and selfishness engaged, prescribed in solemn documents, and guaranteed by institutions which work impersonally without fear or favor.
>
> (Sumner 1889b, p. 5)

The perversity of economic justice

Sumner's objection to the "socialistic and semi-socialistic propositions" being advanced at the time is that they would violate certain basic principles of morality and ethics, *viz.*, "[t]o every one his own; that responsibility should be equal to liberty; that rights and duties are correlative; and that those should reap the consequences who have set in action the causes," principles not in conflict with those adumbrated by Mill, Stephen, and Spencer (Sumner 1887a, p. 1). Both social and political equality must be understood to involve concomitant obligations: if all are equal, each must be so treated, and each must accept responsibility for the effects of his actions on himself and on others.

Yet, Sumner notes, the principles which are said to underlie the social compact are contradictory in their actual employment. All men are equal, and still there are those who are of such a constitution as to be incapable of discharging the duties to which all are to be held, be it because they are "weak, ignorant, undisciplined, poor, vicious, or otherwise unfit." This implies "that the strong, learned, well-trained, rich, and virtuous" must be called to a leadership role, a role which is itself said to be aristocratic and anti-democratic (Sumner 1887a, p. 1).

From this dual tension emerges the notion that the better-off elements of the society (the minority) have an obligation to the worse-off (the majority), the latter being the true source of legitimacy in a democracy. The fact that some in the society have succeeded while others have not is taken as evidence of an inherent inequity; material gains are seen not as the result of diligence and discipline, but as blessings and privileges to which desert cannot be attributed. The new theology, the doctrine Sumner criticizes, holds that it is the "educated men and others who have enjoyed exceptional advantages, or who have acquired any of those forms of training which make men better, not than other men, than they would themselves have been without the expenditure of capital and [l]abor" who "have a duty to perform – viz., to lead, guide, and instruct the real rulers" (Sumner 1887a, pp. 1–2). This leads to a perverse juxtaposition. If one succeeds, if he completes his education, secures gainful employment, is morally disciplined, in other words fulfills the "duty which is incumbent on all, and is enjoined on all, without exception," while another sees no need to so structure his life, the former shall be prevented from realizing the enjoyment of the fruits of his industry as they shall redound to the latter. After all, it is the *responsibility* of the successful minority to instruct the masses as to the "right" course of action to be pursued; if the masses do not heed the lesson, the fault is not theirs, but must lie with the minority who failed to make the instruction sufficiently clear (p. 2).

Wealth and success, then, no longer appear as the rewards achieved in the fulfillment of one's duty. Rather, "wealth is a duty and a responsibility," to be held in trust for others. Reward and desert have become disconnected, as obligation has become divorced from the ethic of the community (Sumner 1887a, p. 2). This Sumner sees as a perverse social result. To the extent that the State supports, even promotes, such an end by subsidizing the idle at the expense of the industrious, it advocates poverty as a social policy. The "social doctors" see to it that those who have will support those who have not, irrespective of the circumstances of their poverty. The mantra of the State and its self-styled social physicians Sumner states clearly: "Poverty is the best policy. If you get wealth, you will have to support other people; if you do not get wealth, it will be the duty of other people to support you" (Sumner 1883, p. 22).[18]

Property

Property and marriage

For Sumner, the institution of property ranks first in importance; it "is the most fundamental and complex of social facts, and the most important of human interests" (Sumner 1888, p. 2).

As part of his critique of Socialism, Sumner likens the institution of private property to the institution of marriage. While any connection between the two would appear to be tenuous at best, Sumner offers a rather interesting character- ization in making his point.

First, both the institution of private property and the institution of marriage are essential to the maintenance of society: marriage equates with reproduction, property with nutrition, "and no society could exist without both." Thus Sumner can conclude that both are institutions "in exactly the same sense and in exactly the same degree" (Sumner 1888, p. 2).

Second, consider the family as it existed in primitive, tribal societies. In these early communities, the family unit (we are told) is comprised of the mother and her children, the father having the responsibility not for the welfare of his family but, along with the other males in the society, for the welfare of the tribe. (Sumner also allows that, in many cases, the father was actually "a man of another tribe," someone literally from outside the group (Sumner 1888, p. 2).) In terms of the group as a whole, the organization "is that of the hordes which possess property in common" (p. 2), with property to be defined in the broadest possible terms. The males of the tribe are responsible for its protection and survival; the females are responsible for the care of the children, with the under- standing that the children, as with the property, are common assets of the tribe. Such an explanation is quite at one with that of Friedrich Engels. In Engels's explication of the anthropological record, in the most primitive state, the division of labor was sexual: males provided food for the family as well as protection for the community, while females cared for the household; each held control of the implements of their respective domains of specialization, while sharing as common property that which was the result of common production (Engels 1884, p. 259). Thus we have a primitive communism, or communalism, a system ideally suited to the time, place, and circumstance of its creation.

Whence arises a difficulty. There are those, notes Sumner, who idealize the primitive state, who argue that the property relations of these primitive cultures are ideal for *all* times, places, and circumstances, and should be acknowledged as thus. If only we could appreciate the equity and fairness inherent in the primitive property arrangements of these tribal communities, we would see that they are the only legitimate form of ownership. If primitive man saw in communal property relations a most effective and efficient, not to mention fair and equitable, means to the allocation of resources, does this not suggest that communal ownership is somehow "purer" and more natural than private ownership, an arrangement that modern societies would do well to emulate?

To this line of thinking Sumner retorts: "if the primitive forms of property bear any authority as to the proper forms of property, why do not the corresponding facts in regard to primitive marriage and the primitive family carry with them authority for the criticism of existing family institutions?" (Sumner 1888, p. 2). Both have their genesis in the folkways and the mores, and one can readily see in the historical record changes in both relations that are reflective of changes in these fundamental social belief structures.[19] Indeed, in primitive societies women were seen as property, as "drudges or slaves"; they are seen to have been "assimilated to property to such a degree that the rights which the men have in respect to the women are logically developed from the notion of property in the wives" (p. 2). (As noted above, Engels, writing at about the same time, concludes that this reading of the record is incorrect, as he maintains an equality between the sexes.) Marriage, then, as a social institution, developed as a means of solidifying the property relation, and so is an institution that had in its genesis rule by force and compulsion.

So, it is no more justifiable to conclude that, because the institution of private property emerged through some sort of compulsion, it is somehow illegitimate, than it is to suggest that, because the institution of marriage developed along similar lines, its legitimacy too is suspect. In fact, notes Sumner, the emergence of the family as an institution – itself derivative from the institution of marriage – created the conditions needed for the alteration in property relations that followed the evolution of society from primitive communism to capitalism. It was only when women began to be "esteemed" as women that they lost the mantle of slave. It was at this point that women began to share in the fruits of inherited wealth, as the men who had previously been content to share the common stock perceived a need for private holdings to which each may "dispose of and give away to the wife and children who possessed a special and lasting claim on him" (Sumner 1888, p. 2). The institution of the family, then, provided the impetus to the institution of private property, as the maintenance of a cohesive family unit was seen to depend in no small measure on the need to protect a lineage through inheritance.[20]

Capitalism

Sumner sees in the advance of capitalistic society the means of social cooperation. Early man as hunter-gatherer was at the mercy of the vicissitudes of nature; his existence depended on his ability to amass what meager fruits happened to be immediately available. With capital, the situation reversed. The ability to *produce* goods gave man an element of control over nature, reducing the variability inherent in the hunter-gatherer society, as he harnessed the forces of nature to his own ends. The mere shaping of the first tools was enough to set in motion the evolutionary process which led to the modern economic form, as each discovery and invention prompted the next. "Every step of capital won made the next step possible, up to the present hour" (Sumner 1883, p. 54).

Capital – "labor accumulated, multiplied into itself" – is the single most important element in the development of civilization (Sumner 1883, p. 54). The modern liberal order, "based on liberty, on contract, and on private property," is the result of the transformations brought about by the employment of capital; likewise the institutions of the modern social order, an order indistinct from the economic order upon which it is supported, derived from and are sustained by these very transformations. This is quite a Marxian understanding of the genesis and evolution of the modern social and economic structure, as one may identify in Sumner's analysis of the social metamorphosis brought about by the replacement of labor by capital a kinship with Marx's analysis (in the *Communist Manifesto* as well as in Chapter XXXII of *Capital*) of the transformation of the feudal system of production to the capitalist (without of course the attendant negations and exploitative relationships). The gradual evolution of the social order from primitive to capitalistic was made possible by "a gradual emancipation of the mass of mankind from old bonds both to Nature and to their fellow-men" (Sumner 1883, p. 56). The early, mostly tribal, societies were ill-equipped to handle the complexities resulting from the need to provide for larger populations. The modern capitalist order, by contrast, characterized by a highly evolved division of labor, is ideally suited to the complexities of large, interdependent societies. It requires no central authority to control its movements, and works along no organized or predetermined plan, and yet it succeeds in allocating resources and distributing products in the most efficient form imaginable, as it induces each to undertake a role in the promotion of the larger effort. Capitalism "is a great social co-operation," an "automatic and instinctive" mechanism. It is "this great co-operative effort" that Sumner sees as "one of the great products of civilization – one of its costliest products and highest refinements, because here, more than anywhere else, intelligence comes in, but intelligence so clear and correct that it does not need expression" (p. 58).[21]

Remarks

While having gained a reputation as a strident ideologue and promoter of a philosophy of extreme individualism, Sumner appears the very antithesis of the characterization. The individual cannot be construed as acting outside his social environment, for it is the environment which gives him structure and the domain within which he must function. One cannot envision any reasonable, just, moral society populated by unencumbered individuals, as the social order is impossible in the absence of such encumbrances. But Sumner actually goes further, arguing that man is *incapable* of acting in isolation from the group, for his very psychology is group-dependent: his every activity is motivated by the structures of his community.

The folkways and the mores are as instrumental in socializing individuals as they are in producing social institutions. As the institutions are the embodiment of custom and tradition, so the individuals in a society are conditioned by these same factors. So ingrained are the traditions that we are not even aware of their import, and yet each of us, no matter how much we perceive ourselves as masters of our own domain, are under their sway.

As to Sumner's reputation, it may be of some interest to note the assessment of a student and disciple, and so we shall allow Keller the last word:

> [I]t could be asserted that William Graham Sumner was the last great anthropologist – taking the term in his own broad sense, for he defined anthropology as the science that makes a study of the human group, of its relation to its habitat, and of membership in it. We now have somatic anthropologists, prehistoric archeologists, economists, political scientists, sociologists, and so on; but Sumner knew a great deal about all the social sciences, and was an expert on several.... I do not mean that he spread out beyond the field of the social sciences as some of our venerable scientific fathers have done, but that he covered more completely and thoroughly than anyone is likely soon again to do the several divisions of the field.
>
> (Keller 1910, p. 118)

Notes

1   His insistence upon using Spencer's *The Study of Sociology* as a textbook brought him into direct conflict with Yale's president, Noah Porter. For a recitation of the incident, see Harris Starr (1925). Starr also insists than Sumner was not, in fact, a faithful disciple of Spencer: "The rather widespread opinion that Sumner was a disciple of Herbert Spencer is more than half false. He neither owed as much to Spencer nor was in as close agreement with him as is generally assumed" (Starr 1925, p. 392).

2   Richard Hofstadter, for one, presses the case for Sumner as "[t]he most vigorous and influential apostle of American social Darwinism" (Hofstadter 1941, p. 457). Norman Erik Smith (1979) presents the case against such a contention.

3   Norman Smith (1979) shows this to be inconsistent with Sumner's own approach to the subject, as Sumner acknowledged the transcendent nature of culture, ethics, and learning as he rejected the application of natural selection to the social realm.

4   Sumner does, however, allow that certain actions otherwise viewed as taboo may nonetheless continue to be practiced to the extent that they have been "conventionalized." See Sumner 1906, pp. 68–70.

5   Sumner actually prefers to use the Greek "ethica," and so to identify the study of social norms with the word "ethology," but considers these terms to have been appropriated to other interests. See Sumner 1906, pp. 37–8.

6   Sumner actually goes so far as to suggest they live "a purely instinctive life just like animals" (Sumner 1906, p. 45).

7   Sigmund Freud notes that the word "taboo" is taken from the Polynesian, where it refers to "something unapproachable." The restrictions covered by taboo

are distinct from religious or moral prohibitions. They are not based upon any divine ordinance, but may be said to impose themselves on their own account. They differ from moral prohibitions in that they fall into no system that declares quite generally that certain abstinences must be observed and gives reasons for that necessity. Taboo prohibitions have no grounds and are of unknown origin. Though they are unintelligible to *us*, to those who are dominated by them they are taken as a matter of course

(Freud 1913, pp. 24–5)

8 Note also the following from Holmes with respect to morality:

My aim and purpose have been to show that the various forms of liability known to modern law spring from the common ground of revenge. In the sphere of contract the fact would hardly be material outside the cases which have been stated.... But in the criminal law and the law of torts it is of the first importance. It shows that they have started from a moral basis, from the thought that some one was to blame.

It remains to be proved that, while the terminology of morals is still retained, and while the law does still and always, in a certain sense, measure legal liability by moral standards, it nevertheless, by the very necessity of its nature, is continually transmuting those moral standards into external or objective ones ..."

(O. W. Holmes 1881, pp. 37–8)

9 This thesis is argued in some detail by Richard Schwartz (1980).
10 Schwartz (1980) points to the enactment of civil rights legislation in the United States in the 1960s, the acceptance of which took a much longer period of time in the southern states than in the northern and western parts of the country. One might also mention the post-Civil War civil rights acts, the failure of which necessitated the passage of additional legislation a century later.
11 Cf. Habermas:

Moral norms regulate interpersonal relationships and conflicts between natural persons who are supposed to recognize one another both as members of a concrete community and as irreplaceable individuals. Such norms are addressed to persons who are individuated through their life histories. By contrast, legal norms regulate interpersonal relationships and conflicts between actors who recognize one another as consociates in an abstract community first produced by legal norms themselves.

(Habermas 1998, p. 112)

12 As Donald Pickens (1968) demonstrates, Sumner's view here is consistent with, and may have derived from, the philosophy of Adam Ferguson. In Ferguson's terms, "[t]he history of the individual is but a detail of the sentiments and thoughts he has entertained in the view of his species: and every experiment relative to this subject should be made with entire societies, not with single men" (Ferguson 1767, p. 10).
13 This essay, entitled "Individualism," was delivered as a sermon on 11 March 1871, but had not been published until 1992.
14 "A democracy, then, becomes immoral, if all have not equal political duties" (Sumner 1883, p. 32).
15 For Sumner this would violate the physical principle of the conservation of energy: "The law of the conservation of energy is not simply a law of physics; it is a law of

the whole moral universe, and the order and truth of all things conceivable by man depends upon it" (Sumner 1919, p. 473).

16 See Marshall's letter to Sumner in Whitaker 1996, vol. I, p. 185.

17 Cf. Green:

> The pure desire for social good does not indeed operate in human affairs unalloyed by egoistic motives, but on the other hand what we call egoistic motives do not act without direction from an involuntary reference to social good – 'involuntary' in the sense that it is so much a matter of course that the individual does not distinguish it from his ordinary state of mind'.
>
> (Green 1879–80, p. 99)

18 "The man who has done nothing to raise himself above poverty finds that the social doctors flock about him, bringing the capital which they have collected from the other class, and promising him the aid of the State to give him what the other had to work for. In all these schemes and projects the organized intervention of society through the State is either planned or hoped for, and the State is thus made to become the protector and guardian of certain classes" (Sumner 1883, p. 21).

19 "Property, marriage, and religion are the most primary institutions. They begin in folkways" (Sumner 1906, p. 54). "Property and marriage are in the mores. Nothing can ever change them but the unconscious and imperceptible movement of the mores" (p. 76).

20 One should note that this explanation reverses the order as maintained by Engels. For Engels, it was the emergence of private property over common property that led to alterations in the marriage relationship, as "marriage became more than ever dependent on economic considerations" (Engels 1884, p. 186). Consequently,

> full freedom of marriage can become generally operative only when the abolition of capitalist production, and of the property relations created by it, has removed all those secondary economic considerations which still exert so powerful an influence on the choice of a partner.
>
> (p. 188)

21 Compare this with Sumner's view of Socialism:

> The projects of the socialists are based on the dogmas that man is born free and good, when he is, in fact, born helpless, and good or bad, as he works out his destiny; that the responsibility for vice and crime is on society, when, in truth, it is in the individual; that nature meets men at the outset with gratuitous bounty, which some appropriate to the exclusion of others, when, in fact, nature holds back every thing, and surrenders only to force and labor; that man is born endowed with "natural rights," when, in truth, nothing can be affirmed universally of the state of man by nature save that he is born to struggle for his own preservation, with nothing but the family to help him, and nothing but liberty, or the security of using his own energies for his own welfare, as a fair claim upon his fellow-men; that work is pleasant, or, under some circumstances, might be so, when, in truth, work is irksome; that men universally may be made, by some conventional agreement or sentimental impulse, to work for others to enjoy the product, or to save in order to give away; that they may be led universally to lay aside talents, health, and other advantages; that we can increase consumption and lessen production, yet have more; that all have an equal right to the product of some; that talents are the result of chance, which intelligence ought to correct, when, in truth, talents are the reward, from generation to generation, of

industry, temperance, and prudence; that the passions need no control, and that self-denial is a vice. This is the socialistic creed, and from it it follows that a man has a "natural right" to whatever he needs; that his wishes are the measure of his claims on his fellow-men; that, if he is in distress, somebody is bound to get him out; that somebody ought to decide what work every one should do, regardless of aptitude; to distribute the products equally, regardless of merit, and to determine consumption, regardless of taste or preference. As this "some one" must be a pure despot, or, in fact, a god, all socialistic schemes annihilate liberty. Most of them are atheistic, and reject any other god than the master of society.

(Sumner 1878, pp. 892–3)

6 Mises and the triumph of libertarian ideas

Based on the philosophies of those with whom we have so far dealt, the inclusion of the Austrian economist Ludwig Edler von Mises (1881–1973) may appear to be peculiar. His 1912 *Theorie des Geldes und der Umlaufsmittel* (*Theory of Money and Credit*) is still highly respected as *the* statement of the Austrian theory of money and the business cycle, as it established him as the leader of the successor genera-tion to Böhm-Bawerk. His attack on Socialism – both in his 1922 *Die Gemeinwirtschaft: Untersuchungen über der Sozialismus* (translated as *Socialism*) and in the famous socialist calculation debate – established his credentials as an advo-cate of the free-market philosophy. Yet Mises is generally regarded as the most articulate spokesman, not of the *liberal* position, but of the *libertarian* point of view; his 1949 masterwork, *Human Action*, is widely regarded as one of the most profound statements of the principles of this philosophy.[1] His perception of man as a rational being in pursuit of rationally determined ends, and his insistence on a strict *laissez-faire* attitude predicated on the belief that the best social outcomes are the result of unfettered human interaction, are not inconsonant with the views of those considered above, and yet not even Spencer and Sumner, gener-ally held to be ardent believers in the *laissez-faire* philosophy, seem to come close to the attitude of Mises.

As an economist and social philosopher, Mises has not always enjoyed the status due him. He is typically excluded from studies of the philosophies of liber-alism and individualism, as though his voluminous writings added so little to the dialogue. Those who bother to examine his philosophy at all typically resort to simplistic (and even *ad hominem*) attacks rather than serious appraisal.[2] In recent years, however, he has gained dramatically in stature. Vernon Smith, for example, a major figure in the field of experimental economics, appraises him as "the leading economic thinker of the 20th century who saw what must be the mainsprings of the extended order," and suggests that "no one was better at articulating the primacy of the individual and the need to define and nurture individual rights" (V. Smith 1999, p. 208).[3] In the present context, Mises is offered, not only for his own insights into the nature of man, but also to serve as a counter to the thought of Hayek, a means by which better to appraise the latter's liberalism.

Individualism and liberalism defined

We must begin our look at Mises and his libertarian outlook by defining two of the more important terms, *viz.*, individualism and liberalism, in the sense in which he employs them. Individualism is defined rather simply as "a philosophy of social cooperation and the progressive intensification of the social nexus" (Mises 1996, p. 152). It is manifest in the philosophy of Utilitarianism, a philosophy opposed to all manner of collectivist and universalist thought, as it exalts personal judgments of value over absolutes, and makes the pursuit of personal ends the sole criterion in the formation of social order.

Liberalism is handled within the same context. As a product of a utilitarian philosophy, it is "the first political movement that aimed at promoting the welfare of all, not that of special groups" (Mises 1978, p. 7). Liberalism is not to be construed as a philosophy of utopianism, for it is concerned solely with the *material* and not the *psychic* welfare of mankind (p. 4). More importantly, it is the only approach one can accept on the basis of rational deliberation.[4] Each individual strives to the fulfillment of certain ends, and these ends may be seen as common to each and to all. Apart from the desire to acquire the basic articles essential to survival, all wish "to be able to pass their lives under the most favorable physiological conditions possible" (Mises 1981a, p. 38). At the same time, each is (or becomes) aware of the fact that, in order to gain that which he desires, he must engage in cooperative relations with others around him: it is among the most basic of all understandings that cooperation is more productive, in terms of the satisfaction of individual wants, than is isolated labor. Finally, in terms of the *form* of production – the terms of ownership – it is an undeniable truth that, even if only in terms of output potential and hence social product, private ownership is the most effective and the most efficient form to the fulfillment of wants. One can then only conclude, "strictly by adherence to the canons of scientific procedure" alone, "that private ownership of the means of production is the only practicable form of social organization." From this it follows, again from an application of the "scientific method," that "liberalism must appear as the only policy that can lead to lasting well-being," both for the individual and for the society as a whole (p. 39).

At its most basic level, liberalism is a philosophy that

> aims at a political constitution which safeguards the smooth working of social cooperation and the progressive intensification of mutual social relations. Its main objective is the avoidance of violent conflicts, of wars and revolutions that must disintegrate the social collaboration of men and throw people back into the primitive conditions of barbarism ...
>
> (Mises 1996, p. 153)

Liberalism is not value-neutral; on the contrary, "[i]t presupposes that people prefer life to death, health to sickness, nourishment to starvation, abundance to poverty" (p. 154). Despite this obvious normative element, liberalism to Mises "is based upon a purely rational and scientific theory of social cooperation," one that "does not refer in any way to sentiments, intuitive creeds for which no logically sufficient proof can be provided, mystical experiences, and the personal awareness of superhuman phenomena" (p. 155).[5]

Liberalism is a political philosophy tied inextricably to economic evolution, that is, it is a doctrine that comes to importance as a result of fundamental alterations in the structure of production.

Division of labor

Among the more obvious Spencerian elements of Mises's philosophy is his emphasis on the central place of the concept of the division of labor, a concept which informs much of his economic and political writing. The sentiments of sympathy and friendship, Mises proposes, are the result of the felt need for cooperation: they develop as a result of the understanding of the need for a division of labor, "one of the great basic principles of cosmic becoming and evolutionary change" (Mises 1996, p. 145). It is the division of labor, as we shall see below, which serves as the basis for Mises's understanding of social order and the resolution of the apparent conflict between the social and the personal.

Division of labor defined

The very idea of the division of labor requires some explanation. For Mises, the central biological concepts of evolution, specialization of function, and the struggle for existence manifest in the survival of the fittest, all had their origins in the *social* sciences. Darwin in his autobiography credits his reading of Malthus's *Essay on Population* with having provided him with "a theory by which to work" (Darwin 1969, p. 120); Durkheim, in his *Division of Labor in Society* (1893), credits Christian Wolff and Henri Milne-Edwards (among others) with having applied the "law" of the division of labor to biological organisms as well as to society – the concept of the division of labor he affirms was a "generality" of the economists, but that it was the biologists who refined the principle to areas in which the economists "had been incapable of suspecting" (Durkheim 1893, p. 2). Biology "borrowed" these important concepts and redefined them so as to allow application to the description of biological processes; it did not proceed by analogy, incorporating economic principles into the corpus of the biological sciences, but actually made "profitable use of what it had gained" (Mises 1981b, p. 257). In so doing, these social motifs took on a "scientific" significance from which they could not be separated. The implication is that when the social sciences attempted to resurrect these concepts, they could not divorce them from their biological meanings, and did not even try.

Yet in attempting to reincorporate these now biological principles into their lexicons, economics and sociology failed to recognize the significance of some of the most important of these, especially the division of labor. The division of labor is "the essence of the organism," that structure which "makes the parts become members," through which "we recognize the unity of the system, the organism." It "is the *tertium comparationis* (basis for comparison) of the old simile," a "general law," the "fundamental principle of all forms of life" (Mises 1981b, p. 258). But social scientists must be cognizant of the differences in usage of the principle between their fields and that of biology: they must understand that the division of labor as it relates to cellular specialization is fundamentally different from a process through which rational and intentional individuals form into ever more complex social collectives.

As to its use in the social sciences, the division of labor is that principle that allows one to explain the manner in which social organization evolves. Thus there is much to the claim "that the happy accident which made possible the birth of civilization was the fact that divided labour is more productive than labour without division," leading to the conclusion that "the extension of the division of labour is economic progress" (Mises 1981b, p. 266). An application of this principle to the social sciences *must*, if it is to avoid being a mere naive application of a biological metaphor, identify (1) the way in which (rather, the "law" by which) "society originates and transforms itself," and (2) the "causal connection between the stages constituting the sequence" (pp. 266–7). Theories of psychosocial development fail because they are incapable of demonstrating "the inner and necessary connection between evolution of the mind and evolution of society." Too often, in these approaches, the changes that are of the most significance are interpreted "as facts acting on society from outside," and not "as the workings of a constant law" (p. 266). On the other hand, "stage" theories typically "do not go beyond establishing a definite sequence of events," and so "give no proof of the causal connection between the stages constituting the sequence." They are not evolutionary theories, in so far as they fail to demonstrate movement between the stages, but rather are taxonomies, which succeed only "in establishing parallels between the sequence of events in different nations" (p. 267).

In all, Mises argues that one must be cognizant of the *continuity* of evolutionary development. Yet one cannot offer this as a basis for assuming either that evolutionary development is a continuous, uninterrupted process, or that the development of each nation must follow along identical paths (meaning that stage theories of development are case-specific, as they relate to the peculiar historical episodes in the development of particular economies). The evolution of the division of labor, which Mises sees as coeval with social evolution, has clearly not been continuous but has been punctuated, and has even at certain periods and in certain contexts exhibited retrogression; once the division of labor has "advanced" to a higher stage, the behaviors and institutional frameworks with which this new phase is associated are retained, and serve as a template for future development elsewhere.

While one may uncover instances of this mis-characterization of the role of the division of labor and its role in social evolution throughout writings in economics and sociology, Mises is especially critical of the portrayal of the concept in Marx's materialist conception of history, which maintains that "the development of social ideology" is intimately connected with "the stage of technical evolution which has been attained" (Mises 1981b, p. 269). The error in such a perspective is that it attempts to construct a theory of social evolution that ignores the critical component of the division of labor, replacing it with techniques of production, the very thing the theory is designed to *explain*. By contrast, Ferguson's argument relating the emergence of production techniques (the separation of arts and professions) to the alteration of social conditions is much more in line with Mises's own understanding. Here we have the division of labor given central importance as the engine of social evolution, with technical innovation following from the conditions thus engendered.[6]

Labor specialization and the formation of society

The origin of the division of labor is manifest in two essential facts: human beings are unequal in abilities, and "the external conditions of human life" display an endless variety (Mises 1981b, p. 259). Mises argues in support of Spencer (and against Durkheim and Comte) that the division of labor evolves, not from the "struggle for existence," as a means to secure cooperation, but rather as a result of the need to ensure greater efficiency in production (p. 260 n. 7). Were all men of the same ability, the resources of the earth so distributed as to be readily accessible to all, and the labor required in altering the resources to consumption use of the most simple type, each could easily provide for his own needs, without the need of any social involvement.

Were this the case, were cooperation not essential for existence, society would not exist. Instead of a cooperative union, there would form merely "transient" alliances set to the completion of specific tasks (Mises 1981b, p. 260). That this is not the case is abundantly clear (Mises 1996, p. 158). "Animal man" evolved into "human being" (or "social man") precisely because he was capable of ascertaining that, in order most efficiently and effectively to supply his own needs in a world of scarce resources and limited natural abilities, he must of necessity avoid conflict and cooperate.[7] Society exists precisely because of the realization among its members that any individual sacrifices made "for the maintenance of social cooperation" are only temporary, that for each the "renunciation of a momentary benefit" is a more-than-adequate trade-off "for the sake of an advantage that endures throughout the continued existence and evolution of the division of labor" (Mises 1981a, p. 42). It is not necessary to invoke the specter of the "moral law" as the source of cooperation, to insist that each must, on moral grounds and contrary to the dictates of his own self-interest, subordinate himself to the interests of the collective. Rather, it is sufficient that each understands and accepts that society is possible only "through the actions of individuals cooperating in the attainment of ends that they severally aim at, in order to take advantage of the higher productivity brought about by the division of labor" (p. 42). Absent such a directing force as the division of labor, society could (and would) never have come about; the importance of the division of labor is precisely the fact "that it turns the independent individual into a dependent social being" (Mises 1981b, p. 270). Thus the "consciousness of kind" or "sense of community" which is often offered as antedating, and indeed fostering, human social interactions, is itself little more than "the acknowledgment of the fact that all other human beings are potential collaborators in the struggle for survival because they are capable of recognizing the mutual benefits of cooperation" (Mises 1996, p. 144).

The division of labor in fostering greater efficiency and productivity then directly induces sociality, as the interests of the individual are seen as coincident with the interests of the society as a whole. To put it more emphatically, the very notion of society is incomprehensible, absent an apprehension of this most important of all principles: "It leads men to regard each other as comrades in a joint struggle for welfare, rather than as competitors in a struggle for existence. It makes friends out of enemies, peace out of war, society out of individuals" (Mises 1981b, p. 261).

The notion of will is critical in the formation of society. Man is a social being, "already a member of a social body when he appears as a thinking, willing creature," and such an acknowledgment is sufficient testament to his social nature (Mises 1981b, p. 258). Following Fichte, Mises concludes that, as "[t]he development of human reason and the development of human society are one and the same process," it then follows that "[s]ociety is the product of thought and will" and cannot exist in the absence of either. "Its being lies within man, not in the outer world. It is projected from within outwards" (p. 258). It is the division of labor which allows us to conceive of society as an organism, not from its organic nature that we identify division of labor, and the division of labor follows directly from rational thought and individual will. It emerges with the realization that "material needs could not be supplied in isolation," and is made possible only when man "has achieved a development of reason and of the perceptive faculty that would have been impossible except within society." It is the division of labor and the social cooperation engendered which in fact makes individuals human, "for humanity exists only as a social phenomenon and mankind transcended the stage of animality only in so far as co-operation evolved the social relationships between the individuals" (p. 259). As each individual is a "willing creature" who seeks in his actions the satisfaction of desires, society as a collection of individuals, the existence of which is dependent upon (and in fact defined with respect to) cooperation, can exist "only where willing becomes a co-willing and action co-action." Society is nothing but a linking of individual wills for the attainment of some goal; it "is not an end but a means, the means by which each individual member seeks to attain his own ends" (p. 264).

But this is not a strict enough definition for, if it were, society would be little more than a name for any grouping allowing even a temporary benefit. It must also be acknowledged that, in seeking the attainment of some goal, the will and action of each must be coincident with, or at least not in conflict with, the wills and actions of others within the community. Each then, to some extent, employs the wills and actions of others to the achievement of his own purpose (Mises 1981b, p. 264). Thus, for Mises, the division of labor completes the effort by Kant to explain the origin of sociality by reference to the Doctrine of the Harmony of Interests, while avoiding the antagonism between the impulse to cooperate and the impulse to a solitary life. With the principle of the division of labor, "nothing remains of the antithesis between individual and society" (p. 265).

The social order

Man as a social being

As mentioned above, of the utmost importance to Mises is the manner in which the division of labor is responsible for transforming man as independent, rational individual into man as "dependent social being." It is undeniable that, with few exceptions, "all people agree in considering some kind of social cooperation between men the foremost means to attain any ends they may aim at" (Mises 1957, p. 37). Indeed, "social cooperation" is a manifestation of the "spiritual and intellectual unity of all species of *homo sapiens*," as it is "the best means of satisfying the biological urge, present in every living being, to preserve the life and health of the individual and to propagate the species" (pp. 37–8). Mises considers social cooperation to be "a natural phenomenon," consistent with the very nature of man. Indeed, mankind is unique among biological species in his understanding that social cooperation produces a better individual result than does competition:

> In resorting to this mode of expression and asserting that conscious association is in conformity with human nature, one implies that man is characterized as man by reason, is thus enabled to become aware of the great principle of cosmic becoming and evolution, viz., differentiation and integration, and to make intentional use of this principle to improve his condition.
>
> (Mises 1957, p. 38)

The fact of acting conditions man to be a *social* creature: "man emerges from his prehuman existence already as a social being," this as a consequence of the fact that he engages in *action* (Mises 1996, p. 43). This emergence of the social being, though, takes place under conditions in which the ability for rational thought and deliberation, and the consciousness of the human will, are less than fully developed, that is, under conditions in which man is "under the influence of blind instinct" (Mises 1981b, p. 265). Society, in the sense of the community structures that serve to socialize the individual, pre-dates any ability for conscious and rational formulation, and appears to have been the result of an instinct to cooperation more than of any rational process of creation. Man did not *invent* society, if by such is meant engagement in a conscious effort to erect structures through which interpersonal interactions could be facilitated, as might, for instance, be the case consistent with a social compact.

Mises finds it impossible to differentiate society from the individuals comprising it, and, interestingly enough, admits that, while the "social collective comes into being through the actions of individuals," this is not to suggest "that the individual is temporally antecedent" to society (Mises 1996, p. 43). Here we see shades of Sumner, as well as a seeming concession to parts of the communitarian argument. In fact, Mises goes further than Sumner, stating explicitly that indeed "society is –

logically or historically – antecedent to the individual." This must be so for society to have the influence on the undeveloped, pre-rational human will which he asserts comes into being. But, as if to anticipate the charge of communitarianism, he severely qualifies this statement, limiting its import to the rather obvious observation that "[i]ndividual man is born into a socially organized environment" and so society itself is nothing more than "the combination of individuals for cooperative effort," a label designating "[t]he total complex of the mutual relations created by … concerted actions" (p. 143). To view society as something distinct from the individuals comprising it – to consider society as having an "autonomous and independent existence" – is tantamount to suggesting that society is somehow more than the sum of its parts; to attempt to identify the individual as somehow independent of society is tantamount to suggesting that action can be defined in the absence of society (p. 143). Neither contention, Mises asserts, is valid. Society is concerted action; there is no independent *social* interest, and no *individual* interest that does not at least in part take into consideration *social* consequences. While action is always individual, one can nonetheless always define a social element in "a certain orientation of the actions of individual men" (p. 143).

It is in acting in cooperation with others that the individual actor takes on the character of the social animal. Here Mises demonstrates a divergence from the views of, among others, Smith and Spencer.[8] For both Smith and Spencer, the moral sense and the sympathetic sentiment are of critical import in impelling man to social cooperation; they act as forces essential to social action. For Mises, by contrast, "sympathy and friendship," sentiments that represent "the source of man's most delightful and most sublime experiences," of such singular importance to the essential nature of man that "they lift the animal species man to the heights of a really human existence," are not to be understood as products of an innate sense, after the manner of the intuitionist ethicists. They are rather a *consequence* of society, the "fruits of social cooperation" (Mises 1996, p. 144).

> [A]s a member of society, a man must take into consideration, in everything he does, not only his own immediate advantage, but also the necessity, in every action, of affirming society as such…. In requiring of the individual that he should take society into consideration in all his actions, that he should forgo an action that, while advantageous to him, would be detrimental to social life, society does not demand that he sacrifice himself to the interests of others. For the sacrifice that it imposes is only a provisional one: the renunciation of an immediate and relatively minor advantage in exchange for a much greater ultimate benefit. The continued existence of society as the association of persons working in cooperation and sharing a common way of life is in the interest of every individual.
>
> (Mises 1978, pp. 33–4)

It is at best a desire to manufacture an idealized past that has led some, particularly those antagonistic to the social relations of the modern era (read capitalist society and the division of labor which has made possible these relations), to encourage a reversion to a romanticized vision of society. Marx and Adam Müller are singled out as representatives of a movement to devolve social relations in an effort to produce a more community-oriented (less alienated) individual, freed from the bonds of servitude to which he has been subjected as a result of labor specialization. Müller, for one, in his 1809 *Über das Ganze der Staatskunst*, portrays the State as an organic whole; as Carl Schmitt interprets Müller, the Romantic attitude holds the State to be

> the embodiment of psychic and intellectual life; and all oppositions – especially the opposition of the estates (nobility, clergy, and bourgeoisie) necessary for the articulation of the organism, but also the opposition of person and thing – are combined in a grand, vital, and organic unity.
>
> (Schmitt 1925, p. 114)

Mises counters that this can only be granted if labor is regarded as something other than a factor of production, that is, if it is granted that one can "achieve all human aims with only that amount of labour which does not itself cause any discomfort but at the same time relieves the sensation of displeasure that arises from doing nothing" (Mises 1981b, p. 271). It is only with specialized labor that one can realize the benefits from overall productivity that more than offset any diminution in pleasure associated with self-sufficiency. Equally, it is the division of labor which is responsible for the social progress by which each individual has the wherewithal to realize his fulfillment as "a complete human being."

Organism versus organization

Appreciating the genesis of society as cooperation through the need for a division of labor, Mises proceeds to an examination of the means to its manifestation. Here Mises distinguishes between *organization* and *organism*. An organism is a natural and living entity, while an organization is a manufactured collective. In a biological organism, "each cell lives its own life for itself while functioning reciprocally with the others" (Mises 1981b, pp. 261–2). Order, in the sense of the organism itself, is the result of a unity of disparate elements, each intent on "self-existence and self-maintenance," while coalescing to a common purpose (p. 262). An organism is thus characterized by a "mutuality" of actions, a melding of individual wills to a common purpose; it is a living thing, a natural and indeed spontaneous ordering of the individual elements.

An organization, by contrast, requires for its existence a conscious imposition of the will of a creator. Here, "the separate parts are members of the whole only as far as the will of him, who united them, has been effective" (Mises 1981b, p. 262). The constituent parts have no "natural" relationship to one another, no effective links beyond filling the positions into which they are thrown. The demands of "self-existence and self-maintenance" which characterized the individual parts of the organism and make its existence possible are replaced by "instructions" concerning place and function. The will of each part is subservient to the will of the creator, as to allow independent wills would invite the possibility of independent actions and hence a collapse of the collective whole. This is the case with all organization which denies organicism. Those "attempts to coerce the living will of human beings into the service of something they do not want must fail," as any whole must be "founded on the will of those organized" (p. 263). Otherwise, the whole is but an artificial construct, the existence of which is in effect only possible "after the living social organism has been killed" (p. 263).

Moral duty and individual interest

Rational man

Of interest in Mises's social philosophy is his extreme reliance on rationalism as the force compelling social organization. Why cooperate? Very simply, because cooperation serves better to promote our egoistic interests than does isolation and individual effort; man would be irrational to divorce himself from the group, if within the group his needs, desires, wishes, and hopes are furthered more completely. Society becomes the means for the satisfaction of personal ends.[9]

As man accepts that society offers the best means for the attainment of his own selfish desires, he structures the institutions of society in such a way as better to bring about those ends. The institutional forms evolve as the result of conscious decisions respecting the superiority of a division of labor over a singular existence. No moral sense (in the terms offered by Hume and Hutcheson) is necessary by which man may be driven to cooperation, as cooperation and society are identified with the "mutual relations" and "concerted action" that bring them into existence; Mises actually defines moral behavior as "the name we give to the temporary sacrifices made in the interests of social co-operation, which is the chief means by which human wants and human life generally may be supplied" (Mises 1981b, p. 408).[10] While man is born into the social order, and is therefore responsible neither for its genesis nor its structure, one may be tempted to suggest that individuals would be disposed to seek other arrangements for organizing their personal affairs, arrangements more consistent with the pursuit of personal ends. Yet from the fact that this occurs but rarely, we may nevertheless with Mises conclude that, in order to continue to exist in such an order, and to be consistent with the primary axiom that man is rational and deliberative, the individual must continue to find in cooperation a better arrangement than any other alternative; each individual understands through rational reflection that *social* cooperation will produce greater *personal* benefits than can be had in isolation. Each member of the social collective realizes almost at once and instinctively that, by cooperating with others, he will acquire gains beyond his individual effort and, he again appreciates, these gains will accrue to others in future generations (Mises 1996, p. 146). One then need only submit to "autonomous rational morality" and not bother with "heteronomous and intuitionist ethics," a relic of some unenlightened past. "Law and legality, the moral code and social institutions are no longer revered as unfathomable decrees of Heaven. They are of human origin, and the only yardstick that must be applied to them is that of expediency with regard to human welfare" (p. 147).

Mises's utilitarianism

Mises is adamant in his rejection of the concepts of moral duty and the moral conscience as transcendent forces impelling man to a social interest. There is, in effect, no validity in a concept such as absolute ethics. Rational action is coincident with the pursuit by the individual of his own happiness or pleasure, which conduces to the *greatest* happiness or the *greatest* pleasure of the whole, where "pleasure is to be understood as embracing all those things which men hold to be desirable, all that they want and strive for" (Mises 1981b, p. 96). Ethical duties are coincident with human ambitions and desires; "the ethical aim is a means, in so far as it assists in the human struggle for happiness," while serving as a mechanism through which "intermediate aims [are mapped] into a unitary scale of values" and assessed "according to their importance" (p. 356). Eudaemonistic ethics – egoism – and the "ethics of duty" are then one and the same, as pleasure (and any of its synonyms – utility, happiness, satisfaction, *et al.*) "includes all human ends, regardless of whether the motives of action are moral or immoral, noble or ignoble, altruistic or egotistical," a judgment Mises credits Mill with having elucidated in *Utilitarianism* (p. 96 & n. 3). To think otherwise, to assert that the right and the good are transcendent values to which all must submit, is to demand allegiance to means irrespective of consequences (p. 357).

We have already seen that, for Mises, the will and actions of each individual are such as do not conflict with the wills and actions of others in the community. Each in effect comports himself to life in a community setting, fashioning his personal actions in a conscious effort to "affirm the existence and progress of society." Social cooperation is seen as consonant with self-interest, and is indeed accepted as such. The ends of the community *become* the ends of the individuals comprising it; social ends in fact have no meaning beyond individual ends. The individual views the ends of society as merely an extension of his own desires and wants; he does not "renounce the fulfillment of any of his own desires in favour of those of a mystical universe" for the simple reason that the ends of society are not final ends to which each strives, but rather intermediate ends in the personal "scale of values" (Mises 1981b, p. 357).

Thus it follows that, since the self and the egoistic motive are identical with the whole and the altruistic motive, it is no longer meaningful to speak of egoistic motives as opposed to social duties. That which serves the individual *must* be seen as in the service of the whole. Self-interest is a sufficient motive to compel individuals to act in the social interest, and so there need be no special recourse to the fulfillment of one's social or moral duty.

Such an attitude is given greater credence when viewed through the writings of David Gauthier. In *Morals by Agreement*, Gauthier makes the rather Spencerian claim that society may best be viewed as "a co-operative venture for mutual advantage," satisfying certain elementary principles respecting individual benefits and concessions, themselves seen as governing rational agreement (Gauthier 1986, p. 14).[11] The task he seeks to undertake is to "develop a theory of morals as part of the theory of rational choice," arguing along the way that rational principles respecting choice must include impartial constraints on the actions of individuals, these constraints being in the nature of moral principles (pp. 2–3).

To begin this endeavor, one needs to establish a fixed point of departure, to elucidate a set of conditions the fulfillment of which will produce the desired outcome. Gauthier observes that the "perfect market," the ideal of the advocates of *laissez-faire* and unrestricted individualism, in fact produces an outcome consistent with that required of a theory of morals, but does so *without* the express need for constraints on individual behavior. This is in effect the ideal, as it establishes with as few restrictions as possible parameters within which a moral theory can be constructed. The paradigm of the perfectly competitive market is important in elucidating the most important features of the moral society, including rational choice behavior and the conditions necessary to the promotion of social benefit, with a minimum of extraneous side conditions. Most importantly, the perfectly competitive ideal, "were it realized, would constitute a morally free zone, a zone within which the constraints of morality would have no place" (Gauthier 1986, p. 84).

Consider Gauthier's argument in greater detail. Rational action is the seeking of personal interest. In the perfectly competitive market society, rational agents each pursuing personal satisfaction (personal advantage), unconstrained in their actions, will as a consequence of such pursuits realize the mutual benefit of all in the society. Since personal advantage leads in the absence of formal constraints to a mutually advantageous outcome, an outcome of which we would approve were it the product of a society founded on an appropriate set of moral conditions, it then follows that such conditions, such moral constraints on actions, are unnecessary. Further, since the freedom of choice in the perfectly competitive ideal is identical with the freedom enjoyed by the solitary individual (of the Robinson Crusoe economy), this ideal is also impartial. Moral constraint is then unnecessary on both moral and rational grounds (Gauthier 1986, p. 13).

Were the perfectly competitive market to be realized, "as a structure for rational interaction," there would then be no need for morality or any other constraints on action, as utility-maximization alone would suffice in the ordering of the society (Gauthier 1986, p. 84); the utility-maximizing outcome would be the optimal outcome under the ideal of "free interaction." This unbridled pursuit of self-interest, which in the ideal may be termed "moral anarchy," can best be understood in reference to political anarchy: as the political anarchist views the society as consisting of "peaceable, productive, and companionable persons whose interactions are blessedly free of all authority or compulsion," making "the artifice of politics" irrelevant, so the moral anarchist presents a vision of "a society of peaceable, productive, and companionable persons who nevertheless are without conscience," with "the deeper artifice of morality" an irrelevancy (p. 84). But this is not a sufficient basis for the claim made by some advocates of *laissez-faire* that such an outcome is *morally right*. The concept of moral rightness in this instance simply *does not apply*. All the *laissez-faire* proponents need maintain in defending the ideal is that choice in a freely functioning, perfectly competitive market society, in so far as it leads through individual utility-maximization to an optimal outcome, "removes both need and rationale for the constraints that morality provides, which enable us to distinguish choices as right or wrong." Choice itself must be interpreted as amoral, not given to considerations of right and wrong, good and bad (p. 93).

The principles of (1) free activity – the actions of the individuals in the society are not circumscribed – and (2) the absence of external effects – the activities in which the individual engages are those selected by him, not imposed on him by an outside agency – are sufficient in and of themselves to guarantee impartiality in the workings of the system. A set of moral conditions imposed on the society over and above these minimal requirements would be at best counterproductive. In Gauthier's construction, morality is the result of market failure. Moral constraints need be imposed *only* under conditions demanding some correction, conditions, for example, under which coercion is seen as interfering with the functioning of the society. The market, however, excludes these possibilities by definition, and so the imposition of constraints on behavior would not only be an unnecessary burden, but may be viewed as unjust, in granting privilege to some at the expense of others (Gauthier 1986, p. 96).

The oft-cited problem with the idealization of the *laissez-faire* society is that it demands an independence from all associative ties save those of family and friendship. As each is set upon maximizing his personal utility (happiness), independently of and without regard for the interests of others, there can develop no social ties seen as critical to the formation and the continuance of society, a view in fact embraced by Spencer, who is generally regarded as among the premier supporters of *laissez-faire*. Yet the *laissez-faire* doctrine as offered by Gauthier holds that such ties are not critical to the advancement of mutual benefit, as the only social bonds necessary are those which individuals create in the process of pursuing personal advantage. The "mutual uncon-cern" exhibited by the egoists populating this society nevertheless leads to an outcome productive of social welfare; as in Mandeville's hive, private interest conduces to public benefit (although the licentiousness demanded by Mandeville is not countenanced here) (Gauthier 1986, p. 102). One may conclude then that, while the unfettered market is indeed a moral free zone, this depiction can be sustained only if it is recognized that the market rests on a moral predicate, this being the realization by each that his own best interest is fulfilled in egoistic pursuits, conditioned on his internalizing the conse-quences of his actions; the ideal then requires no formal constraints, as market interactions themselves are sufficient to the formation of a natural harmony (p. 13). The *imposition* of affective bonds (even as a first principle) is unnecessary, as in this ideal "the constraints are generated simply by the understanding that they make possible the more effective realization of one's interests, the greater fulfilment of one's preferences" (p. 103). Morality (should one deem it neces-sary to equate this term with the social harmony so engendered) *derives* from a felt need arising solely from self-interest, and not from some pre-existing bond of affection or association; morality needs no affective basis, as "mutual uncon-cern" is sufficient to the fostering of moral constraint, a notion borrowed from Kant. The amoral society, then, populated by unconcerned individuals in rational pursuit of personal advantage, unfettered by bonds of affection or community, is yet capable of generating those moral constraints essential to its functioning and stability.

So with Mises. Mises identifies the division of labor as "the great means for the attainment of all ends," a means perceived through rational deliberation as the one best suited to the fulfillment of human needs (Mises 1957, p. 56). To the extent that social cooperation is undoubtedly the best means to achieve desired personal ends, and that this arrangement is so obviously superior to competition for resources that all recognize it as such, it is abundantly clear that this alone is sufficient to the orga-nization of individuals into social unions; "no unanimity with regard to value judgments is required to make it work" (p. 56). Before one can engage in those higher pursuits which are taken as indicative of a civilized culture – art, literature, philosophy, the sciences – one must first satisfy those most basic of wants, *viz.*, the provision of food, clothing, and shelter. It is social cooperation which allows these most basic wants to be fulfilled, and so on utilitarian grounds alone such an arrangement should be agreed upon by all (p. 57). There is no need for moralizing sentiments, as the sole criterion underlying the utilitarian appraisal of conduct is that "there can be no other standard ... but the desirability or undesirability of its effects" (p. 57). To proceed otherwise, to insist upon adherence to ethical principles without due consideration of the consequences, "is mere fancy" (p. 58).

Yet, despite his stance that cooperative arrangements are the most effective means for the attainment of ends, Mises argues that this is not sufficient justification for *collectivist* measures. Specifically, Utilitarianism is a doctrine which "dispels the notion that society, the state, the nation, or any other social entity is an ultimate end and that individual men are the slaves of that entity" (Mises 1957, p. 58). Social cooperation allows the fulfillment of individual desires, but is not designed to that purpose and has no meaning apart from those engaged in the effort. Collectivism, by contrast, proceeds on the assumption that the group has an interest of its own, independent of and antagonistic to that of the members. At least in the form considered by Mises, collectivist philosophy holds the group to have a real existence, with the members of the collective existing for the sake of the whole (p. 58).

That this is fallacious is readily shown. If the individual and the group are in conflict, the existence of the latter can only be secured through the threat of punishment, hardly an efficient social mechanism. In addition, if indeed cooper-ative social groups are to be understood as ends in themselves and not as means to the satisfaction of ends, does this not imply that the proponents of collectivism are introducing a personal value judgment under the guise of an absolute stan-dard? Social cooperation emerged as individuals recognized the benefits it offered. Collectivist arrangements ignore this personal and subjective calculus, and instead demand individual sacrifices to what they perceive as a higher end (Mises 1957, p. 59). To Mises, this substitution of an absolute standard of value for individual, personal judgments is anathema to a free society.

Collectivism is a doctrine of war, intolerance, and persecution. If any of the collectivist creeds should succeed in its endeavors, all people but the great dictator would be deprived of their essential human quality. They would become mere soulless pawns in the hands of a monster.

(Mises 1957, p. 61)

The need for restraint

As noted above, for Gauthier, morality (as opposed to moral constraint) is the result of market failure; it is a *restraint* on self-interest and so is necessary *only* when the predicate conditions fail to hold. The need for a constructed morality is seen to apply in those instances in which optimality and utility-maximization diverge, instances in which some form of externality is present which interferes with rational choice. Utility-maximization may produce an equilibrium outcome which is not optimal – it may be possible to increase the utility of some (or all) without decreasing the utility of any. As the pursuit by each individual of maximum utility (happiness) may actually lead to a situation in which *total* utility is less than optimal, moral constraint serves as a means to the provision of greater mutual benefit. Only if the natural harmony of the ideal cannot be realized will it be necessary to impose an artificial harmony in the form of conditions respecting the coordination of actions. Morality is the device constructing this artificial harmony. Thus the perfectly competitive ideal and the cooperative society "share the non-coercive reconciliation of individual interest with mutual benefit" (Gauthier 1986, p. 14).

Specifically, cooperation arises in those instances in which the market fails in its task of fulfilling the requirements of individuals. In the presence of externalities, such as the free-rider (one who receives a benefit without incurring a cost) or parasite (one who receives a benefit but burdens another with the cost) problem, the moral argument for the *laissez-faire* ideal breaks down (Gauthier 1986, p. 96); mutual advantage derives not from personal choice but from a social contract wherein justice depends upon cooperation. In contrast with the unfettered *laissez-faire* society, the cooperative society is inconsistent with a moral free zone, and in fact requires the imposition of moral restraints. While the *laissez-faire* ideal requires no formal role for morality, cooperation, Gauthier offers, "is the domain of justice" (p. 113). As does Spencer, Gauthier allows that self-interest and scarcity are insufficient as grounds for cooperation; what is essential is an *awareness* of the *variability of scarcity* – as each becomes conscious of the desires of others for resources, a consciousness which translates into an awareness of the potential for conflict engendered by competition for a limited supply, each also develops a consciousness of the benefits to be gained by cooperation in the possibility of producing more for all (p. 114). Market failure, to the extent that it prevents each from realizing his optimal outcome (since we have seen that the definition of market failure is a divergence of optimality from utility-maximization), forces a change in strategy, away from independent actions and toward cooperative endeavors.

Competition as defined by Gauthier has two attributes: consistent with the unfettered market process, it is impartial; in contrast to the market process, the optimal outcome *requires* constraints on action (Gauthier 1986, p. 150). Competition is in effect "the visible hand restraining persons from taking advantage of their fellows, but restraining them impartially and in a way beneficial to all" (pp. 150–1).

The justification for the state

Yet, as one might expect, there arises a problem, one with which Mill and others also struggled. The rational individual must, if he is to fulfill his own desires, fulfill also those of society as a consequence; it is the ability to reason which impels him to this end. The social and the individual interest – "moral duty and selfish interest" – are so interconnected that the rational man "cannot deny society without denying himself" (Mises 1981b, pp. 357–8). The difficulty lies in the possibility that the person may not appreciate this connection; reason is not infallible and so "society cannot always trust the individual to see which are his true interests" (p. 358). As noted above with respect to Mill and Spencer, those lacking the ability for ratiocinative judgment may be placing themselves and their community at risk in making decisions and taking actions without due regard to the deleterious consequences. The "narrow-minded" and the "weak" in society (including, but presumably not limited to, "infants, the aged, and the insane"), those somehow deficient in that mental faculty that allows them to appreciate the advantages to themselves and to others of social cooperation, may very well, if left to their own devices, be placed at the mercy of others seeking personal advantage, or may even themselves, being incapable of understanding the need for concerted action, pose a threat to the social order. It then seems obvious that, for the sake of society as a whole, the majority must be prepared "to hinder, by the application or threat of violent action, minorities from destroying the social order" (Mises 1996, p. 149).

The need for social cohesion, then, animates the need for social coercion. This need for a "social apparatus of compulsion and coercion," essential in restraining conduct to that which serves the individual interest as it furthers the community interest, provides the rationale for the existence of the State and the law. Mises makes the argument for the need for compliance, by coercive means if necessary, on *efficiency* grounds: for any potential gains from social cooperation to be realized, each member of the society must desist from those actions the effects of which may be detrimental to the stability and cohesion of the whole (as well as to himself). This is not to be seen "as a sacrifice to a mythical entity, but as the recourse to the most efficient methods of action, as a price expended for the attainment of more highly valued returns" (Mises 1996, p. 883). Mises is not then prepared to succumb to the proposals of the Anarchists that government as an instrument of education (writ large) and coercion is unnecessary: were it true that each individual were indeed capable of knowing his own wants and desires, and in seeing in social cooperation the means to the most effective fulfillment of those needs and desires, government would be unnecessary, as each would of his own accord be led to actions reinforcing social cooperation and away from those actions harmful to social order. Government and the law derive from the realization that this is not the case, and so self-interest dictates the need for a mechanism through which may be secured the preservation of the collective whole and, in consequence, the protection of the individual. Liberalism concedes the need for a system of laws established for the maintenance of the social order, even as it sees in such an order a means to the circumscription of the control of the State. Liberalism does not, then, seek the dissolution of the State; it *does* reject the idea of the State of Hegel and Marx, as representative of the general social and political will.[12] According to the liberal doctrine, "the aim of the moral law is to impel individuals to adjust their conduct to the requirements of life in society, to abstain from all acts detrimental to the preservation of peaceful social cooperation and to the improvement of interhuman relations" (p. 157). The State, then, as "essentially an institution for the preservation of peaceful interhuman relations," while restricted in its control over individual actions, nonetheless "must be prepared to crush the onslaughts of peace-breakers" (p. 149).[13]

The social whole: instrumental or real?

In his discussions of the evolution of society, Mises appears to offer both an instrumentalist and a realist interpretation. The instrumentalist interpretation is the one most closely associated with Mises's political and social philosophy. On this reading, "[s]ociety is the outcome of conscious and purposeful behavior.... The actions which have brought about social cooperation ... do not aim at anything else than cooperation and coadjuvancy with others for the attainment of definite singular ends" (Mises 1996, p. 143). Society exists because it is useful; social collectives form and dissolve as need dictates, as those constituting society seek alternative means for the realization of their personal ends.

We see an explicit understanding of the realist interpretation of Mises in *Human Action*. The whole and its parts are "correlative," and so it is nonsensical to attempt to dissociate the one from the other, e.g., to attempt to apprehend actions of the individual as independent of his place in the society, or to attempt to fathom social change absent a consideration of the motives and desires of the individuals comprising the society. Likewise, Mises bristles at the very notions of realism and nominalism as being somehow in competition as explanation of the structure of the social whole. These approaches he considers remnants of medieval Scholasticism, having no application to the analysis of the origin of the structure of society. It is simply undeniable "that in the sphere of human action social entities have real existence. Nobody ventures to deny that nations, states, municipalities, parties, religious communities, are *real* factors determining the course of human events" (Mises 1996, p. 42; emphasis added). This is indeed a central tenet of methodological individualism, which has "as one of its main tasks [in the study of collective wholes] to describe and to analyze their becoming and their disappearing, their changing structures, and their operation" (p. 42).

This may appear to contradict Mises's observation, mentioned above, that the social group is defined only by the activities of its members. In fact, Mises actually condemns what he terms "the propensity to hypostatize, i.e., to ascribe substance or real existence to mental constructs or concepts" (Mises 1962, p. 78). Mises "resolves" the contradiction by noting that society is but a shorthand term for "the cooperation of individuals united in endeavors to attain definite ends," and so is descriptive of a social form; it is not a designation of a real and substantive construct with interests above and beyond those that have caused its animation (p. 78). The whole is nothing but "a particular aspect of the actions of various individuals and as such a real thing determining the course of events," "real" in the sense of being capable of producing tangible effects on its members. Yet the existence of the whole – the society, the collective – is known only through a connection of acts and consequences:

> It is illusory to believe that it is possible to visualize collective wholes. They are never visible; their cognition is always the outcome of the understanding of the meaning which acting men attribute to their acts.... Not our senses, but understanding, a mental process, makes us recognize social entities.
>
> (Mises 1996, p. 43)

In sum, then, Mises does not deny the *existence* of the social collective; he merely rejects its *status* as an independent structure. To understand the collective, one must first seek to understand the motives of individuals, for the collective has no independent motivation and no independent end.[14] Mises's ontological individualism simply prevents him from acknowledging that the "collective whole" can have any independent claim beyond those of the individuals comprising it.[15]

Justice

In his remarks on the origin of justice, Mises takes a cue from such Utilitarians as Bentham and Spencer. Social cooperation is possible because of the realization among those in the society that it is "the means for the attainment of all their ends" (Mises 1957, p. 51). Here we come to consider the idea of justice. Mises rejects the notion of justice as an end in itself, as he rejects any notion of an absolute standard, including standards derived from intuitionist ethics. With Mill he holds intuitive ethics to be a "normative quasi science," which takes its precepts "as if their adoption as a guide to action would not affect the attainment of any other ends considered desirable" (pp. 52–3). Those who advocate such a position have never bothered to inquire as to the consequences of such moral standards, but "silently assumed either that these consequences will be beneficial or that mankind is bound to put up even with very painful consequences of justice" (p. 53).

The difficulty thus is a failure to recognize the true nature of justice. Justice and the attribute of the adjective "just" as applied to conduct are manifestly connected with social order; beyond the bounds of the social community, such a concept as the just has no meaning. In those instances in which each has as his sole concern survival, justice and just conduct are meaningless concepts; the need for self-preservation alone is sufficient grounds for ignoring the consequences to others with whom we are in competition of our actions. It is only in society that one is compelled to consider in his conduct the external consequences, and it is only in this setting that just and unjust have any relevance. The very fact of being in a society, the need for social cooperation, compels man "to abstain from conduct incompatible with life in society. Only then does the distinction between what is just and what is unjust emerge." It then follows that "[t]he ultimate yardstick of justice is conduciveness to the preservation of social cooperation," with social utility being the standard (Mises 1957, p. 54).

Justice then is nothing but "a utilitarian precept designed to make social cooperation under the division of labor possible." The laws governing action in a society are entirely instrumental, "means for the realization of definite ends" (Mises 1996, p. 720). The good and the right have no basis other than that of pure utility. Murder, for example, is not *morally* wrong; it is wrong *only* to the extent that it interferes with the ability to pursue the satisfaction of other desires, desires the fulfillment of which requires the cooperation of others in a society (p. 174). To the extent that individual action is identified as a means and not an end in itself, "we call an action good or evil only in respect of the consequences of the action. It is judged according to its place in the system of cause and effect" (Mises 1981b, p. 359). For Mises, the categorical imperative of Kant,[16] by which actions are accounted as ends in themselves, is a pernicious doctrine, and must lead to the destruction of eudaemonian ethics (pp. 388–9).[17]

Yet, while insisting that it is illegitimate to attempt to derive standards of conduct from some ephemeral concept such as natural law, Mises is prepared to accept that justice, and by extension notions of good and right, are themselves social norms "uncontested and safe against any criticism" (Mises 1996, p. 720). This requires some examination. Justice, notes Mises, is "logically" only *de lege lata* – literally, "from law passed," the law *as it is*; it is by no means *de lege ferenda* – "from law *to be* passed," the law as it *ought to be*, as reflective of a change in circumstance (p. 721). Law is positive, not normative. Justice refers not to the consistency of the laws with some "natural" standard of right and good, an ideal to which the legislator appeals in forming rules of just conduct, nor does it refer to norms consistent with and protective of individual natural rights, minimum standards to which all are entitled by virtue of their status as human beings. Justice has only to do with social utility, and so only rightly is concerned with ends. With Bentham, Mises agrees that the goal is to promote that which "best serves the promotion of human welfare and happiness" (p. 175), and so "the issue is not justice, but social expediency and social welfare" (p. 721).

Consequently, right and good are not defined with respect to some ancient notions of virtue, but rather "the social system ... determines what should be deemed right and what wrong" (Mises 1996, p. 721). One is then led to conclude in purely utilitarian fashion that "[c]onduct suited to preserve social cooperation is just, conduct detrimental to the preservation of society is unjust. There cannot be any question of organizing society according to the postulates of an arbitrary preconceived idea of justice. The problem is to organize society for the best possible realization of those ends which men want to attain by social cooperation" (Mises 1957, p. 54).

From this understanding of the origin of justice, Mises is led to conclude that "there are no irreconcilable conflicts between selfishness and altruism, between economics and ethics, between the concerns of the individual and those of society" (Mises 1957, pp. 54–5). The identification of desirable ends, for the realization of which justice is but one means, does not proceed haphazardly or arbitrarily, but rather results from an awareness by all of the efficacy of cooperation. "Society could not have come into existence or been preserved without a harmony of the rightly understood interests of all its members" (p. 55).

Remarks

Mises has been presented here as a significant figure, in the sense that he, after a fashion, extends notions inherent in the social philosophies of Spencer and Sumner, especially the importance of rationality in human action and the need to maintain an attitude of *laissez-faire* in social relations, and gives central place (*à la* Mill, Stephen, and Spencer) to the mechanism of the utilitarian calculus. Yet his approach is far more dependent than either Spencer or Sumner (or indeed Mill and Stephen) on the efficacy of human reason in the establishment and maintenance of order.

Despite this attitude, Mises still manages to accept as critical to his theory those very elements of human nature that dispose man to social life. As with the others thus far examined, Mises holds this social nature to be the defining element in man, so much so that he develops his theory of individualism around this basic core. The primary difference is that Mises accepts that sociality is so much part of the constitution of man that he is disposed to it by his very nature, and so anything interfering with the pursuit of individual action is, *ipso facto*, interfering with the whole of society.

As mentioned above, Mises is employed here as both a complement and a contrast to Hayek, with whom we shall deal next. Mises stresses the role of reason in the social order, while limiting the need for any structures which may have the effect of impeding human action; Hayek de-emphasizes the role of reason, and focuses attention on the role of moral rules. Thus it is to Hayek that we turn in the next chapter.

Notes

1   We use here the 1996 ("fourth") edition.
2   A particularly egregious example is Rick Tilman's *Ideology and Utopia in the Social Philosophy of the Libertarian Economists*. The closest Tilman gets to a serious appraisal of Mises is in his statement that

> [v]on Mises is best known in many quarters for his incapacity to make elementary ideological and political distinctions and for his willingness to inflict this on

his political opponents.... [I]n order to get at his substantive contributions it is
necessary to sidestep massive deposits of ideology.

(Tilman 2001, p. 25)

No particulars are offered in substantiation.

3 Smith also notes that many of Mises's conjectures have been confirmed in experimental studies.

4 "Liberalism does not say that men always act intelligently, but rather that they ought, in their own rightly understood interest, always to act intelligently" (Mises 1978, p. 5)

5 Mises is quick to interject that this in no way suggests that liberalism is antithetical to religion. Liberalism is hostile to *theocracy*, but neutral with respect to belief systems that do not pretend to extra-religious interferences.

6 Ferguson states that:

> [A] people can make no great progress in cultivating the arts of life, until they have separated, and committed to different persons, the several tasks, which require a peculiar skill and attention. The savage, or the barbarian, who must build and plant, and fabricate for himself, prefers, in the interval of great alarms and fatigues, the enjoyment of sloth to the improvement of his fortune: he is, perhaps, by the diversity of his wants, discouraged from industry; or, by his divided attention, prevented from acquiring skill in the management of any particular subject.
>
> The enjoyment of peace, however, and the prospect of being able to exchange one commodity for another, turns, by degrees, the hunter and the warrior into a tradesman and a merchant. The accidents which distribute the means of subsistence unequally, inclination, and favourable opportunities, assign the different occupations of men; and a sense of utility leads them, without end, to subdivide their professions.
>
> (Ferguson 1767, p. 172)

7 "Evolution from the human animal to the human being was made possible by and achieved by means of social cooperation and by that alone" (Mises 1981b, p. 259).

8 Mises also criticizes those within the social Darwinist movement as having misrepresented Darwin's views on evolution. *Bellum omnium contra omnes* is not the natural condition of society. Rather, the "struggle for survival" is to be understood as a metaphor, referring to "the tenacious impulse of beings to keep alive in spite of all factors detrimental to them." For man, the best means to survival is intentional social cooperation (Mises 1957, pp. 39–40).

9 On this, see especially Mises 1944, pp. 542–3.

10 "To behave morally, means to sacrifice the less important to the more important by making social co-operation possible" (Mises 1981b, p. 408).

11 Specifically, Gauthier requires both a minimax criterion – whereby the "greatest concession" by the individual is as small as possible – and a maximin criterion – whereby the "least relative benefit" is as large as possible (Gauthier 1986, p. 14).

12 Mises writes:

> It is therefore absurd to maintain that Liberalism, Utilitarianism and Eudaemonism are "inimical to the State." They reject the idea of Etatism, which under the name State adores as God a mysterious being not comprehensible to human understanding; they dissent from Hegel, to whom the State is "divine will"; they reject the Hegelian Marx and his school who have replaced the cult of "State" with the cult of "Society"; they combat all those who want the State or "Society" to perform tasks other than those corresponding to that social order which they themselves believe the most proper to the end in view.
>
> (Mises 1981b, p. 358)

13 Mises makes the case as well in *Socialism*: "Liberalism does not contest the need of a legal order when it restricts the field of State activity, and certainly does not regard the State as an evil, or as a necessary evil" (Mises 1981b, p. 46). Also, "if the laws are sufficiently severe to ensure that, as a general rule, our peace is not disturbed, then we feel ourselves independent of the evil intentions of our fellows, at any rate to a certain extent" (p. 170). Finally, the State and its legal apparatus

> are not something outside the individual, demanding from him actions which run counter to his own interests, forcing him to serve alien purposes. They merely prevent the misguided, asocial individual, blind to his own interests, from injuring his fellow men by a revolt against the social order.
>
> (p. 358)

14 Peter Boettke and Virgil Storr emphasize that Mises is committed to a Weberian method of *Verstehen* and so is not the atomist he is often portrayed (although his commitment to methodological *individualism* is consistent with that of Weber). Man is neither over-socialized nor under-socialized (Boettke and Storr 2002, pp. 174–5).

15 Colin Bird (1999) takes Mises to task on this claim (see especially his Chapter 2).

16 This will be discussed at greater length in Chapter 7, as the categorical imperative is an important aspect of Hayek's social philosophy.

17 Mises is adamant in his contention that acceptance of the categorical imperative provides a foundation for Socialism (1981b, pp. 388–91).

7 Hayek and the form of the liberal community

The economist and social philosopher Friedrich August von Hayek (1899–1992) is the last of the figures with whom we shall deal, and perhaps (with a bow to Mill) the most influential of the group. A student of Mises in Vienna, Hayek made significant contributions early in his long career to economic theory: at least for a time his *Prices and Production* (1931) and *Geldtheorie und Konjunkturtheorie* (*Monetary Theory and the Trade Cycle*) (1933) were hailed as major efforts (his contributions only to be eclipsed for a time by the publication in 1936 of John Maynard Keynes's *General Theory of Employment, Interest and Money*), and he played a central role in the debate over the efficacy of economic calculation in a socialist organization of production. Yet the scope of his interests was great, as his voluminous writings covered not merely economic theory, but social theory, political and legal philosophy, and even theoretical psychology.

Hayek's reputation extends far beyond the academic, for he is generally regarded as one of the premier advocates of the liberal philosophy in the twentieth century. He consistently, throughout his life and career, championed the ideals of individualism and the moral requirement of a liberal political and economic order. *The Road to Serfdom*, *The Constitution of Liberty*, and *Law, Legislation, and Liberty* are among the most important works in the library of liberal thought.

As with the others with whom we have dealt, at the heart of Hayek's social philosophy is a regard for the socially constituted nature of man. This is a point which is often neglected in considerations of Hayek's political and social philosophy. Fellow liberals may acknowledge it, but focus attention on his individualism; communitarians and even conservatives may acknowledge it, but highlight the negative aspects of his liberalism. It is to an examination of this aspect of Hayek's thought that we now turn.

The principles of liberalism

On Hayek's definition, the fundamental principle of liberalism is "that in the ordering of our affairs we should make as much use as possible of the spontaneous forces of society, and resort as little as possible to coercion" (Hayek 1944, p. 21). It is "a doctrine about what the law ought to be," and to this end seeks "to persuade the majority to observe certain principles" (Hayek 1960, pp. 103–4).

Before pursuing this further, it is necessary to understand Hayek's distinction between *rules* and *orders*.[1] To this end, to allow a treatment of the different ways in which Hayek employs these terms, it will be useful if not instructive to direct the presentation, first to rules and orders in their most general application, and then to rules and orders as regulators of conduct.

Spontaneous orders

Essential to Hayek's understanding of complex phenomena is the notion of order. Order represents

> a state of affairs in which a multiplicity of elements of various kinds are so related to each other that we may learn from our acquaintance with some spatial or temporal part of the whole to form correct expectations concerning the rest, or at least expectations which have a good chance of proving correct.
>
> (Hayek 1973, p. 36)

Orders may be of two types: spontaneous or endogenous (also known as "grown" order), and directed or exogenous (also known as "made" order); Hayek, for the sake of precision, also at times denotes the first as *kosmos*, the second as *taxis* (Hayek 1968, Sec. I; 1973, p. 37). The directed order or *taxis* is purposeful, deliberate, intentional, and end-defined. The exogeneity refers to the fact that the order is imposed from without in an effort to secure a specific result.

Of import to social theory is the spontaneous order[2] – a concept defined by Ferguson and employed to great result by Spencer and even (perhaps unwittingly) by Sumner as well. So significant is the concept for Hayek that he identifies the "insight" that order is not necessarily the result of human design as representing "the beginning of social theory" (Hayek 1968, p. 10).[3] The spontaneous order or *kosmos* does not derive from human intention. Not being the result of conscious design, such an order cannot be said to have a purpose, as it represents little more than an unintended outcome of the process of social evolution. The relations within spontaneous orders are of such an abstract nature that the orders themselves "will not be intuitively perceivable and not recognizable except on the basis of a theory accounting for their character" (Hayek 1973, p. 39).[4] The spontaneous order, then, is merely a descriptive term for what we perceive to be "individual elements adapting themselves to circumstances which directly affect only some of them, and which in their totality need not be known to anyone" (p. 41); we ascertain its existence by identifying recurring patterns or regularities. Society is an example of a spontaneous order, comprised of smaller organized units each with specific and identifiable common purposes, but nonetheless itself without direction or even a discernible end.[5]

Rules and orders in society

While we cannot know the full measure of the social order, we can understand the *rules* underlying it, and so indirectly we may apprehend "the general character of the order which will form itself" (Hayek 1973, p. 41); to the extent that we can force a change in the rules underlying the order, we may effect a change in the "character" (but not in the "detail") of that order. We may in effect "determine their abstract features," while leaving "the particulars to circumstances which we do not know" (p. 41).

The elements of which the order is constituted must follow certain rules corresponding to their place within the order. These rules need not be (and typically are not) formally stated, nor need they be even completely apprehended by those under their dominion. The rules are typically known by the fact of their being adhered to, not by virtue of their expression as connected with a defined purpose. Rules "are genuine social growths, the result of a process of evolution and selection, the distilled essence of experiences of which we ourselves have no knowledge" (Hayek 1967c, p. 243).

Hayek identifies two types of rule which, not surprisingly, correspond to the distinction between *kosmos* and *taxis*, the two forms of order (Hayek 1968, Sec. II). The first, *nomos*, is defined as "a universal rule of just conduct applying to an unknown number of future instances and equally to all persons in the objective circumstances described by the rule." The *nomos* is then by definition an abstraction and so is end-independent. The second type of rule, *thesis*, is an explicit, end-directed criterion, devised for the regulation and direction of specific actions within a formal institutional or organizational setting (p. 15).[6]

Tribal societies can be distinguished from modern society by the manner in which the rules are known and the objects to which they apply. The tribal society is "end-connected," a purposive union dedicated to the advancement of concrete ends; it is a *taxis*, and the rules governing its order fall within the parameters of *thesis*. The modern, Great (or Open) Society, by contrast, is "rule-connected," or "means-connected," its purpose being "the purely instrumental one of securing the formation of an abstract order which has no specific purposes but will enhance for all the prospects of achieving their respective purposes" (Hayek 1976, p. 110); it is a *kosmos*, and the rules governing its order (or, rather, that *should* govern its order) are universal and abstract, i.e., *nomos*. End-independence of rules is essential for any society extending beyond the tribal community. Justice as equal treatment derives from this critical distinction, that actions must be judged by their correspondence to rules, and not with respect to their consequences alone (p. 39). This is the *rule of law*, as opposed to *law* itself – the latter exists in every society, the former only in the *liberal* or *open* society, and defines it as such.[7]

Rule-following

While adherence to rules may produce certain consequences, observance of the rules is not the *result* of these consequences; we do not follow rules merely because in so doing we may achieve some defined good (Hayek 1973, p. 19). The rules directing the spontaneous order, as they are universal and abstract, cannot be viewed as mechanisms established to the promotion of an end, which would require that they be amenable to articulation and the end to which they would be directed be known and socially accepted (if not explicitly agreed to). Rather, rules, as they correspond to *nomos*, are but practices, remnants of a "cultural heritage," itself nothing more than "a complex of practices or rules of conduct which have prevailed because they made a group of men successful but which were not adopted because it was known that they would bring about desired effects" (p. 17). They are social norms. It is unnecessary for one to be able to fathom the foundation of the prevailing structures – institutions and practices – to understand the rationale for their existence, for all that is required is that the structures serve some instrumental purpose; to the extent that the structures allow those operating within them to accomplish their goals, they are viewed as relevant and even successful.

The essential rules of human society are those conducive to the preservation and continuance of the social order. While within the order each individual will react to circumstances in a manner peculiar to his own nature and understanding, society can exist only to the extent that the individuals accept as binding constraints the rules governing social intercourse (Hayek 1973, p. 44), i.e., the *nomos* of the *kosmos*. This suggests at least a modicum of conformity: while different individuals need not react identically to a given set of circumstances, yet it is necessary to social stability that they all conform to the strictures of the society, adhere to the social norms, with the effect being a limitation of action and behavior to within an acceptable, set range. "In other words, the responses of the individuals to the events in their environment need be similar only in certain abstracts [sic] aspects to ensure that a determinate overall order will result" (p. 44).

To ensure such conformity, Hayek observes that rules may be of three types: (1) those which are obeyed because individuals perceive their environment in a similar way; (2) those which are part of a cultural tradition; and (3) those which *must* be obeyed (by force if necessary) in the interest of the general order (Hayek 1973, p. 45). The last instance is the domain of the law, and is offered as a form of exogenous order – a system of abstract principles designed to codify those reasonable customs and norms ("presuppositions of an ongoing order") essential to the "existing order of actions" (p. 98) – to be contrasted with the endogenous orders represented in morals and customs.[8] Law, then, as a set of "enforced rules of conduct," is as much a product of the evolution of society as norms and customs; this is law as *nomos*, the "rule of law," as there are no specific identifiable ends to which the abstract principles are directed. It is *legislation*, "the deliberate making of law," that is a constituted order – law as *thesis* – and by this very fact it is "the one fraught with the gravest consequences, more far-reaching in its effects even than fire and gun-powder" (p. 72).[9]

In volume two of *Law, Legislation, and Liberty*, subtitled *The Mirage of Social Justice*, Hayek extends his discussion of the concepts of rules and orders, here with reference to the means of ensuring the collective interests of the Great Society. Rules (*nomos*), as noted, are in general abstract principles which serve to *guide* individual behavior, but otherwise promote no specified end;[10] orders (*thesis*, or commands) are edicts designed to *compel* behavior to a determinate and pre-ordained end. Rules frame individual action by maintaining "spheres of responsibility," identifying "certain attributes which any such action ought to possess" (Hayek 1976, p. 14); orders coerce in an effort to promote an outcome. In Hayek's sense, rules fashion choice by limiting the possible actions one may choose to those which custom, habit, and tradition (as "informal" rules) have designated as morally correct (they in effect promote negative liberty, permitting what is not expressly prohibited).[11] As such, this "holding of common values, may secure ... that a pattern or order of actions will emerge which will possess certain abstract attributes" (p. 14); the rules themselves, as they serve "the preservation of an equally abstract order," must be seen not as independent ends to be pursued or means to the achievement of ends, but rather "as ultimate values, indeed as the only values common to all and distinct from the particular ends of the individuals" (pp. 16–17).[12] The communitarian philosopher Charles Taylor actually expresses it well:

> Rules operate in our lives, as patterns of reasons for action, as against merely constituting causal regularities.... Express rules can only function in our lives along with an articulated sense encoded in the body. It is this habitus that 'activates' the rules.
>
> (Taylor 1995, pp. 179–80)

In like fashion, MacIntyre holds that "rule-following is an essential constituent of some of those virtues that both we ourselves and others must have," and that a "failure to observe certain rules may be sufficient to show that one is defective in some important virtues" (MacIntyre 1999, p. 109).[13] Man is an inherently social agent, acting within the confines of the community, and it is this frame to responsible action provided by rules as common values that is most important in promoting this sociality and sense of community, while at the same time respecting individuality and free choice.

The "protected sphere"

It is important to note here before proceeding further the scope accorded to rules. Hayek in essence agrees with Mill as to the need of each individual for a protected sphere into which intrusion by the State or the community is prohibited (as we shall see below). While Hayek notes in *The Constitution of Liberty* "that when we obey laws, in the sense of general abstract rules laid down irrespective of their applica-tion to us, we are not subject to another man's will and are therefore free" (Hayek 1960, p. 153), he later clarifies his position, in response to objections by, among others, Lionel Robbins (1961) and J. C. Rees (1963), that the imposition of general, abstract rules may actually unduly restrict individual liberty. Specifically, in *Rules and Order*, the first volume of *Law, Legislation, and Liberty*, Hayek maintains that "only such actions of individuals as affect other persons, or, as they are traditionally described, actions towards other persons … will give rise to the formation of legal rules."[14] In those instances in which the actions of individuals have no external consequences, the actions "can never become the subject of rules of conduct that will concern a judge" (Hayek 1973, p. 101).

The point of enumerating rules of just conduct is "to tell people which expectations they can count on and which not"; it is not to be an exercise in the creation of protective bubbles around individuals, designed to secure them from any and all repercussions of the actions of others but, rather, is limited to the minimization of foreseen negative effects (and even here the role is limited to socially destructive effects) (Hayek 1973, p. 102). The rules serve merely to "define a domain of the individuals (or organized groups) with which others are not allowed to interfere" (Hayek 1976, p. 37). While the rules may, as they are seen to apply equally to all, in effect result in the formation of individual spheres – areas of liberty within which the individual is protected from intrusion by the coercive actions of the State and from the direct violation of others in the society – it is in following rules and recognizing one's obligations to the whole that such domains are demarcated.

This requires some further comment. To limit coercion – "the control of the essential data of an individual's action by another" – it is necessary that each individual be allowed a certain domain within which he is free from the interferences of others; the recognition of such a protected sphere gives rise to the notion of "rights" (Hayek 1960, p. 139). Yet Hayek does not wish to argue that this domain of protected activity is set by the dictates of the society (as he suggests Mill had done), for this would suggest that society determines the range of actions each may be free to pursue. To be free, to have the ability to use one's talents to one's own ends, demands that individuals "have some voice in the determination of what will be included in their personal protected sphere" (p. 140).

This recognition of the need for a certain degree of separation of individuals from one another and from the intrusion of the State leads to an understanding of the need for "general rules governing the conditions under which objects or circumstances become part of the protected sphere of a person or persons." The rules act as the means by which each may "shape the content of his protected sphere," as it allows "all members to recognize what belongs to their sphere and what does not" (Hayek 1960, p. 140).

Where Hayek disagrees with Mill is in the latter's attempt at defining such a sphere of individual liberty on the basis of the liberty or "harm" principle, as he argues that Mill presupposes such a sphere, and so does not appreciate that it is *derivative* of a system of rules and accompanying duties. There will always, notes Hayek, be *some* external consequence of any action, and so to make a distinction on this basis is of little use. All Hayek requires in a protected sphere is that individuals may "keep certain of the data of their actions from the control of others," the defining criterion being "whether the actions of other people that we wish to see prevented would actually interfere with the reasonable expectations of the protected person" (Hayek 1960, p. 145).

Yet Hayek's view coincides with that of Mill in that both demand that, where the only one affected by an action is the actor himself, where there is no external consequence, there is no legitimate reason for limiting or prohibiting the action. Public discomfort or moral reprehension is not a sufficient cause for the restriction of actions, the consequences of which are confined to the actor alone. Should other individuals find the actions reprehensible, each is free to express his disapproval, so long as the coercive force of the State is not called upon to enforce such opinions (Hayek 1960, p. 146).

Duty and obligation

Important in this understanding of rules of just conduct is the Kantian notion of duty – "that action to which someone is bound," or obligation – "the necessity of a free action under a categorical imperative of reason" (Kant 1797, p. 15).[15] This is significant in that Hayek resurrects Kant's ideal of the categorical imperative as indicative of "one criterion to which particular rules must conform in order to be just" (Hayek 1960, p. 197).[16] For Kant, duty (as "the unconditional ought") unites with freedom of choice through the device of self-constraint, making the choice of *performing* one's duty an ethical choice. In fact, in Kant's view, ethics *connects* free choice with duty, as it provides "an end of pure reason which it represents as an end that is also objectively necessary, that is, an end that, as far as human beings are concerned, it is a duty to have." This end – "an object of the choice" – must "be given *a priori*, independently of inclinations" (Kant 1797, p. 146). But this still requires a determination of *ends* that are also *duties*. Kant specifies two: (1) self-perfection, the "cultivation" of understanding and will "so as to satisfy all the requirements of duty," and (2) the happiness of others. In performing these duties, the individual acts so as to promote not only his own interest, but also the best interests of the community (pp. 150–1).

With this we return to Hayek. For Hayek, the essential virtues of the liberal (individualist) society are "independence, self-reliance, and the willingness to bear risks, the readiness to back one's conviction against a majority, and the willingness to voluntary cooperation with one's neighbors," of which the latter is especially important (Hayek 1944, p. 233). The concern of the liberal philosopher, then, is "to find a set of institutions by which man could be induced, by his own choice and from the motives which determined his ordinary conduct, to contribute as much as possible to the needs of all others" (Hayek 1948, pp. 12–13). Of critical importance to Hayek's position are the twin ideals of liberty and individual responsibility, ideals which echo the Kantian sentiment. Hayek regards it as almost axiomatic that a "free society will not function or maintain itself unless its members regard it as right that each individual occupy the position that results from his action and accept it as due to his own action" (Hayek 1960, p. 71). Freedom of choice and personal responsibility for one's actions together form "the air in which alone moral sense grows and in which moral values are daily re-created in the free decision of the individual" (Hayek 1944, p. 231). Freedom is not valuable in and of itself, but has value to the extent that it provides the means to the fulfillment of our plans. Freedom aims for "the enlargement of those capacities in which man surpasses his ancestors and to which each generation must endeavor to add its share – its share in the growth of knowledge and the gradual advance of moral and aesthetic beliefs" (Hayek 1960, p. 394). As such, it follows a presumption of reasonable or rational behavior, which of necessity includes the acceptance of individual responsibility. The assignment of responsibility compels one to view one's actions in the light of their consequences; it serves the function "of a convention intended to make people observe certain rules" (p. 75). This is of such great import that Hayek maintains it as a pillar upon which liberty rests: "the argument for liberty can apply only to those who can be held responsible" (p. 77). But this responsibility itself redounds to freedom of choice.

Consider this contention further. The freedom to act, if it is to have meaning, must be broad enough to allow wrongdoing, i.e., to allow one to decide on an unpopular or even illegal course of action; it cannot be confined to "action in conformity with moral rules," for otherwise the actions are not freely taken but are rather the result of coercion (Hayek 1960, p. 79). For a "free society" to function, its members cannot be constrained to behave in some agreed-upon "right" fashion, but rather must be "in some measure guided by common values" or standards of judgment, described by Adam Smith as "certain general rules concerning what is fit and proper either to be done or to be avoided" (A. Smith 1790, Part III, Ch. 4, Sec. 7, p. 159).[17] Each individual in a society has a personal "scale of values" (a "protected sphere") which gives him his identity and with which the State or the community must not interfere. The only legitimate device available then to channel behavior to more desirable ends is a sense of moral duty, "the only principle by which the bulk of mankind are capable of directing their actions" (p. 162).[18] It is indeed to this duty that one must look for a socially correcting influence. One may agree with Hart – that "[r]ules are conceived and spoken of as imposing obligations when the general demand for conformity is insistent and the social pressure brought to bear upon those who deviate or threaten to deviate is great" (Hart 1994, p. 86) – and as a consequence acknowledge that responsibility and a sense of moral esteem combine, with the least amount of formal coercion, to *limit* one's free choice of actions, to restrain one through moral opprobrium from performing those activities which may have socially harmful consequences (to the extent that they impinge on the "protected spheres" of others).[19] Responsibility and obligation and the onus of social disapproval thus combine to compel rational action as they guide choice to the pursuit of socially acceptable ends.[20]

While this may appear to be a restraint on freedom of action, it is so only to the extent that it is a *personal* or *own* restraint, one derived from an understanding and acceptance of one's moral duty. It is this responsibility "to one's conscience, the awareness of a duty not exacted by compulsion, the necessity to decide which of the things one values are to be sacrificed to others, and to bear the consequences of one's own decision" that is "the very essence of any morals which deserve the name" (Hayek 1944, pp. 231–2). (Hayek denies the legitimacy of *social* or *collective* responsibility.) It is in effect an evolved form of social custom, "a device that society has developed to cope with our inability to look into other people's minds and, without resorting to coercion, to introduce order into our lives" (Hayek 1960, p. 77). (It is significant that, in this passage, Hayek explicitly maintains that order is introduced into "our" lives, and not "their" lives, thereby suggesting that responsibility is indeed not coercive.) Our awareness of a moral duty is inherent in our constitution, part of our socially embedded nature: "It is part of the ordinary nature of men ... and one of the main conditions of their happiness that they make the welfare of other people their chief aim" (p. 78).[21] Yet the acceptance of personal responsibility and the feeling of obligation is nonetheless a free act, and not the product of a coercive state, demanding conformity to a social norm. Actions are free to be taken so long as one is willing to bear the *consequences* of those actions, including the onus of social ostracism and the potential loss of personal advantage deriving from the inability to achieve desired objectives. The important point is that personal responsibility born from moral duty is inextricably entwined with free, individual action in a liberal society.[22]

The social order

The social nature of man

These notions of duty, responsibility, and rule-following inform Hayek's social philosophy and provide the foundation for the Good Society. Hayekian individualism[23] is "primarily a *theory* of society, an attempt to understand the forces which determine the social life of man" (Hayek 1948, p. 6; emphasis in original). More importantly, it is a theory of social order predicated on an understanding of man as socially constituted, his "whole nature and character" deriving from his social existence (p. 6). Its fulfillment requires "the universal acceptance of general principles as the means to create order in social affairs" (p. 19), its essence being "respect for the individual man *qua* man" (Hayek 1944, p. 17). This is clearly at odds with the positions of Anna Galeotti and Geoffrey Hodgson, both of whom view Hayek as an "extreme" individualist. In Galeotti's view, Hayek holds that individuals are "defined privately, independently from the body politic." She contrasts Hayek with Rousseau, who "focuses on the importance of social cohesiveness for preserving the good political community" in his promotion of the "general will" (Galeotti 1987, p. 164). Hodgson maintains that Hayek has a "molecular view of the modern economy," and even goes so far as to identify his social philosophy as "a kind of totalitarian liberalism" (Hodgson 1993, p. 185). Yet this ignores Hayek's explicit rejection of those philosophies that postulate "the existence of isolated or self-contained individuals" (Hayek 1948, p. 6). Given Hayek's denial of the unencumbered self, and his depiction of rationalist individualism as a pernicious variant, such readings cannot be sustained.[24]

Hayek's individualism thus stands in stark contrast to atomistic approaches which isolate man from society, approaches which provide "no cohesion other than the coercive rules imposed by the state," such that "all social ties [are merely] prescriptive" (Hayek 1948, p. 23). An illuminating example of such an approach as repudiated by Hayek can be found in the *sociology* of Freud.[25] For Freud, society is a creation of man, established in an effort to oppose the power of the individual, "to set limits to man's aggressive instincts and to hold the manifestations of them in check by psychical reaction-formations" (Freud 1930, pp. 69–70). Thus he considers there to be a conflict between the twin urges of individual happiness and social union, as "the two processes of individual and of cultural development must stand in hostile opposition" (p. 106). Hayek's view is in a sense more in line with Max Weber's (1947) concept of "social action," and Durkheim's understanding of man as "a sociable animal," his consciousness deriving from "the nature of the group" of which he is part (Durkheim, 1893, pp. 285, 287).[26] Indeed, consistent with Weber's "social relationship" – whereby individuals subjectively account for the actions of others in orienting their own actions, and Durkheim's "social solidarity" – an amorphous moral phenomenon manifested (in this case, objectified) in the law and custom, we have Hayek's conception of the necessity of the individual *voluntarily* submitting himself to social rules, "noncompulsory conventions of social intercourse ... essential ... in preserving the orderly working of human society" (Hayek 1948, p. 22). (Hayek explicitly condemns the notion of solidarity "in the true sense of unitedness in the pursuit of known common goals," a position he attributes to Durkheim and other "constructivists," but does accept it as it refers to "common purpose." To accept solidarity in the "true sense" would be to acknowledge the existence of known ends, and that indeed "such a common scale of ends is necessary for the integration of the individual activities into an order" which, as we have seen, Hayek denies (Hayek 1976, p. 111).) For all three, social relations inform custom and ultimately codified law as if through a community (or collective, as Durkheim prefers) consciousness (whether directed toward a known end or merely common purpose). In addition, as Steve Fleetwood argues, the positions of Weber and Durkheim, taken together, seem to inform Hayek's social philosophy: Weber's "voluntarism" allows that agency generates structure, while Durkheim's "reification" allows that structure constrains agency. Hayek takes the additional step of completing the circle (Fleetwood 1997, pp. 130, 147). This should not, however, be seen in any case as a movement away from individualism.[27] One should not conclude, as does Rees, for example, that Hayek's emphasis "could induce us to look upon individual liberty as subordinate to higher social purposes" (Rees 1963, p. 352). To the contrary, for Weber, Durkheim, and Hayek, it is a realization that "egoistic" individualism is an oxymoron: it is simply not possible to envisage the individual apart from his social and cultural moorings.[28] Of the greatest importance for the individual is not the freedom to act indiscriminately, in selfish pursuit of his own well-being, but rather the "freedom some person may need in order to do things beneficial to society. This freedom we can assure to the unknown person only by giving it to all" (Hayek 1960, p. 32).

As the social nature of man is then understood, the matter ultimately reduces to the structure of the social order itself, specifically to the method of social cohesion.

The choice is between surrendering to the "blind forces of the social process and obeying the orders of a superior," between choice within an impartial and impersonal framework, and coercion leading ultimately to the absence of choice. To Hayek, the former provides the only means of sustaining individual freedom within the community for, while accepting the centrality of self, this method at the same time acknowledges the critical fact that actions are not taken in a vacuum. Choice is constrained, not ceded to a controlling authority. Submitting to the "anonymous and seemingly irrational forces of society" at least *allows* one a choice of acting within the limits provided by the rules, a choice that is not granted to those constrained by orders; individualism constrained by rules actually *promotes* freedom (Hayek 1948, p. 24). It is the demand for a *constructed* morality, the product of a known intelligence that seeks to direct individual action and define individual initiative, that Hayek sees as a surrender of individualism and freedom.

Rationalism and anti-rationalism

In *The Constitution of Liberty*, Hayek makes the case quite forcefully. Convention and custom, those spontaneous and undesigned rules to which we voluntarily adhere, provide the pattern for the "orderliness of the world in which we live," our shared moral values being the most significant of these. For a free society to function, there must be a conformity to such strictures (although we need not be aware that we are so conforming, as the values are often mere "unconscious patterns of conduct," demonstrating an adherence to "firmly established habits and traditions"). Hayek in fact holds it to be

> a truth, which all the great apostles of freedom outside the rationalistic school have never tired of emphasizing, that freedom has never worked without deeply ingrained moral beliefs and that coercion can be reduced to a minimum only where individuals can be expected as a rule to conform voluntarily to certain principles.
>
> (Hayek 1960, p. 62)[29]

It is here that one sees a distinction between rational (including, but not limited to, utilitarian) and anti-rational approaches to liberalism. To the rationalist (who views the world through the lens of the scientific tradition), custom and habit have little meaning, as institutions emerge as warranted, the result of deliberate design; this approach aims at a constructed morality suited to a known and identifiable collective purpose.[30] To the anti-rationalist (the moralist), tradition and collective institutional memory are essential, with purposive institutions developing spontaneously through an evolutionary selection process that is inherently tradition-bound. The very nature of civil society is received custom, in contrast to the State, which is a constructed organizational form. This approach allows that a common sense of morality develops as the outgrowth of an evolutionary process which then serves to inform action. Yet it is only to the anti-rationalist tradition that morality has any place in informing conduct, as these institutional structures channel the baser instincts of man to the ultimate pursuit of the socially beneficial; as Herbert Simon observes, "institutions provide a stable environment for us that makes at least a modicum of rationality possible" (Simon 1983, p. 78). Thus, in advancing the anti-rationalist posture, Hayek is advocating "not an abdication of reason but a rational examination of the field where reason is appropriately put in control" (Hayek 1960, p. 69).

The rationalist tradition, by contrast, is inherently teleological, as it perceives the question of "collective interest" as one reducible to human understanding and hence rational deliberation to an identifiable end. This is most clearly evident in Hobbes and Hegel, but takes very different forms. For Hobbes, civil society is an intentional construct, the contract upon which it is established the result of human deliberation. For Hegel, the State is "objective spirit," and thus is not the result of rational deliberation: one cannot simply *decide* whether to belong to the State, for the very nature of the individual is determined through his relations *to* the State; the individual gains "objectivity, truth, and ethical life" only in so far as he is a member of this universal order. Rationality is "the unity and interpenetration of universality and individuality," or alternatively "the unity of objective freedom (i.e. of the universal substantial will) and subjective freedom (as the freedom of individual knowledge and of the will in its pursuit of particular ends)" (Hegel 1821, §258). The Hegelian form of rationalism has a particularly disturbing element. As Carl Jung so eloquently states, this form of scientific rationalism "robs the individual of his foundations and his dignity," leading him to "become a mere abstract number in the bureau of statistics" as he is reduced to "the role of an interchangeable unit of infinitesimal importance" (Jung 1990, p. 9). For Jung, the intrusion of scientific rationalism destroys individual moral responsibility and indeed the "moral and mental differentiation of the individual," replacing it with an abstract notion of "public welfare" coincident with the provision of mere satisfaction (p. 8).[31] Morality becomes little more than an anachronism. It is indeed within this context that one sees the profundity of Michael Polanyi's observation, that "moral rules control our whole selves rather than the exercise of our faculties, and to comply with a code of morality, custom and law, is to live by it in a far more comprehensive sense than is involved in observing certain scientific and artistic standards" (Polanyi 1962, p. 215).[32]

Morality

This requires some further elaboration. Morals, Hayek maintains (following Hume), "are not a product but a presupposition of reason, part of the ends which the instrument of our intellect has been developed to serve" (Hayek 1960, p. 63); "ought" is not derivable from "is."[33] The rules governing social intercourse are the embodiment of the knowledge of a given epoch – the customs, folkways, mores, and traditions of a culture which serve to fashion habits of thought and so restrain action but which are nonetheless themselves only imperfectly understood (and so represent tacit knowledge). These moral principles thus must be (for the purposes of understanding their genesis) antecedent to the institutional structure, as they serve the function of standards of cooperative conduct and so are, in one sense at least, *ex ante* rationally determined and rationally accepted (in the sense that, in establishing the terms for the construction of the moral order, we accept these conditions as necessary, all the while being oblivious of their constitution).[34] While they indeed "govern our lives," it is still true that "we can say neither why they are what they are nor what they do to us: we do not know what the consequences of observing them are for us as individuals and as a group" (p. 64). They are as much a part of our nature as is language. Jung phrases it most succinctly, when (in contrast to the beliefs of the Freudian school) he states that morality, "the instinctive regulator of action," "is a function of the human soul, as old as humanity itself. Morality is not imposed from outside; we have it in ourselves from the start – not the law, but our moral nature without which the collective life of human society would be impossible" (Jung 1966, p. 27).

These shared values (including the institutional structure) define ends, establishing bounds to agency. Tony Lawson stresses the fact that the social structure is presupposed by human agency, so that "individual agents draw upon social structure as a condition for acting, and through the action of individuals taken in total the structures are *reproduced* or *transformed*" (Lawson 1994, p. 150; emphasis in original).[35] Yet as we exist *within* the bounds of these structures or principles, these rules of play, while we can effect a transformation (an evolutionary change), we cannot effect their wholesale reconstruction, nor can we entertain more than incremental alterations.[36]

At the level of the individual, all this is merely to say that ends are constitutive of self, and so the self must be socially embedded. The unencumbered and emotivist self has no place in Hayekian liberalism (or, for that matter, in Jungian psychology); there seems to be no real inconsistency between Hayek and MacIntyre, for example, on the importance of practices, narrative unity, and tradition in providing the means for situating the individual socially. Yet Hayek goes even further, distancing himself from the standard liberal theology (as defined by communitarians) as he explicitly rejects teleological explanations and the rationalist possibility that a system of morality *can* be synthesized,[37] for such a constructed morality implies that social interactions are mere extensions of personal preference orderings, and so are independent of the rules of the game.

Utilitarianism

Utilitarianism is a case in point. In Hayek's estimation, whereas "utility" in its original use "expressed an attribute of *means* – the attribute of being capable of potential uses," the term itself eventually became associated with the *ends* to be realized (Hayek 1976, p. 18; emphasis in original). The means employed to an end came to be seen as indicative of the significance of the end itself. An action taken in pursuit of a goal which is seen as conducive to the promotion of happiness may suggest that happiness is of great importance to the actor; happiness is endowed with utility. The more complex the means, the more important must be the ends to which they are directed; if the ends can be known, the utility of the means to those ends can then be derived (p. 18).

The notion that ends – the effects or consequences of any action – can be known beforehand, and so actions can be directed to the furtherance of the greatest happiness, is associated with Bentham (and to an even greater extent with Henry Sidgwick and G. E. Moore), and to act-Utilitarianism (also denoted by Hayek as "particularistic" Utilitarianism). Act-Utilitarianism allows a judgment of the rightness of each individual action "according to the utility of its known effects," which in turn allows that rules may be disregarded as irrelevant (Hayek 1976, p. 19). By contrast, rule-Utilitarianism (also denoted "generic" Utilitarianism), associated with William Paley, focuses attention on *types* of actions. Each of these utilitarian approaches has for Hayek a fatal flaw. While act-Utilitarianism, in basing approval of acts on their known effects, requires "a factual assumption of omniscience," an assumption which, "if it were ever true, would make the existence of those bodies of rules which we call morals and laws not only superfluous but unaccountable and contrary to the assumption," rule-Utilitarianism cannot pretend to "treat all rules as fully determined by utilities known to the acting person," since it is obvious that "the effects of any rule will depend not only on its being always observed but also on the other rules observed by the acting persons and on the rules being followed by all the other members of the society." The utility of any single rule is dependent upon its consistency with other pre-existing rules, justification of which (in terms of consideration of utility) cannot be made; one cannot, in effect, employ utility to justify the *entire system* of rules, since their justification depends on factors independent of utility (p. 20).

Utilitarianism fails, in the end, because it cannot incorporate the uneliminable element of ignorance as a justification for rules. Rules are necessary precisely because of man's ignorance of the consequences of his actions. Utilitarianism takes as a fundamental postulate the absence of this ignorance, and yet seeks to erect an edifice essential only to its elimination.

We must at this point consider a cogent criticism directed at what appears to be a latent Utilitarianism in Hayek. Rees notes that, despite his professed hostility to Utilitarianism, Hayek in fact makes his argument along "severely utilitarian lines." Specifically, when Hayek states that it is not freedom to pursue personal desire which is important, but only the "freedom some person may need in order to do things beneficial to society" (Hayek 1960, p. 32), Rees insists that by such a statement Hayek "either rejects or ignores the view that the individual has a right to live his own life in his own way irrespective of whether he adds something to the stock of human knowledge or helps to promote social improvement" (Rees 1963, p. 351). But this interpretation conflates the utilitarian with the communitarian or even conservative strain in Hayek.

For the utilitarian, social utility derives from individual utility, which then serves to produce a rational social morality. Morality ultimately redounds to some measure of social preference. Yet a problem arises, this being the possibility that, in maximizing *social* utility – promoting "the greatest happiness of the greatest number" – it may be necessary to restrict liberty, to disadvantage certain identifiable segments of the population; one group may be required to lose so the society can realize an even greater gain. The promotion of the social interest as the maximization of social utility can then result in an immoral outcome, as segments of the community are (however temporarily) denied the rights and freedoms enjoyed by others.[38] The welfare of the majority is given precedence over the rights of the individuals in the minority. So long as we allow that the addition to social utility defines morality, there is nothing to prevent such an outcome, as there is no objective moral standard by which we may judge situations.[39] Utilitarianism and all other synthetic moral systems are thus actually inconsistent with morality, since morality must *inform* preference, not be the *product* of it.[40] The very fact of human nature *derives from*, and is not the *cause of*, our shared morality (Hayek 1960, pp. 64–5).

This objection applies to all forms of act-consequentialism, not merely Utilitarianism.[41] Specifically, Hayek sees in the notion of "social consciousness" the same pernicious influences evident in rationalism, extended to the social realm. The socially conscious individual must be supposed to act with full knowledge of the social consequences of his actions, and must seek to maximize some result taken to be the "social good." The problem, of course, is that in *defining* social consciousness we are still left with the prospect of relying on individual judgment and hence individual preference respecting *specific* cases. Social consciousness is therefore little more than an attempt to substitute reason for general moral rules, a prospect made infinitely more difficult because, while moral rules established by habit and custom (from "behind the veil of ignorance") are effective as they apply to all in a dispassionate and fair manner, any attempt at *constructing* morality based on rational preference would require everyone involved to accept those preferences, with full knowledge of the consequences for themselves and for others.

> The rules of morals are instrumental in the sense that they assist mainly in the achievement of other human values; however, since we only rarely can know what depends on their being followed in the particular instance, to observe them must be regarded as a value in itself, a sort of intermediate end which we must pursue without questioning its justification in the particular case.
>
> (Hayek 1960, p. 67)

The only recourse is an affirmation that shared moral rules of conduct and the acceptance of these rules by the members of the society – shared values not susceptible to deconstruction and rational demonstration – form the basis of community. In Sandel's terminology, the community (in the strong sense) "must be constitutive of the shared self-understandings of the participants and embodied in their institutional arrangements, not simply an attribute of certain of the participants' plans of life" (Sandel 1998, p. 173). But this is equally expressive of Hayek's understanding as well. While the individual is clearly at the center of the Hayekian order (as has been noted), Hayek nonetheless explicitly argues in favor of this central tenet of communitarianism, that of the socially constituted self, whose "whole nature and character" are determined by the community of which he is a part.

Social wholes

Here we come to consider Hayek's understanding of "social wholes," and to motivate this discussion it is necessary to introduce some additional concepts. Wholes are structures the existence of which is not determinable from a mere analysis of their constituent parts, nor are the constituent parts readily observable. In *The Sensory Order*, Hayek offers a clear statement of the significance of this for the study of man and society. Here he maintains a distinction between objective reality (the "physical world") and our subjective apprehensions of that reality (the "phenomenal world"), holding

> that it is possible to construct an order or classification of events which is different from that which our senses show us and which enables us to give a more consistent account of the behaviour of the different events in that world.
>
> (Hayek 1952, p. 173)

Science, then, is not merely a descriptive discipline, but rather is constructive, relational, and taxonomic, as it involves a constant search for classes and categories and seeks connections between and among events (p. 174).

Yet while Hayek eschews any concern with essences, as one can only relate a sense-datum to an order or class, this does not mean that he is not concerned with structure: the *objects* of knowledge may indeed be real structures existing independently of our apprehension of them. All Hayek argues is that we are capable of experiencing *only* the phenomenal world, which is at best a "first approximation" of the "true" reality – an objective order which we assume exists and underlies the phenomenal order – all the while cognizant of the fact that our ordering of these phenomena "try and approach ever more closely towards a reproduction of this objective order" through successive alterations in our classes and categories (Hayek 1952, p. 173). Structure is not simply imposed by the imagination upon the objects of our perception, but rather the mind categorizes phenomena and then uses this material to refine further its categories (and this is part and parcel of the learning process), until the underlying structures, which themselves cannot be perceived, are made apparent. In this Hayek would appear to be in agreement with the position of the transcendental realist philosopher Roy Bhaskar:[42]

> It is through our acquired skills of perception that we come to be in a position to formulate propositions concerning the behaviour of things, to identify and describe the flux of events. But it is through our manipulative powers that, by interfering with the course of nature (this flow of events), we are able to check the reality and study the operation of the hypothetical generative mechanisms that in the scientific imagination we picture as responsible for their behaviour.
>
> (Bhaskar 1997, pp. 240–1)

For Hayek, then, social wholes (as specific examples of the above) "as such are never given to our observation but are without exception constructions of our mind." They are the categories into which we place our observations. But the import of this is typically misconstrued. We are capable of perceiving only the *actions* of individuals, not the *structures* within which they operate, and it is from these actions (as phenomena) that we surmise or postulate the existence of structural relationships (rules and other ordered relationships). These wholes then

> refer to certain structures of relationships between some of the many things which we can observe within given spatial and temporal limits and which we select because we think that we can discern connections between them – connections which may or may not exist in fact
>
> (Hayek 1979b, pp. 96–7)

Despite the fact that it is so constructed, the "social sphere" is nonetheless critical in promoting

> a certain structural connection between the parts," with the "social wholes ... thus maintained [being] the condition for the achievement of many of the things at which we as individuals aim, the environment which makes it possible even to conceive of most of our individual desires and which gives us the power to achieve them.
>
> (pp. 145–6)

A social whole for Hayek then is not, as Fleetwood maintains, "merely the aggregate of the individuals and their conceptions that can initiate it," nor can the importance of social wholes be minimized in the assertion that they serve as mere "aids to thinking" (Fleetwood 1995, p. 46), for this directly contradicts Hayek's expression of their constitutive authority. Indeed, it seems evident that Hayek's understanding of social wholes parallels that of Lawson, who characterizes them as "typically complex, irreducible, causally efficacious totalities," non-separable, non-sequential, and antecedent to action (Lawson 1997, p. 143). In Lawson's formulation, agency and structure "presuppose each other. Neither can be reduced to, identified with, or explained completely in terms of the other, for each requires the other" (p. 32). Social wholes then are pre-existent structures that serve to fashion conceptions, "not merely a mass of separable events and consequences" (p. 143). To consider them otherwise would be to concede that they constitute *resultants of* action, and not *conditions for* action, which would be counter to Hayek's own claims.

Thus on many different levels one may conclude that Hayek is neither instrumentalist nor sentimentalist; his community is indeed constitutive. Ends are not mere *attributes* of self; they are *constituents* of self. This can be rationalized in another sense. One of Sandel's chief criticisms of Rawls is that the latter routinely regards "community" and "collective" as equivalent. To Sandel this is unacceptable because "community" implies situation (belonging) and so is best understood as representative of "attachments" and "participation," while "collective" implies voluntary association and so is representative of "relationships" and "cooperation" (Sandel 1998, pp. 151–2). Yet it should be noted that Hayek goes to great lengths in justifying the use of the term "community" and in refraining from the use of the term "collective." Community is antecedent to the self, while the collective suggests a rationally constructed organization designed to promote sought-after ends; there is even here an implicit distinction between what Taylor (1995, pp. 190–2) defines as "mediate" and "convergent" goods (where "good" is defined in the broad sense), goods central to a shared social identification versus common goods of instrumental (ego-enhancing) value.[43] Hayek's insistence on the constituted, embedded self is thus sufficient to classify him as promoting a communitarian aim, while continuing to adhere to a liberal (individualist) ontology. It appears, then, that the only characteristic distinguishing Hayek from Sandel (at least in terms of formal construction) is Hayek's insistence that right (justice) take priority over any conception of the "social good."

Social and distributive justice

The good society

Having established that Hayek accepts the communitarian definition of community (or do the communitarians actually come to accept the position of Hayek?), the question remains as to the meaning of this concept in respect of ascribing a "public" or "social" interest. The Good Society, as Hayek envisions it, is "one which we would choose if we knew that our initial position in it would be decided purely by chance," i.e., from behind the veil of ignorance (Hayek 1976, p. 132).[44] While the "rules of just conduct", once established, can indeed change, it is not the case that they may be employed to alter the actual positions of specific persons or groups, but rather only "to improve as much as possible the chances of anyone selected at random" (pp. 129–30). Rules must be of a universal nature, not reducible to individual facts but abstract and applied equally to all. They must be end-independent. To Sandel, however, it is not enough to base arguments respecting social inequality, for example, on notions of fairness alone; one must also take into account the corrupting influences manifested in the actual conditions of poverty and opulence alike. The spirit of community depends to a great extent on a sense of mutuality and shared fate that is impossible in an atmosphere of class conflict. Yet Sandel readily admits that such proposals as might be made to alleviate the inequities in the distribution are meaningless if they rely for their legitimacy on the promotion of a free exercise of choice rather than on the promotion of a community ethic, as the remedies then are little more than palliatives, mere extensions of the liberal philosophy (Sandel 1996, p. 330). The *interest* of the community and the *notion* of community itself are thus intimately bound.

Here the distinction between Hayek and the communitarians is clear indeed. To Hayek, the connection between the priority of the community and the affirmation of a specified community *interest* cannot be made, for the community is a relationship of shared identifications, values, and commitments, not an instrumentality designed for individual or collective purposes. For there to be a "social" interest independent of individual interests would require an acknowledgment of the existence of both identifiable and mutually-reinforcing individual ends, and by extension a prescribed social end. This would presuppose that the community is an organic whole capable of *defining* ends; it would appear to be "a quasi-animate personality from whom everything is expected" (Jung 1990, p. 11). This possibility Hayek denies. Any social order (of which the market is one example) "operates on the principle of a combined game of skill and chance in which the results for each individual may be as much determined by circumstances wholly beyond his control as by his skill or effort" (Hayek 1967b, p. 172). The purpose of the State is thus the limited one of enforcing the rules of play, of "the securing of conditions in which the individuals and smaller groups will have favourable opportunities of mutually providing for their respective needs" (Hayek 1976, p. 2). While the individuals may identify themselves through their community, they nonetheless act independently in pursuit of personal goals; the individual acts within an institutional framework which inculcates a value system that governs conduct, yet at the same time he cannot be said to be acting in concert with others to the fulfillment of an independent community end. Social morality, i.e., the moral framework of the society, defines individual conceptions of right and wrong, and so is critical in framing individual interests. Social morality fashions belief and constrains action, and so acts as a real social structure, albeit undirected and without intent, design, or purpose. Communities indeed shape individual interests as they direct individual action. Yet one important point must not be neglected: to Hayek, the formal community has no end and no independent interest, and little legitimacy beyond the maintenance of an environment conducive to individual initiative.[45] The State, as a manifestation of a *political* community, cannot legitimately employ resources to the attainment of *particular* group ends or to the promotion of "just" deserts, as these are illegitimate impositions; it must reserve concern solely to the purpose of providing "the conditions for the preservation of a spontaneous order which enables the individuals to provide for their needs in manners not known to authority" (p. 2).

Consider in this regard the notions of "social justice" and "distributive justice." To Hayek, "only situations which have been created by human will can be called just or unjust," and so justice "always implies that some person or persons ought, or ought not, to have performed some action" (Hayek 1976, p. 33).[46] But "social justice" has come to be defined by extension "as an attribute which the 'actions' of society, or the 'treatment' of individuals and groups by society, ought to possess" (p. 62), and thus "presupposes that people are guided by specific directions and not by rules of just individual conduct" (p. 69). It is employed solely in an effort "to evaluate the effects of the existing institutions of society" (p. 63). Social justice is animated by a desire to arrive at a measure of social utility as aggregated individual utilities, and then to identify from this aggregate a social morality. But this is clearly illegitimate for, as mentioned above in respect of Utilitarianism, it denies the embeddedness of the self, and the subordination of preferences to morality. Justice can only apply to the correctness of *conduct*, of *actions*, not to the appearance of *consequences*; so long as actions are just, the unforeseen consequences of those actions cannot be interpreted as just or unjust. As an inherently *individual* notion, justice applies solely in respect of adherence to the rules governing *individual* conduct; only *individuals* are capable of acting purposefully, for only *individuals* are goal-directed. Society, by contrast, is neither constructed nor purposive – it does not allocate nor does it prescribe – and so its outcomes are neither intentional nor foreseeable;[47] the very idea of a "social result" has no meaning, as the social order is outcome-neutral. While one may question the legitimacy of the process itself and so characterize the *arrangements* as "unjust," one cannot legitimately so label the *outcomes* of the process once begun (Hayek 1967b, p. 171).[48]

Fairness and equality

Fairness and equality have meaning only in so far as justice is applied consistently and equitably. Social justice, by contrast, has a teleological component, absent from Hayek's procedural justice. Implicit in the design of social justice is "a hierarchy of ends ... a complete ethical code in which all the different human values are allotted their due place." But as an end is (in Kant's phrase) "an object of choice," the existence of such a hierarchy implies that there exists "a comprehensive scale of values in which every need of every person is given its place" (Hayek 1944, pp. 57–8), an obvious impossibility in even the most utopian social complex (an ideal state in which predictability is perfect and certainty is achieved) but nevertheless a necessary condition to the advancement of the utilitarian order. The lack of "a comprehensive scale of values" giving rise to "a complete ethical code" argues against the consequentialism required of social justice, and by extension calls into question the very idea of a purposive society. As Hayek denies that society is purposive, he must ultimately reject the notion of social justice.[49]

The same objection applies to distributive justice. The promotion of a pattern of distribution requires the governing authority to extend its mandate beyond the enforcement of general rules to the promotion of a prescribed end. Nicholas Rescher puts it succinctly enough in suggesting that "[t]he task of a theory of distributive justice is to provide the machinery in terms of which one can assess the relative merits or demerits of a distribution, the 'assessment' in question being made from the moral or ethical point of view" (Rescher 1966, p. 7). To be viable, such a concept must allow a ranking of alternative distributions from among which we may choose, and this is where the problem arises. Distributive justice, to have any validity, demands an *ideal* as the basis for judgments of outcomes. But under *actual* conditions, this cannot be forthcoming absent an imposition by authority. The establishment of a system dedicated to the furtherance of distributive justice is therefore coercive in so far as it *imposes* a given *pattern* of distribution; social ends then supersede individual ends. In contrast to Walzer's assertion – that, by its very nature, "[h]uman society is a distributive community," as "we come together to share, divide, and exchange" (Walzer 1983, p. 3) – for Hayek the only equality that the State can be justified in promoting is equality before the law, and such patterned arrangements as required by distributive justice clearly violate this mandate. Justice resides not in the *pattern* of distribution, but rather in the *mechanism generating* the distribution. Any action taken to "correct" the distribution must be discriminatory, allocating reward not on the basis of value but on the basis of merit.[50] But it is from *value* that obligation arises: "What determines our responsibility is the advantage we derive from what others offer us, not their merit in providing it" (Hayek 1960, p. 97).

Consider the case of social insurance. Sandel criticizes the American system as relying too heavily on voluntarism and too little on a sense of community obligation: the impetus in the organization of the program was not an appeal to the structure of community so much as it was an effort to secure access to the political and economic systems (Sandel 1996, pp. 282–3). Hayek's concern, by way of contrast, accounts for community *and* voluntarism. Protection for the vicissitudes of life Hayek regards as an obvious "duty of the community" (Hayek 1960, p. 285). To the extent that individuals perceive this duty and undertake to make provision for their own welfare, there is no problem. Yet it is obvious that not all will be able or be willing to so provide, and so it becomes "the recognized duty of the public" to "compel" such contributions, the justification being that, in failing to do so, those who opted out would eventually "become a charge to the public" (p. 286).[51] The communal interest in the security afforded by a "safety net" outweighs parochial concerns respecting the sanctity of individual choice.[52] The criterion Hayek maintains is as follows:

> Wherever communal action can mitigate disasters against which the individual can neither attempt to guard himself nor make provision for the consequences, such communal action should undoubtedly be taken.
>
> (Hayek 1944, p. 134)

Thus we see the apparatus of a social institution engaged in the promotion of a community ethic (something which Sandel and Walzer and others trumpet).[53] Yet this role itself is limited, confined to the mere *facilitation* of the development of an institutional structure dedicated to the maintenance of such arrangements, and even then State involvement is to be temporary, to see the process through the transition. The State has the catalytic function of securing the climate for the promotion of social insurance; it is not, however, justified in establishing a permanent central authority to this end, as this compulsory membership requires a degree of coercion beyond the performance of duty.[54]

Which community?

One aspect of the above discussion requires further elaboration. To motivate this exercise, consider the following from Jung:

> All the highest achievements of virtue, as well as the blackest villainies, are individual. The larger a community is, and the more the sum total of collective factors peculiar to every large community rests on conservative prejudices detrimental to individuality, the more will the individual be

morally and spiritually crushed, and, as a result, the one source of moral and spiritual progress for society is choked up…. It is a notorious fact that the morality of society as a whole is in inverse ratio to its size; for the greater the aggregation of individuals, the more the individual factors are blotted out, and with them morality, which rests entirely on the moral sense of the individual and the freedom necessary for this.

(Jung 1966, pp. 152–3)

With this sentiment Hayek appears to be in agreement, so long as the nature of the morality in question is understood. According to Hayek, the Great Society is an outgrowth of earlier tribal societies, and the moral sentiments underlying it derive from these pre-industrial arrangements. The problem, however, lies in the fact that the Great Society is no mere *extension* of the tribal society. Whereas in the small-group society, each individual is aware (or can be readily made aware) of the effects of his actions on others, and the rules established to govern conduct can be made specific to certain actions and may even impose upon each certain social requirements, in the Great Society the arrangements are fundamentally different. As we have seen above, given the complexity of the interactions among individuals as well as considerations of distance and anonymity, the consequences of actions (especially the more remote consequences) may be completely unknown to the actor, and so rules must of necessity concern not specifics of individual cases but rather more general prohibitions and demands. The rules in the Great Society cannot, then, serve to codify a range of legally enforceable social duties and obligations, but can only serve to guide conduct in a general direction. As Hayek notes, the transition from a tribal society to the Great Society came at a cost, this being "a reduction of the range of duties we owe to all others" (Hayek 1976, p. 90). As the range of duties and obligations narrowed, so the common sense of loyalty found in the earlier society came to be seen as irrelevant to the moral order of the new structure. The attempt to extend tribal morality, with its "parochial sentiments," to a more extended, complex social order, means a diminishing of the scope of the common sense of morality: while "tribal" morality holds that "the enforceable duties towards all are to be the same," and so "the duties towards none can be greater than the duties towards all," this ethos is clearly not extendable to the modern social order (p. 146).

Yet such sentiments as guided the tribal order continue to hold sway, and the dilemma of the modern industrial culture is that man has yet to free himself from those earlier "deeply ingrained instincts to let himself be guided in action by perceived needs" (Hayek 1976, p. 146). An early expositor of the communitarian message, John Dewey, laments that the development of modern capitalism, in uprooting the stable social relations that had developed in pre-industrial society, destroyed "the loyalties which once held individuals, which gave them support, direction and unity of outlook on life" (Dewey 1999, p. 26).[55] With this notion Hayek takes exception, as such a position ignores the fact that the evolution of economic relationships led to a commensurate alteration of the moral fabric of society. Hayek in fact regards those who hold views such as

Dewey's as engaged in "a vain attempt to impose upon the Open Society the morals of the tribal society" (Hayek 1976, p. 147).[56] Even modern communitarians recognize that the pluralistic nature of modern society reduces the influence of "tribal" morality; as MacIntyre proclaims, while "versions of the traditional scheme of the virtues survive," it is still the case that the separate and disparate voices "are all too easily interpreted and misinterpreted in terms of the pluralism which threatens to submerge us all" (MacIntyre 1984, p. 226).

MacIntyre, of course, sees salvation in a return to the Aristotelian virtues, wherein society accepts an ideal of the good life towards which we all must strive. For MacIntyre, "my good as a man is one and the same as the good of those others with whom I am bound up in human community. There is no way of my pursuing my good which is necessarily antagonistic to you pursuing yours because *the* good is neither mine peculiarly nor yours peculiarly – goods are not private property" (MacIntyre 1984, p. 229). As a result, for the communitarian at least, the situation as described by Jung simply cannot come to pass: the social morality and the moral sense of the individual are co-extensive, and form the basis of a truly just and free society.

But as we know, large societies are indeed pluralistic, comprised of smaller groupings, each with its own mission and perceived loyalties; pluralism is the result of an inability to arrive at a transcendent *telos*. Even MacIntyre recognizes this fact, seeing in the expansive concept of *Volk* a misconceived attempt to extend community and kinship loyalties to the nation as a whole (MacIntyre 1999, pp. 132–3). The alternative to a reliance on the ancient virtues as the basis of community morality, in Hayek's view, is to acknowledge that a *new* morality has indeed emerged, one consistent with the complexity of the new social order. To accept this is to understand that equality "is possible only under a system in which individual actions are restricted merely by formal rules rather than guided by their known effects" (Hayek 1976, p. 147). Society in the large is fundamentally different from society in the small, yet the evolution of the complex order has proceeded ahead of the evolution of the social ethics demanded of it. In Hayek's estimation, the imposition of "moral rules which can be justified only by a rational insight into the principles on which this order is based," is the sole alternative to a system predicated on "the unreflected 'natural' emotions deeply grounded on millennia of life in the small horde" (p. 147).[57]

This is anathema to MacIntyre and other communitarians, who feel as though, as the basis for moral belief has shifted from the virtues to rules, the individuals within the society have become disengaged. The rules themselves, and not the underlying moral sentiments, come to be viewed as virtuous; he even invokes the name of Adam Smith who, in contrast to Kant, "did in fact allow for one moral area in which rules will not supply us with what we need: there are always borderline cases in which we do not know how to apply the relevant rule and in which niceness of feeling must therefore guide us" (MacIntyre 1984, p. 236). The communitarian critique centers on just these "inherited instincts," these tribal morals, as examples of the virtues made anachronistic by the move to the Open Society but which must be resurrected if the moral society is to flourish.

Yet Hayek understands that the complexity of modern society militates against any attempt at resurrecting a community end, such as is required of a return to the Aristotelian virtues that serve to define the common good, since all such attempts "to turn it [the modern social order] into a community by directing the individuals towards common visible purposes, must produce a totalitarian society" (Hayek 1976, p. 147). In small social groupings, the problem of moral cohesion does not arise because of the closeness of the members and the unity of purpose. Yet this small-group solidarity – the striving for a common purpose – is inapplicable to the dynamics of the new, incompletely evolved social order. Shared identifications, values, and commitments, sentiments that had in the tribal societies become virtues in themselves, no longer are adequate as the basis for community. It is just as evident that they persist in the absence of a clear and demonstrated alternative. What is needed, in Hayek's opinion, is time "to learn the rules of the market," and to leave behind the "intuitive craving for a more humane and personal morals corresponding to ... inherited instincts" (p. 146).

Of significance here is the idea of *directing* interests towards a *community* purpose. This should not be interpreted as a denial of a common sense of *morality* – or even Smith's "niceness of feeling" – for the realization of a duty to adhere to common rules of behavior is the outgrowth of just such a morality. Rather, it is a rejection of the idea of desert. The extended, Great Society cannot promote a specific concept of the good, some agreed-upon common end, for this alone is incapable of serving as a basis for the coalescing of interests in a social complex. It must instead content itself with abstract rules respecting conduct. The moral component is essential; in the modern society, one cannot justify pursuit of a common end through mere reference to a common purpose.

Hayek's ontology

To summarize, to the extent that communitarianism is a social philosophy that identifies the individual as socially constituted, Hayek is indeed a communitarian in the broad sense of that term (and no less so than are Weber and Durkheim). This is enough to sustain the objection to his being associated without qualification with the libertarian strain of liberalism, the egoistic or *laissez-faire* variant which perceives society as individually constituted, and not constituting. For Hayek, the individual is a product of society, and social relationships are critical in molding feelings of community and belonging, as well as instilling a moral vision; doubtless also Hayek would find little disagreement with Jung's claim that "the value of a community depends on the spiritual and moral stature of the individuals composing it" (Jung 1990, p. 18). The genius of Hayek's contribution lies in his understanding that agency and structure are interdependent, "that the structures possessing a kind of order will exist because the elements do what is necessary to secure the persistence of that order" (Hayek 1967a, p. 77).

More significantly, while explicitly adhering to the demand of an *individualist* ontology, Hayek clearly affirms the prerequisites of a *social* ontology lacking in many other liberal theories, a qualification many of his communitarian critics and others (typically philosophers) who have commented on his social theory are loathe to assert.[58] Hayek is thus (as one communitarian writer notes of Wilhelm von Humboldt, for whom Hayek expresses the highest regard) "fully aware of the (ontological) social embedding of human agents but, at the same time, prizes liberty and individual differences very highly" (Taylor 1995, p. 185). This is most clear in Hayek's essay, "Why I Am Not a Conservative," appended as a postscript to *The Constitution of Liberty*. Hayek acknowledges that, despite its emphasis on stasis, continuity, and order in social affairs (and the need for any alteration in the social order to be supervised), conservatism (which also affirms a social ontology) displays "an understanding of the meaning of spontaneously grown institutions such as language, law, morals, and conventions," an apprecia- tion for "which the liberals might have profited" (Hayek 1960, p. 400). As Oakeshott frames it, those disposed to conservatism "know the value of a rule which imposes orderliness without directing enterprise, a rule which concentrates duty so that room is left for delight" (Oakeshott 1991, p. 435). Hayek's objection to conservatism centers on its lack of "an understanding of the general forces by which the efforts of society are co-ordinated" (Hayek 1960, p. 401), which understanding is provided in classical liberalism. Conservatism seems to allow a place for social control, as it affirms the validity of the *thesis* of the *taxis*. For the sake of illustration, for Oakeshott the conservative, the State serves a coordi- nating function as it imposes duties and obligations on those comprising it; for Hayek the liberal, the State has a potentially more coercive role, as it is a rational construct (it is a constituted order imposed upon the spontaneous order of society) established in a conscious effort to ameliorate interpersonal conflict and to guarantee individual liberties.[59] Hayek even goes so far as to identify his own philosophy as lying "midway between the socialist and the conservative" (p. 406), a philosophy which John Gray defines as embodying the conservative view of limited rationality and "the Scottish Enlightenment's conception of man as the creature (and not creator) of social life" (J. Gray 1998, p. 130).[60] In addition, Hayek's repeated and favorable references to Burke highlight his openness to, if not complete acceptance of, conservative principles.[61] So in the end, Hayek promotes a type of institutionalism consistent with his individualist perspective, a form of conservatism tempered by liberal principles. This alone is sufficient to deny the charge that Hayek's brand of liberalism (and its association with an institutionalist objective) is a mere version of sentimentalism or instrumentalism, a charge which has merit when applied, for instance, to the libertarianism of Mises, or at worst a species of Romanticism. One also in this regard sees Hayek's break with libertarianism.

Yet despite some obvious similarities, Hayek parts company in two critical areas with the communitarians who define themselves as such. First, he eschews any devotion to methodological collectivism, finding it antithetical to the position he seeks to justify. While subjectivists and methodological individualists proceed "from our knowledge of the inside of these social complexes, the knowledge of the individual attitudes which form the elements of their structures," by contrast methodological collectivism "treats social phenomena not as something of which the human mind is a part and the principles of whose organization we can reconstruct from the familiar parts, but as if they were objects directly perceived by us as wholes" (Hayek 1979b, pp. 93–4). As Hayek interprets it, methodological collectivism suggests that "all members of society become merely instruments of the single directing mind and … all the spontaneous social forces to which the growth of the mind is due are destroyed" (p. 162). This is essentially a reaffirmation of the position of Jung: "A collective attitude naturally presupposes this same collective psyche in others…. This disregard for individuality obviously means the suffocation of the single individual, as a consequence of which the element of differentiation is obliterated from the community" (Jung 1966, p. 152).

At the same time, the philosophy of Hayek cannot really be understood as methodological individualism, if only because of the central importance he gives to rules as social mechanisms. On Bhaskar's definition – methodological individualism being "the doctrine that facts about societies, and social phenomena generally, are to be explained solely in terms of facts about individuals" (Bhaskar 1998, p. 27) – Hayek is clearly *not* a methodological individualist. Contrary to Fleetwood, Hayek does not maintain that "the social world is constituted solely by individuals' conceptions" (Fleetwood 1995, p. 53), a charge that *would* have validity if applied, for instance, to Mises.[62] Significantly for Hayek, the institutions he suggests are integral in the formation of individual conceptualizations are not merely abstractions into which are placed the facts of experience, but rather are themselves determinative mechanisms. In actuality, then, one may identify in Hayek's position elements of what Joseph Agassi (1960) refers to as institutionalist-individualism, a stance which "accords with the classical individualistic idea that social phenomena are but the interactions between individuals," while "it adds to these factors of interaction the existing inter-personal means of co-ordination as well as individuals' ability to use, reform, or abolish them, on their own decision and responsibility" (Agassi 1960, p. 267).[63] Even Lawson accepts that Hayek came ultimately to accept a "structural ontology," "acknowledging the reality of structure irreducible to events, including social structures that are dependent upon, but irreducible to, the concepts and actions of human agents" (Lawson 1997, p. 150).

Second, there is Hayek's insistence on the primacy of justice in respect of individual liberty, a claim many communitarians feel is antithetical to the concept of community. Hayek's conception is more broadly conceived than is typically acknowledged, for the concept of right, the guarantee of which is seen as the defining characteristic of the liberal polity, is itself a common good. The question then centers on the practical matter of the role of government in directing the polity to the fulfillment of some larger goal. To Hayek, there is no legitimate claim to the interference with individuals in the free engagement in what can be defined as market activity. Where the State or any collective attempts to promote or even to define social ends instead of restricting its functions to the delimiting of a sphere of action, the result is an unwarranted abridgment of individual freedom, leading to coercion and tyranny. One sees here the influence of Humboldt, who sees in the "too extensive solicitude on the part of the State ... the necessary deterioration of the moral character," so that in seeking to extend its reach, the State succeeds only in "limiting the sphere of morality" (Humboldt 1791/2, p. 20). Certainly Hayek is willing to concede a place for State action. In general terms, he acknowledges a government role in activities designed "to provide a favorable framework for individual decisions," such as would "supply means which individuals can use for their own purposes," as well as actions dedicated to "the enforcement of the general rules of law" (Hayek 1960, p. 223). After the fashion of John Stuart Mill, Hayek envisions government activity in other areas, with the proviso that its involvement be "on the same terms as the citizens" (p. 223).

Yet this is the practical aspect of Hayek's social philosophy, with which we have not here been concerned. For his part, Hayek manages to combine the best aspects of individualism and communitarianism. He thus can account for community without the metaphysics inherent in a structured communitarianism, for he simply accepts that individuals will, if left to their own devices, form the very relationships that communitarians declare to be the hallmarks of a social ethic.

Remarks

The attacks on liberalism outlined in Chapter I are taken to be encompassing of *all* variants, including egalitarian liberalism (the focus of the attack) and libertarian liberalism as well (the latter represented by Robert Nozick, Mises,[64] and Murray Rothbard). The question, of course, is whether there can be a *communitarian* or *conservative* liberalism, a philosophy of individualism that explicitly accounts for a transcendent morality. The argument here is that Hayek actually articulated just such a social philosophy, supplementing deontological ethics with elements of a critical ontology (albeit *individualist*, not *social*, as Hayek does not go so far as to reify social relations) which communitarians insist is a necessary component of moral theory. The blanket condemnation of liberalism thus simply cannot be applied to Hayek, as he explicitly accounts for the very elements communitarians regard as essential.

For Hayek, structure shapes agency, which then transforms structure. This is not to deny Hayek's liberalism, for his *bona fides* are well-established and beyond dispute. It is merely to attempt to refute the notion, made explicit by Sandel in his elucidation of the communitarian thesis, that Hayek is representative of the philosophy of "libertarian liberalism," a philosophy that explicitly denies the socially constituted nature of man.

Notes

1   Steve Fleetwood (1995) has an especially interesting discussion of Hayek's employment of rules. See especially his Chapters 7–9. See also William Baumgarth (1978) and Karen Vaughn (1999).

2 Posner opines that "spontaneous" was perhaps for Hayek a poor choice of terminology – "not the happiest term for what he has in mind" – and suggests that "'unplanned' or 'undesigned' would be better and 'evolved' would be best, given his emphasis on the analogy of natural selection" (Posner 2003, p. 276).

3 Hayek actually traces the emergence of the idea of spontaneous order to the teachings of Cato and Cicero, both of whom acknowledged the workings of such an order in the founding of the Roman constitution. See Hayek 1960, pp. 57–8.

4 But see pp. 195–97 as to whether Hayek's understanding of social wholes is real or nominal.

5 It should be noted here that Hayek explicitly rejects Mises's distinction between organism and organization in the present context, noting that an organism is distinct from a spontaneous order in that, in the former, "most of the individual elements occupy fixed places which, at least once the organism is mature, they retain once and for all." Organisms then are more "concrete" than spontaneous orders (Hayek 1973, pp. 52–3).

6 Tönnies assigns both *thesei* and *nomo* to the category of artifice: the former is by adoption, the latter from custom. See Tönnies 1935, p. 211.

7 Hayek 1944, chapter 6, presents one of his earliest discussions of the distinction between law and the rule of law.

8 On the distinction between laws and norms, see Posner (1997). On Hayek's views of custom and its relation to law, see Robert W. Gordon (1994).

9 Hayek attributes this phrase to Berhhard Rehfeldt, *Die Wurzeln des Rechts* (1951). The original German quotation is presented in Hayek 1973, p. 162, n. 1. See also Hayek 1967d, p. 457.

10 Nicholas Rescher likewise observes that "all that a family of moral rules can do is to provide general guidelines. Rule morality in this view can indeed orient and guide but cannot determine and specify action" (Rescher 1987, p. 52).

11 Liberty "does not assure us of any particular opportunities, but leaves it to us to decide what use we shall make of the circumstances in which we find ourselves" (Hayek 1960, p. 19). While Hayek credits T. H. Green with having elucidated the idea of negative liberty, deriving it from the work of Hegel, it is clearly evident in Hobbes's *Leviathan*: "In cases where the Soveraign has prescribed no rule, there the Subject hath the liberty to do, or forbeare, according to his own discretion" (Hobbes 1651, p. 271).

12 In the words of Hart, rules "constitute *standards* by which particular actions may be thus critically appraised" (Hart 1994, p. 33; emphasis in original). (This is a second edition, the first having been published in 1961.)

13 MacIntyre nonetheless is cautious of a too-strict reliance on rules in respect of conduct:

> no rule or set of rules by itself ever determines how to respond rightly. This is because in the case of those rules that are always to be respected … they are never sufficient to determine how we ought to act, while with other rules what always has to be determined is whether in this particular case they are relevant and, if so, how they are to be applied.
>
> (MacIntyre 1999, p. 93)

14 "Law can be expected to attach a sanction to a violation of a good norm when the private benefits of violation are great or the private costs … are slight, so that not everyone obeys the norm all the time, and where in addition the violation inflicts substantial social costs" (Posner 1995, p. 368).

15 "An imperative is a practical rule by which an action in itself contingent is *made* necessary." It "is a rule the representation of which *makes* necessary an action that is subjectively contingent and thus represents the subject as one that must be *constrained* (necessitated) to conform with the rule." The

categorical (unconditional) imperative is one that represents an action as objectively necessary and makes it necessary not indirectly, through the representation of some *end* that can be attained by the action, but through the mere representation of this action itself (its form), and hence directly.

The "categorical imperative" is thus "a morally practical *law*," which "asserts an obligation with respect to certain actions.(Kant 1797, p. 15; emphasis in original)

16 This places Hayek in conflict with Mises who, as we saw, rejects the categorical imperative as leading to a socialist order.

17 Note Rescher: "The prospect of conflict in out-of-the-ordinary cases is the price that any set of rules – moral codes included – pays for the sort of simplicity that is essential to its capacity to function effectively in the guidance of conduct" (Rescher 1987, p. 53).

18 The notion of socially stabilizing custom is clearly evident in Max Weber's sociology:

The stability of merely customary action rests essentially on the fact that the person who does not adapt himself to it is subjected to both petty and major inconveniences and annoyances as long as the majority of the people he comes in contact with continue to uphold the custom and conform with it.

Similarly, the stability of action in terms of self-interest rests on the fact that the person who does not orient his action to the interests of others ... arouses their antagonism or may end up in a situation different from that which he had foreseen or wished to bring about. He thus runs the risk of damaging his own interests.

(Weber 1947, p. 123)

19 Cf. Burke, a member of Hayek's pantheon: "When antient opinions and rules of life are taken away, the loss cannot possibly be estimated. From that moment we have no compass to govern us; nor can we know distinctly to what port to steer" (Burke 1790, pp. 172–3).

20 Rationality means, in this instance, "no more than some degree of coherence and consistency in a person's action, some lasting influence of knowledge or insight which, once acquired, will affect his action at a later date and in different circumstances" (Hayek 1960, p. 77). It is in this context that Fleetwood (1995) considers Hayek to have adopted a form of procedural rationality.

21 In this Hayek seems to be in agreement with Adam Smith: "The wise and virtuous man is at all times willing that his own private interest should be sacrificed to the public interest of his own particular order or society" (A. Smith 1790, Part VI, Sec. ii, Ch. 3, p. 235).

22 Throughout his discussions of freedom and liberty, Hayek seems less the classical liberal than what Quentin Skinner (1998) refers to as a "neo-roman" liberal. For the neo-roman, individual liberty is not simply non-interference in personal matters, but more significantly freedom from a *condition* of restraint or dependence. Thus Thomas Hobbes and Isaiah Berlin could agree that one is as free in a commonwealth as in an absolute monarchy, as it is the *extent* of the law that matters, while for some, such as Thomas More and James Harrington, the *source* of the law is at least as important, if not more so.

23 Hayek makes a distinction between "true" and "false" individualism. "False" individualism "is the product of an exaggerated belief in the powers of individual reason and of a consequent contempt for anything which has not been consciously designed by it or is not fully intelligible to it" (Hayek 1948, p. 8). "True" individualism, by contrast, "is a product of an acute consciousness of the limitations of the individual mind which induces an attitude of humility toward the impersonal and anonymous social processes by which individuals help to create things greater than they know" (p. 8). The "rational man" condemned by the communitarians is in reality *not* the subject of "true" individualism.

24 By contrast, John Gray (1998) appears to interpret Hayek correctly, as he notes that, for Hayek, morality is "partly constitutive" of life.

25 As evidence of Hayek's disdain for Freud, note the following:

> Through his profound effects on education, Sigmund Freud has probably become the greatest destroyer of culture. Although in his old age, in his *Civilisation and its Discontents*, he seems himself to have become not a little disturbed by some of the effects of his teaching, his basic aim of undoing the culturally acquired repressions and freeing the natural drives, has opened the most fatal attack on the basis of all civilization.
>
> (Hayek 1979, p. 174)

26 "[B]ecause individuals form a society, new phenomena occur whose cause is association, and which, reacting upon the consciousness of individuals, for the most part shapes them. This is why, although society is nothing without individuals, each one of them is much more a product of society than he is the author" (Durkheim 1893, p. 288, n. 16). Note Marx: "Man ... is not only a social animal, but an animal that can be individualised only within society" (Marx 1859, p. 189).

27 It is interesting to note that Durkheim distinguishes, as does Hayek, two types of individualism: egoistic and moral. Egoistic individualism is predicated on atomism, and is consistent with act-Utilitarianism; it is within the purview of "[Herbert] Spencer and the economists," and represents an attempt at "crass commercialism which reduces society to nothing more than a vast apparatus of production and exchange" (Durkheim 1973, p. 44). By contrast, moral individualism – "the individualism of Kant and Rousseau, of the idealists" – is akin to communitarianism, and holds that individuals are bound in society by a set of common beliefs, while society itself is pluralistic, comprised of a profusion of social communities which serve to provide identity to their members (p. 45). For a communitarian interpretation and defense of Durkheim's sociology, see Mark Cladis (1992).

28 While there are indeed elements of similarity between Hayek and Durkheim, it is clear that Hayek does not accept completely Durkheim's organicism nor the scientism evident in his embracing of natural scientific methods.

29 Murray Rothbard (1998) takes issue with Hayek's definition of coercion, devoting an entire chapter (Chapter 28) to the topic. See also Baumgarth (1978), especially pp. 15–20.

30 The limitation of rationalism seems rather obvious – one simply cannot plan for every conceivable consequence of every action, or even know all such actions that are capable of leading to a particular consequence. But this has not deterred some from making the most bizarre claims in attempting to refute Hayek. Consider the following from an avowed Misesian, Hans-Hermann Hoppe: "Every action involves the purposeful employment of scarce means, *and every actor can always distinguish between a successful and an unsuccessful action*" (Hoppe 1994, p. 77; emphasis added); and "Acting is always conscious and rational" (pp. 77–8). He further criticizes Hayek for denying "at least the possibility of recognizing *all* indirect causes and consequences of human action" (p. 93; emphasis added). For these statements to be valid would require perfect foresight and extreme cognitive abilities, attributes which simply do not exist. In addition, Hoppe is oblivious to a critical distinction: Hayek concentrates his critique of rationalism on the impossibility of discerning unintended *social* consequences of *individual* actions, thus providing the intellectual argument against social planning. Hoppe's critique conflates this with an inability on the part of Hayek to acknowledge the possibility of individual rational *behavior* (as expressed in utility maximization), a charge which cannot be leveled at Hayek.

Furthermore, Mises himself considers the terms "rational" and "irrational" to be "inappropriate and meaningless," as they "imply a judgment about the expediency and adequacy of the procedure employed [to the attainment of ends]." This is so because "human reason is not infallible and ... man very often errs in selecting and applying means" (Mises 1949, pp. 18, 20).

31 One sees another parallel between Hayek and Jung, this in their general attitudes toward science: "[S]cience conveys a picture of the world from which a real human psyche appears to be excluded – the very antithesis of the 'humanities'." As Jung sees it, this leads to a situation in which "[t]he moral responsibility of the individual is then inevitably replaced by the policy of the State" (Jung 1990, p. 8).

32 Kukathas maintains that Hayek's project fails because of his "assumption that it is rationalism, particularly as it is manifested in the attempt to give a deductively sound justification for a morality, that is the source of all that is hostile to the Open Society" (Kukathas 1989, p. 19). Yet Hayek does not abandon rationalism or reason, but rather denies the possibility of a *constructed* morality.

33 Reason "is no motive to action, and directs only the impulse received from appetite or inclination, by showing us the means of attaining happiness or avoiding misery" (Hume 1777, p. 294). See also McCann (1999).

34 The use of the term "rational" in this instance follows Gauthier: "Moral principles are those to which our rational selves would agree, *ex ante*, for the regulation of our cooperative interactions" (Gauthier 1990, p. 272). We *would agree* as to their necessity, but are not required even to *understand* the way in which they function.

35 It must be noted that Lawson attributes to Hayek a "hermeneuticist/subjectivist" posture, which effectively leads him "to reduce structure to agency" (1994, p. 150). Yet such a position is at odds with Hayek's ontology, and can be justified only if one is already convinced that Hayek is a committed positivist.

36 Here we see the basis for Hayek's rejection of socialist calculation and arguments for social design, as these constraints make it impossible to effect purposeful constructions.

37 This is in stark contrast to the position of the political philosopher C. B. Macpherson, who proclaims "the facts of human capacities and needs contain enough data for the deduction of a system of obligation and rights" (Macpherson 1962, p. 83). For Macpherson, democracy is an end in itself, a form of moral order. Yet his liberal vision must be seen as diametrically opposed to that of Hayek for, while he accepts the socially constituted self as central, he nonetheless looks to rational structure as the appropriate vehicle for social cohesion. This allows the derivation of Marxian conclusions respecting property, and more importantly (but perhaps unwittingly) establishes a theoretical justification for a totalitarian order.

38 The classic example concerns the outbreak of a communicable disease. In this instance, the population as a whole is protected by the quarantine of the affected group, until the outbreak is halted. This is a position also embraced by Mises.

39 As Rescher suggests, Utilitarianism does not allow for the judgment of "vicarious" affects, which judgment would allow us "to set up moral criteria as an arbiter over the points of view of individuals" (Rescher 1975, p. 93).

40 Rescher notes, "Morality and utility-maximization go their own separate ways. The utilitarian policy of providing for the greatest good of the greatest number may perhaps afford a plausible *political polity*, but it just is not a plausible *morality*" (Rescher 1989, p. 83; emphasis in original). But note Mises: "Everything that serves to preserve the social order is moral; everything that is detrimental to it is immoral" (Mises 1978, p. 34).

41 Despite Hayek's dismissal of both act- and rule-Utilitarianism, some have nonetheless still attempted to classify him within the rule-utilitarian camp. As Brian Lee Crowley notes, Hayek argues that the rules on a society which tend to the direction of "good"

social acts also contribute to "the prosperity and continuation of the evolutionary order." All Hayek then argues is that "rational analysis" cannot be employed in an attempt to establish a foundation for these rules. On this basis, Crowley portrays Hayek as an "irrational or anti-rational rule-utilitarian" (Crowley 1987, p. 56). Likewise, John Gray esteems Hayek to be a "system" utilitarian, to the extent that "the proper rôle of utility is not prescriptive or practical but rather that of a standard of evaluation for the assessment of whole systems of rules or practices" (J. Gray 1998, p. 59).

42 It is not clear that Hayek can be classed as a full-fledged transcendental (critical) realist, but there is much in his writings to suggest at least a close affinity. To give just one example, Bhaskar notes that "experiences and the things and causal laws to which it affords us access are normally out of phase with one another" (Bhaskar 1997, p. 25), while Hayek allows that

> [t]here exists … no one-to-one correspondence between the kinds (or the physical properties) of the different physical stimuli and the dimensions in which they can vary, on the one hand, and the different kinds of sensory qualities which they produce and their various dimensions, on the other.
>
> (Hayek 1952, p. 14)

43 Cf. Hayek's position to the instrumental position of Humboldt: "It is through a social union … based on the internal wants and capacities of its members, that each is enabled to participate in the rich collective resources of all the others" (Humboldt 1791/2, p. 11).

44 This has led some, such as Viktor Vanberg (1986) and Robert Sugden (1993), to observe that Hayek actually is a contractarian.

45 Cf. Jung:

> Happiness and contentment, equability of mind and meaningfulness of life – these can be experienced only by the individual and not by a State, which, on the one hand, is nothing but a convention agreed to by independent individuals and, on the other, continually threatens to paralyse and suppress the individual.
>
> (Jung 1990, p. 60)

46 Note the Freudian component:

> The first requisite of civilization, therefore, is that of justice – that is, the assurance that a law once made will not be broken in favour of an individual.… The further course of cultural development seems to tend towards making the law no longer an expression of the will of a small community.… The final outcome should be a rule of law to which all – except all those who are not capable of entering a community – have contributed by a sacrifice of their instincts, and which leaves no one – again with the same exception – at the mercy of brute force.
>
> (Freud 1930, p. 49)

47 Hoppe (1994) condemns the very notion of spontaneous order as presented by Hayek, while lionizing Mises for his recognition that society is but the totality of relations engendered by individual, rational actions. But, as we saw above, Mises presents nothing if not an example of what is now generally recognized as a Hayekian spontaneous order!

48 Hayek's views on social justice have been attacked recently (although largely ineffectually and without incident) by, among others, David Johnston (1997) and Steven Lukes (1997). But see Edward Feser (1997) for a point-by-point critique of the critics.

49 While Hayek is unhappy with the concept of "social justice," he nonetheless expresses some regard for the road taken to its advancement, particularly that of Rawls. Specifically, he accepts the validity of the idea of a "veil of ignorance" behind which

the social contract is initiated, since it is entered into without regard to prescribed social ends (although, oddly enough, the initiation of a social contract would require that individuals voluntarily agree to place themselves in society, so the connotation is that the individual is antecedent to community). In establishing the basic rule framework, one of the first conditions is "that only such rules as can be applied equally to all should be enforced" (Hayek 1976, p. 97). Hayek in fact expresses his justification for the concept in very Rawlsian terms: "Man has developed rules of conduct not because he knows but because he does not know what all the consequences of a particular action will be" (pp. 20–1). Once established, rules of law and society are binding on all, and must "be obeyed irrespective of the known effects of the particular action" (p. 21). Hayek rejects, however, Rawls's egalitarianism as somehow short-circuiting the process of social evolution (see Hayek 1988).

50 A particularly misguided interpretation of Hayek's approach is that of Ted Honderich (1990). Honderich allows that principles of distributive justice are predicated on *need*, not *merit*, and so Hayek is mistaken in rejecting them. But he fails to realize that those advocating such a notion in fact equate need with merit in the very manner in which they identify the "classes" in question – the existing distribution is somehow morally suspect, and thus those at the lower end have a moral claim on the whole.

51 Given Hayek's position on this question, it is difficult to fathom the following preposterous claim of Alain de Benoist (1998, p. 76):

> [Adam] Smith operates on a macro-economic level: although operating in an apparently disorderly manner, individual acts end up miraculously contributing to the collective interest or to everyone's well-being. This is why Smith allows for public intervention when individual aims do not bring about collective well-being. Hayek does not allow for this exception.

52 Here (and elsewhere in *The Constitution of Liberty*), Hayek incurs the wrath of Rothbard. Rothbard considers that Hayek's treatise

> can in no sense provide the criteria or the groundwork for a system of individual liberty.... For Hayek, government – and its rule – of law *creates* rights, rather than ratifies or defends them. It is no wonder that, in the course of his book, Hayek comes to endorse a long list of government actions clearly invasive of the rights and liberties of the individual citizens.
>
> (Rothbard 1998, p. 229).

53 Hayek's State can be differentiated from the more libertarian construct of Nozick. Nozick considers his "minimal state" to be "the most extensive state that can be justified" without violating individual freedom and individual rights (Nozick 1974, p. 149). To this end, the State has no authority beyond the limited sphere of the provision of public safety. While communities *within* the State may impose limitations upon members, since these restrictions are agreed to as a condition of membership, the more extensive collective (the State) is proscribed in its role (pp. 320–1).

54 Mises regards the establishment of a system of social security as eliminating incentives to avoid penury, sickness, and injury (Mises 1949, p. 835). It also, to the extent that its financing is controlled by government, can adversely affect capital markets (pp. 843–4). Interestingly, Stephen Holmes notes that communists have also consistently opposed programs of social welfare, "which they considered a subtle ploy to dampen the fighting spirit of the working classes." These policies were seen "as blocking the path to collectivism, as irredeemably liberal" (S. Holmes 1995, p. 37).

55 This book is a collection of essays originally published in the *New Republic* in 1929–1930.

56 For Dewey, "[a]ssured and integrated individuality is the product of definite social relationships and publicly acknowledged functions" (Dewey 1999, p. 27). Yet, as Dewey perceives it, "individuals do not find support and contentment in the fact that they are sustaining and sustained members of a social whole" (p. 28). He thus seems unprepared to acknowledge that the self is socially constituted, but rather appeals to social engineering to construct such a communal being. Dewey's conclusion is that a "new" individual must emerge, one "whose pattern of thought and desire is enduringly marked by consensus with others, and in whom sociability is one with cooperation in all regular human associations" (p. 44).

57 This does not, of course, imply that the rules are rationally *determined*.

58 Cf. Lawson, who interprets Hayek as having an "empiricist ontology ... that is augmented by the concepts and beliefs of others." Lawson suggests that Hayek came eventually to accept a "structured ontology," "acknowledging the reality of structure irreducible to events, including social structures that are dependent upon, but irreducible to, the concepts and actions of human agents" (Lawson 1997, p. 150). See also Lawson, 1996.

59 On this see also Andrew Gamble (1996), especially Chapter 5. On Hayek's liberalism and the conservatism he challenged, see Leonard P. Liggio (1994), and the comments by Christopher T. Wonnell (1994) and Butler Shaffer (1994).

60 Stephan Boehm, in his comments on an early draft of the essay from which this chapter developed, points out that Hayek consistently eschews "the middle." However, Hayek himself shows no such concern. In any event, the problem lies with the relevant continuum: if the continuum extends from libertarianism to communism, then neither liberalism nor communitarianism represents an end point.

61 Although Carl Schmitt regards Burke as at least sympathetic to the Romantics. To Schmitt, Burke's philosophy "marks a historical connection between the Whig aristocrat Shaftesbury and the German romantic Adam Müller" (Schmitt 1925, p. 58).

62 "Men coöperate and are eager to intensify coöperation exactly because they are anxious to pursue their selfish interests" (Mises 1944, p. 543).

63 Chandran Kukathas classifies Hayek as a "molecular individualist," an approach which "asks what rights and obligations there must be if society is to be sustained and the security or freedom of the individual preserved" (Kukathas 1989, p. 125).

64 Although Mises, as we have seen, does also reflect on man as a social being.

Conclusion

Here we have seen that, within liberal philosophical thought as defined in the writings of our chosen exemplars, there has consistently been an emphasis on the *social* nature of man. On the liberal view, the individual is not taken to be asocial or pre-social, egoistic, hedonistic, or selfish, unencumbered by connections and dispositions toward his fellow man. Rather, it is recognized that society *defines* the individual. The very understandings of individualism and individuality arise from the nature of *social* relations. Community is thus an integral part of liberal political and social thought. The fullness and complexity of liberalism simply cannot be comprehended or even appreciated without apprehension of this significant fact.

While liberalism shares with conservatism and communitarianism this understanding of the essential communal nature of man, both conservatism and communitarianism are constructed so as to avoid what they perceive to be the chief conflicts of liberalism. Consider the communitarian argument against liberalism. The caricatured liberal accepts the predicate of an unconstituted self, for whom social obligation is secondary to personal rights. He rejects holism and organicism in favor of atomism, positing as the basic unit of analysis an egoistic individual situated outside his social milieu: there is a divergence of agency and structure. Having thus characterized liberalism, communitarian writers center their attacks on the insufficiency of the atomic postulate, and then proceed to question the justification of the social contract, the minimal state, and the central place of right and justice (distributive and procedural) within the social order. They argue that liberal approaches to social order fail because they lack an ontology that would permit the formation of a moral society. Any and all liberal communities must, by virtue of the manner of their institution, be tenuous, as they lack the indispensable moral foundation, such as would be exemplified in a community of individuals actuated by moral sentiments. Liberalism thus defined fails because it cannot comprehend that justice and fairness are *social* concerns, and so cannot be understood absent an acceptance of a transcendent social group consciousness.

Now consider the conservative argument. Here the caricatured liberal (as defined, e.g., by Kekes) advocates individual autonomy in action. He perceives the individual as excessively rational, with actions purposeful and constrained by the ability to assess fully the consequences of actions; man is a utility maximizer of the highest order, a true *homo economicus*. Finally, the conservative's liberal is committed to the ideal of pluralism as a defining core value. There exists no single set of accepted fundamental beliefs and values; instead, autonomous communities each hold to value systems that may together be incompatible. Yet these very elements which serve to define liberalism also provide the means to its failure. Insisting on greater individual autonomy as an answer to social evils ignores the possibility that evil as much as good is an object of choice, for it assigns to good and evil no relative moral value but assumes that always and everywhere the one is preferred to the other. In addition, the commitment to pluralism as a core value is simply incongruous, as pluralism in and of itself represents a *denial* of any basic core value.

These understandings of liberalism, however valid they may be as characterizations of a modal type, are not consistent with the social philosophy espoused by the writers discussed herein. Specifically, the various liberal philosophies reviewed here share many of the features of conservatism and communitarianism. Even communitarian and conservative terminology can be found in these works, employed to the same effect and to the same vision: man is a social being, his individuality defined through his obligations to self and others, which obligations are not imposed so much as accepted as right and proper conduct. By accepting as a premise the social nature of being, the liberal as here contemplated needs not posit a *social* ontology. Of those with whom we have dealt, Spencer comes closest to such a reification of society. As to the others, it is enough to accept an *individual* ontology, with the understanding that individuals are socially constituted, i.e., they are social beings relationally bound to others. A society, then, is comprised of individuals *and* their relations to one another, where relations include duties and obligations, predicated on benevolence, solidarity, and sociality.

Yet despite the commonalities, there is still room for a great deal of disagreement on key points, as one might expect. Mill and Stephen agree with respect to the basic utilitarian principles that underlie the liberal social order, but disagree with respect to the role of coercion and the constitution of the value structure (pluralistic versus absolutist). Spencer and Sumner grant to the individual a degree of sociality with which communitarians and conservatives could readily agree, but disagree among themselves as to the nature of values and to the extent to which society has a real as opposed to a nominal existence. Mises and Hayek likewise situate the individual with the social order, but disagree as to the role of reason and rationality in the process, as they disagree as to the role of the State.

In the end, perhaps, the Scottish philosophers represent still an intellectual force to be reckoned with. Their estimation of the individual and his relation to the social whole continues to inform liberal social and political thought. However much that philosophy may be denigrated and mischaracterized, the central tenets continue to hold.

Bibliography

Agassi, Joseph (1960) "Methodological Individualism", *The British Journal of Sociology*, vol. 11, no. 2 (September), pp. 244–70.

Archard, David (1990) "Freedom Not to Be Free: The Case of the Slavery Contract in J. S. Mill's *On Liberty*", *Philosophical Quarterly*, vol. 40, no. 160 (October), pp. 453–65.

Baumgarth, William P. (1978) "Hayek and Political Order: The Rule of Law", *Journal of Libertarian Studies*, vol. 2, no. 1, pp. 11–28.

Benoist, Alain de (1998) "Hayek: A Critique", *Telos*, vol. 29, no. 4 (no. 110, Winter), pp. 71–104.

Bentham, Jeremy (1843) *Anarchical Fallacies; Being an Examination of the Declarations of Rights Issued During the French Revolution*, in John Bowring, ed., *The Works of Jeremy Bentham*. Vol. II. Edinburgh: William Tait.

—— (1988) *The Principles of Morals and Legislation*. Amherst, N.Y.: Prometheus Books.

Bhaskar, Roy (1997) *A Realist Theory of Science*. London: Verso.

—— (1998) *The Possibility of Naturalism: A Philosophical Critique of the Contemporary Human Sciences*. Third edn. London: Routledge.

Bird, Colin (1999) *The Myth of Liberal Individualism*. Cambridge: Cambridge University Press.

Boettke, Peter J. and Virgil Henry Storr (2002) "Polity, Society and Economy in Weber, Mises and Hayek", *American Journal of Economics and Sociology*, vol. 61, no. 1 (January), pp. 161–91.

Bork, Robert H. (1996) *Slouching Towards Gomorrah: Modern Liberalism and American Decline*. New York: Regan Books.

Brandt, Richard B. (1992) *Morality, Utilitarianism, and Rights*. Cambridge: Cambridge University Press.

Burke, Edmund (1790 [1986]) *Reflections on the Revolution in France*. Edited, with an Introduction by Conor Cruise O'Brien. Harmondsworth: Penguin Books.

Cladis, Mark S. (1992) *A Communitarian Defense of Liberalism: Emile Durkheim and Contemporary Social Theory*. Stanford: Stanford University Press.

Coats, Wendell John (1985) "Michael Oakeshott as Liberal Theorist", *Canadian Journal of Political Science*, vol. 18 (December), pp. 777–87.

Colaiaco, James A. (1983) *James Fitzjames Stephen and the Crisis of Victorian Thought*. New York: St. Martin's Press.

Copleston, Frederick (1994) *A History of Philosophy*. Vol. VIII: *Modern Philosophy: Empiricism, Idealism, and Pragmatism in Britain and America*. New York: Doubleday.

Crowley, Brian Lee (1987) *The Self, the Individual, and the Community: Liberalism in the Political Thought of F. A. Hayek and Sidney and Beatrice Webb*. Oxford: Clarendon Press.

Darwin, Charles (1969) *The Autobiography of Charles Darwin, 1809–1882*. Edited by Nora Barlow. New York: Norton.

—— (1991) *The Correspondence of Charles Darwin*. Vol. 7: 1858–1859. Edited by Frederick Burkhardt and Sydney Smith. Cambridge: Cambridge University Press.

Devlin, Patrick (1965) *The Enforcement of Morals*. London: Oxford University Press.

Dewey, John (1904) "The Philosophical Work of Herbert Spencer", *The Philosophical Review*, vol. XIII, no. 2 (March), pp. 159–75.

—— (1999) *Individualism, Old and New*. Amherst, N.Y.: Prometheus Books.

Dorfman, Joseph (1935) *Thorstein Veblen and His America*. New York: Victor Gollancz.

—— (1959) *The Economic Mind in American Civilization*. New York: Viking.

Dugger, William M. and Howard J. Sherman (2000) *Reclaiming Evolution: A Dialogue Between Marxism and Institutionalism on Social Change*. London: Routledge.

Durkheim, Emile (1893 [1997]) *The Division of Labor in Society*. Translated by W. D. Halls. New York: Free Press.

—— (1973) *On Morality and Society*. Edited, with an Introduction by Robert N. Bellah. Chicago: University of Chicago Press.

Dworkin, Gerald (1971) "Paternalism", in Richard A. Wasterstrom, ed., *Morality and the Law*. Belmont, CA: Wadsworth Publishing.

Dyzenhaus, David (1992) "John Stuart Mill and the Harm of Pornography", *Ethics*, vol. 102, no. 3 (April), pp. 534–51.

Eaton, Ralph M. (1921) "Social Fatalism", *The Philosophical Review*, vol. 30, no. 4 (July), pp. 380–92.

Edgeworth, Francis Ysidro (1881 [1995]) *Mathematical Psychics and Other Essays*. San Diego: James and Gordon.

Engels, Friedrich (1884 [1990]) *The Origin of the Family, Private Property and the State. In the Light of the Researches by Lewis H. Morgan*. In Vol. 26 of *Karl Marx/Frederick Engels: Collected Works*. New York: International Publishers.

Feinberg, Joel (1973) *Social Philosophy*. Englewood Cliffs, N. J.: Prentice-Hall.

Ferguson, Adam (1767 [1995]) *An Essay on the History of Civil Society*. Edited by Fania Oz-Salzberger. Cambridge: Cambridge University Press.

Feser, Edward (1997) "Hayek on Social Justice: Reply to Lukes and Johnston", *Critical Review*, vol. 11, no. 4 (Fall), pp. 581–626.

Fleetwood, Steve (1995) *Hayek's Political Economy: The Socio-Economics of Order*. London: Routledge.

—— (1997) "Critical Realism: Marx and Hayek", in Willem Keizer, Bert Tieben and Rudy van Zijp, eds, *Austrian Economics in Debate*. London: Routledge.

Franco, Paul (1990) "Michael Oakeshott as Liberal Theorist", *Political Theory*, vol. 18, no. 3 (August), pp. 411–36.

Freud, Sigmund (1913 [1950]) *Totem and Taboo: Some Points of Agreement between the Mental Lives of Savages and Neurotics*. Standard edn. Translated and edited by James Strachey. New York: W. W. Norton.

—— (1930 [1961]) *Civilization and Its Discontents*. Standard edn. Translated and edited by James Strachey. New York: W. W. Norton.

Friedman, Jeffrey (1994) "The Politics of Communitarianism", *Critical Review*, vol. 8, no. 2 (Spring), pp. 297–340.

Galeotti, Anna Elisabetta (1987) "Individualism, Social Rules, Tradition: The Case of Friedrich A. Hayek", *Political Theory*, vol. 15, no. 2 (May), pp. 163–81.

Gamble, Andrew (1996) *Hayek: The Iron Cage of Liberty*. Boulder: Westview Press.

Gardbaum, Stephen A. (1992) "Law, Politics, and the Claims of Community", *Michigan Law Review*, vol. 90, no. 4 (February), pp. 685–760.

Gauthier, David (1986) *Morals by Agreement*. Oxford: Clarendon Press.

—— (1990) *Moral Dealing: Contract, Ethics, and Reason*. Ithaca: Cornell University Press.

Giddens, Anthony (1984) *The Constitution of Society*. Berkeley: University of California Press.

Goodin, Robert E. (1998) "Review Article: Communities of Enlightenment", *British Journal of Political Science*, vol. 28, part 3 (July), pp. 531–58.

Gordon, Robert W. (1994) "Hayek and Cooter on Custom and Reason", *Southwestern University Law Review*, vol. 23, no. 3, pp. 453–60.

Gray, John (1995) *Liberalism*. Second edn. Minneapolis: University of Minnesota Press.

—— (1996) *Mill on Liberty: A Defence*. London: Routledge.

—— (1998) *Hayek on Liberty*. Third edn. London: Routledge.

Gray, T. S (1985) "Herbert Spencer: Individualist or Organicist?", *Political Studies*, vol. XXXIII, no. 2 (June), pp. 236–53.

Green, T. H (1879–80 [1986]) "Lectures on the Principles of Political Obligation", in Paul Harris and John Morrow, eds, *T. H. Green: Lectures on the Principles of Political Obligation and Other Writings*. Cambridge: Cambridge University Press.

—— (1881 [1986]) "Lecture on Liberal Legislation and Freedom of Contract" (Delivered 18 January), in Paul Harris and John Morrow, eds, *T. H. Green: Lectures on the Principles of Political Obligation and Other Writings*. Cambridge: Cambridge University Press.

Habermas, Jürgen (1996) *Between Facts and Norms: Contributions to a Discourse Theory of Law and Democracy*. Cambridge, MA: MIT Press.

—— (1998) *The Inclusion of the Other: Studies in Political Theory*. Edited by Ciaran Cronin and Pablo de Greiff. Cambridge, MA: MIT Press.

Hamowy, Ronald (1978) "Law and the Liberal Society: F. A. Hayek's Constitution of Liberty", *Journal of Libertarian Studies*, vol. 2, no. 4, pp. 287–97.

Hart, H. L. A. (1963) *Law, Liberty, and Morality*. Stanford: Stanford University Press.

—— (1994) *The Concept of Law*. Second edn. Oxford: Clarendon Press.

Hayek, Friedrich A. von (1944) *The Road to Serfdom*. Chicago: University of Chicago Press.

—— (1948) *Individualism and Economic Order*. Chicago: University of Chicago Press.

—— (1952) *The Sensory Order*. Chicago: University of Chicago Press.

—— (1960) *The Constitution of Liberty*. Chicago: University of Chicago Press.

—— (1967a) "Notes on the Evolution of Systems of Rules of Conduct", in F. A. Hayek, ed., *Studies in Philosophy, Politics and Economics*. London: Routledge and Kegan Paul.

—— (1967b) "The Principles of a Liberal Social Order", in F. A. Hayek, ed., *Studies in Philosophy, Politics and Economics*. London: Routledge and Kegan Paul.

—— (1967c) "What is 'Social'? – What Does it Mean?", in F. A. Hayek, ed., *Studies in Philosophy, Politics and Economics*. London: Routledge and Kegan Paul.

—— (1967d) "The Constitution of a Liberal State", *Il Politico*, vol. XXXII, no. 3 (September), pp. 455–60.

—— (1968) *The Confusion of Language in Political Thought, with Some Suggestions for Remedying It*. Occasional paper no. 20. London: Institute of Economic Affairs.

—— (1973) *Law, Legislation, and Liberty*. Vol. I: *Rules and Order*. Chicago: University of Chicago Press.

—— (1976) *Law, Legislation, and Liberty*. Vol. II: *The Mirage of Social Justice*. Chicago: University of Chicago Press.

—— (1978) "The Atavism of Social Justice", in F. A. Hayek, ed., *New Studies in Philosophy, Politics, Economics, and the History of Ideas*. Chicago: University of Chicago Press.

—— (1979a) *Law, Legislation, and Liberty*. Vol. III: *The Political Order of a Free People*. Chicago: University of Chicago Press.

—— (1979b) *The Counter-Revolution of Science: Studies on the Abuse of Reason*. Second edn. Indianapolis: Liberty Press.

—— (1988) *The Fatal Conceit*. London: Routledge.

Hegel, G. W. F. (1821 [1991]) *Elements of the Philosophy of Right*. Edited by Allen W. Wood; translated by H. B. Nisbet. Cambridge: Cambridge University Press.

Hiskes, Richard P. (1983) "Spencer and the Liberal Idea of Community", *The Review of Politics*, vol. 45, no. 4 (October), pp. 595–609.

Hobbes, Thomas (1651 [1981]) *Leviathan*. Edited by C. B. Macpherson. Harmondsworth: Penguin.

Hodgson, Geoffrey M. (1993) *Economics and Evolution: Bringing Life Back into Economics*. Cambridge: Polity Press.

Hofstadter, Richard (1941) "William Graham Sumner, Social Darwinist", *New England Quarterly*, vol. 14, no. 3 (September), pp. 457–77.

Holmes, Oliver Wendell, Jr. (1881 [1991]) *The Common Law*. New York: Dover.

Holmes, Stephen (1993) *The Anatomy of Antiliberalism*. Cambridge, MA: Harvard University Press.

—— (1995) *Passions and Constraint: On the Theory of Liberal Democracy*. Chicago: University of Chicago Press.

Honderich, Ted (1990) *Conservatism*. London: Hamish Hamilton.

Hoppe, Hans-Hermann (1994) "F. A. Hayek on Government and Social Evolution: A Critique", *The Review of Austrian Economics*, vol. 7, no. 1, pp. 67–93.

Humboldt, Wilhelm von (1791/2 [1993]) *The Limits of State Action*. Edited by J. W. Burrow. Indianapolis: Liberty Fund.

Hume, David (1739/40 [1969]) *A Treatise of Human Nature*. Edited by Ernest C. Mossner. Harmondsworth: Penguin.

—— (1777 [1975]) *Enquiries Concerning Human Understanding and Concerning the Principles of Morals*. Edited and Introduced by L. A. Selby-Bigge; revised third edn by P. H. Nidditch. Oxford: Clarendon Press.

Huxley, T. H. (1871) "Administrative Nihilism", *The Fortnightly Review*, vol. X (NS), no. 59, (November 1), pp. 525–43.

Infantino, Lorenzo (1998) *Individualism in Modern Thought: From Adam Smith to Hayek*. London: Routledge.

James, William (1904) "Herbert Spencer", *Atlantic Monthly*, vol. XCIV, no. 66 (July), pp. 99–108.

Johnston, David (1994) *The Idea of a Liberal Theory: A Critique and Reconstruction*. Princeton: Princeton University Press.

—— (1997) "Hayek's Attack on Social Justice", *Critical Review*, vol. 11, no. 1 (Winter), pp. 81–100.

Jung, C. G. (1966) *Two Essays on Analytical Psychology*. Second edn. Translated by R. F. C. Hull. Princeton: Princeton University Press.

—— (1990) *The Undiscovered Self*. Translated by R. F. C. Hull. Princeton: Princeton University Press. [This is excerpted from *Civilization in Transition*, vol. 10 of Jung's *Collected Works*.]

Kant, Immanuel (1797 [1996]) *The Metaphysics of Morals*. Translated and edited by Mary Gregor. Cambridge: Cambridge University Press.

Kekes, John (1997) *Against Liberalism*. Ithaca, NY: Cornell University Press.

—— (1998) *A Case for Conservatism*. Ithaca, NY: Cornell University Press.

Keller, Albert G. (1910) "Anthropologic Miscellanea: William Graham Sumner", *American Anthropologist*, vol. 12 (NS), no. 1 (January–March), pp. 118–19.

Kirk, Russell (1952) "The Foreboding Conservatism of Stephen", *Western Political Quarterly*, vol. 5, no. 4 (December), pp. 563–77.

Kukathas, Chandran (1989) *Hayek and Modern Liberalism*. Oxford: Clarendon Press.

Kymlicka, Will (1988) "Rawls on Teleology and Deontology", *Philosophy and Public Affairs*, vol. 17, no. 3 (Summer), pp. 173–90.

Laveleye, Emile de (1885) "The State versus the Man", *Contemporary Review*, vol. XLVII, no. 4 (April), pp. 485–508.

Lawson, Tony (1994) "Realism and Hayek: A Case of Continuing Transformation", in M. Colonna, H. Hagemann and O. F. Hamouda, eds, *Capitalism, Socialism, and Knowledge: The Economics of F. A. Hayek*, Vol. II. Aldershot: Edward Elgar.

—— (1996) "Hayek and Keynes: A Commonality", *History of Economics Review*, no. 25 (Winter/Summer), pp. 96–114.

—— (1997) *Economics and Reality*. London: Routledge.

Levy, David M. (2001) *How the Dismal Science Got its Name: Classical Economics and the Ur-Text of Racial Politics*. Ann Arbor: University of Michigan Press.

Liggio, Leonard P. (1994) "Law and Legislation in Hayek's Legal Philosophy", *Southwestern University Law Review*, vol. 23, no. 3, pp. 507–30.

Lippincott, Benjamin (1938) *Victorian Critics of Democracy: Carlyle, Ruskin, Arnold, Stephen, Maine, Lacey*. Minneapolis: University of Minnesota Press.

Locke, John (1698 [1988]) *Two Treatises of Government*. Edited by Peter Laslett. Cambridge: Cambridge University Press.

Lukes, Steven (1997) "Social Justice: The Hayekian Challenge", *Critical Review*, vol. 11, no. 1 (Winter), pp. 65–80.

Lyons, David (1994) *Rights, Welfare, and Mill's Moral Theory*. New York: Oxford University Press.

McCann, C. R., Jr. (1999) "Schumpeter, Democracy, and the Scottish Enlightenment", *Journal of Institutional and Theoretical Economics*, vol. 155, no. 4 (December), pp. 573–93.

—— (2002) "F. A. Hayek: The Liberal as Communitarian", *The Review of Austrian Economics*, vol. 15, no. 1 (March), pp. 5–34.

McCloskey, H. J. (1963) "Mill's Liberalism", *Philosophical Quarterly*, vol. 13, no. 51 (April), pp. 143–56.

—— (1966) "Mill's Liberalism – A Rejoinder to Mr. Ryan", *Philosophical Quarterly*, vol. 16, no. 62 (January), pp. 64–8.

MacIntyre, Alasdair (1984) *After Virtue*. Second edn. Notre Dame, Indiana: University of Notre Dame Press.

—— (1988) *Whose Justice? Which Rationality?* Notre Dame, Indiana: University of Notre Dame Press.

—— (1999) *Dependent Rational Animals*. La Salle, Ill.: Open Court.

Macpherson, C. B. (1962) *The Political Theory of Possessive Individualism*. Oxford: Oxford University Press.

Mandeville, Bernard de (1732 [1924]) *The Fable of the Bees: or Private Vices, Publick Virtues*. Edited by F. B. Kaye. Oxford: Clarendon Press.

Marx, Karl (1859 [1970]) *A Contribution to the Critique of Political Economy*. Edited and Introduced by Maurice Dobb. New York: International Publishers.

—— (1887 [1996]) *Capital*. Vol. 35 of *Karl Marx/Frederick Engels: Collected Works*. First English edn from the third German edn. Translated by Samuel Moore and Edward Aveling, and edited by Frederick Engels. New York: International Publishers.

Menger, Carl (1883 [1985]) *Investigations into the Method of the Social Sciences, with Special Reference to Economics.* Edited by Louis Schneider; translated by Francis J. Nock. New York: New York University Press.

Mill, John Stuart (1829 [1963]) "Letter to Gustave d'Eichthal". Reprinted in *Collected Works of John Stuart Mill.* Vol. XII: *The Earlier Letters of John Stuart Mill, 1812–1848.* Edited by Francis E. Mineka. Toronto: University of Toronto Press.

—— (1838 [1987]) "Bentham", in Alan Ryan, ed., *John Stuart Mill and Jeremy Bentham: Utilitarianism and Other Essays.* Harmondsworth: Penguin.

—— (1840 [1987]) "Coleridge", in Alan Ryan, ed., *John Stuart Mill and Jeremy Bentham: Utilitarianism and Other Essays.* Harmondsworth: Penguin.

—— (1852 [1987]) "Whewell on Moral Philosophy", in Alan Ryan, ed., *John Stuart Mill and Jeremy Bentham: Utilitarianism and Other Essays.* Harmondsworth: Penguin.

—— (1859 [1989]) "On Liberty", in Stefan Collini, ed., *On Liberty and Other Writings.* Cambridge: Cambridge University Press.

—— (1861) "Utilitarianism", *Fraser's Magazine for Town and Country*, vol. LXIV, no. 382 (October), pp. 391–406; no. 383 (November), pp. 525–34; no. 384 (December), pp. 659–73.

—— (1865 [1977]) *Considerations on Representative Government.* Third edn. In J. M. Robson, ed., *Collected Works of John Stuart Mill*, vol. XIX: *Essays on Politics and Society.* Toronto: University of Toronto Press.

—— (1869) "Thornton on Labour and Its Claims", *The Fortnightly Review*, vol. V (NS), no. 29 (May), pp. 505–518; no. 30 (June), pp. 680–700.

—— (1871 [1987]) *Principles of Political Economy.* Fairfield, NJ: Augustus M. Kelley.

—— (1879) "Chapters on Socialism", *The Fortnightly Review*, vol. XXV (NS), no. 146 (February 1), pp. 217–37; no. 147 (March 1), pp. 373–82; no. 148 (April 1), pp. 513–30.

Miller, William L. (1972) "Herbert Spencer's Theory of Welfare and Public Policy", *History of Political Economy*, vol. 4, no. 1 (Spring), pp. 207–31.

Mises, Ludwig von (1944) "The Treatment of 'Irrationality' in the Social Sciences", *Philosophy and Phenomenological Research*, vol. 4, no. 4 (June), pp. 527–46.

—— (1957) *Theory and History: An Interpretation of Social and Economic Evolution.* New Haven: Yale University Press.

—— (1962) *The Ultimate Foundation of Economic Science: An Essay on Method.* Princeton, NJ: D. Van Nostrand Co., Inc.

—— (1978) *Liberalism: A Socio-Economic Exposition.* Second edn. Translated by Ralph Raico. Kansas City: Sheed Andrews and McMeel, Inc.

—— (1981a) *Epistemological Problems of Economics.* Translated by George Reisman. New York: New York University Press.

—— (1981b) *Socialism: An Economic and Sociological Analysis.* Indianapolis: Liberty Fund.

—— (1996) *Human Action: A Treatise on Economics.* Fourth (revised) edn. San Francisco: Fox and Wilkes.

Moore, G. E. (1903 [1993]) *Principia Ethica.* Revised edn. Edited and with an Introduction by Thomas Baldwin. Cambridge: Cambridge University Press.

Mosca, Gaetano (1939) *The Ruling Class (Elementi di Scienza Politica)* Fourth edn. Translated by Hannah D. Kahn; edited by Arthur Livingston. New York: McGraw-Hill.

Nozick, Robert (1974) *Anarchy, State, and Utopia.* New York: Basic Books.

Oakeshott, Michael (1991) *Rationalism in Politics and Other Essays.* Expanded edn. Indianapolis: Liberty Fund.

Paul, Ellen Frankel (1983) "Herbert Spencer: The Historicist as a Failed Prophet", *Journal of the History of Ideas*, vol. 44, no. 4 (October/December), pp. 619–38.

Perrin, Robert G. (1995) "Émile Durkheim's *Division of Labor* and the Shadow of Herbert Spencer", *Sociological Quarterly*, vol. 36, no. 4, pp. 791–808.

Pickens, Donald K. (1968) "William Graham Sumner: Moralist as Social Scientist", *Social Science*, vol. 43, no. 4 (October), pp. 202–9.

Polanyi, Michael (1962) *Personal Knowledge: Towards a Post-Critical Philosophy*. Corrected edn. Chicago: University of Chicago Press.

Posner, Richard A. (1995) *Overcoming Law*. Cambridge, MA: Harvard University Press.

—— (1997) "Social Norms and the Law: An Economic Approach", *American Economic Review, Papers and Proceedings of the Hundred and Fourth Annual Meeting of the American Economic Association*, vol. 87, no. 2 (May), pp. 365–9.

—— (1999) *The Problematics of Moral and Legal Theory*. Cambridge, MA: Belknap/Harvard.

—— (2003) *Law, Pragmatism, and Democracy*. Cambridge, MA: Harvard University Press.

Rawls, John (1971) *A Theory of Justice*. Cambridge, MA: Harvard/Belknap.

—— (1993) *Political Liberalism*. New York: Columbia University Press.

—— (1999) *The Law of Peoples, with "The Idea of Public Reason Revisited"*. Cambridge, MA: Harvard University Press.

—— (2001) *Justice As Fairness: A Restatement*. Edited by Erin Kelly. Cambridge, MA: Belknap/Harvard.

Rees, J. C. (1963) "Hayek on Liberty", *Philosophy*, vol. XXXVIII, no. 146 (October), pp. 346–60.

Reisman, David (1999) *Conservative Capitalism: The Social Economy*. London: Macmillan.

Rescher, Nicholas (1966) *Distributive Justice: A Constructive Critique of the Utilitarian Theory of Distribution*. Indianapolis: Bobbs-Merrill.

—— (1975) *Unselfishness: The Role of the Vicarious Affects in Moral Philosophy and Social Theory*. Pittsburgh: University of Pittsburgh Press.

—— (1987) *Ethical Idealism: An Inquiry into the Nature and Function of Ideals*. Berkeley: University of California Press.

—— (1989) *Moral Absolutes: An Essay on the Nature and Rationale of Morality*. New York: Peter Lang.

Rizzo, Mario (1999) "The Coming Slavery: The Determinism of Herbert Spencer", *The Review of Austrian Economics*, vol. 12, no. 2 (November), pp. 115–30.

Roach, John (1957) "Liberalism and the Victorian Intelligentsia", *Cambridge Historical Journal*, vol. 13, no. 1, pp. 58–81.

Robbins, Lionel (1961) "Hayek on Liberty", *Economica*, vol. XXVIII, no. 109 (February), pp. 66–81.

Rothbard, Murray N. (1998) *The Ethics of Liberty*. New York: New York University Press.

Ruse, Michael (1986) *Taking Darwin Seriously: A Naturalistic Approach to Philosophy*. Oxford: Basil Blackwell.

—— (1995) *Evolutionary Naturalism: Selected Essays*. London: Routledge.

Ryan, Alan (1964) "Mr. McCloskey on Mill's Liberalism", *Philosophical Quarterly*, vol. 14, no. 56 (July), pp. 253–60.

—— (1997) "Introduction", in Alan Ryan, ed., *Mill*. New York: W. W. Norton.

Sandel, Michael (1984) "The Procedural Republic and the Unencumbered Self", *Political Theory*, vol. 12, no. 1 (February), pp. 81–96.

—— (1996) *Democracy's Discontent: America in Search of a Public Philosophy*. Cambridge, MA: Belknap/Harvard.

—— (1998) *Liberalism and the Limits of Justice*. Second edn. Cambridge: Cambridge University Press.

Schmitt, Carl (1925 [1986]) *Political Romanticism*. Second edn. Translated by Guy Oakes. Cambridge, MA: MIT Press.

Schwartz, Richard D. (1980) "Mores and the Law: Taking Sumner Seriously", *Behavior Science Research*, vol. 15, no. 3, pp. 159–80.

Scruton, Roger (2002) *The Meaning of Conservatism*. Third edn. South Bend, IN: St. Augustine's Press.

Shaffer, Butler (1994) "Comments on Leonard Liggio's 'Law and Legislation in Hayek's Legal Philosophy'", *Southwestern University Law Review*, vol. 23, no. 3, pp. 539–46.

Simon, Herbert A. (1983) *Reason in Human Affairs*. Stanford: Stanford University Press.

Skinner, Quentin (1998) *Liberty Before Liberalism*. Cambridge: Cambridge University Press.

Skipper, Robert (1993) "Mill and Pornography", *Ethics*, vol. 103, no. 4 (July), pp. 726–30.

Smart, J. J. C. (1973) "An Outline of a System of Utilitarian Ethics", in J. J. C. Smart and Bernard Williams, *Utilitarianism: For and Against*. Cambridge: Cambridge University Press.

Smith, Adam (1790 [1982]) *The Theory of Moral Sentiments*. Sixth edn. Edited by D. D. Raphael and A. L. Macfie. Indianapolis: Liberty Press.

Smith, K. J. M. (1988) *James Fitzjames Stephen: Portrait of a Victorian Rationalist*. Cambridge: Cambridge University Press.

Smith, Norman Erik (1979) "William Graham Sumner as an Anti-Social Darwinist", *Pacific Sociological Review*, vol. 22, no. 3 (July), pp. 332–47.

Smith, Vernon L. (1999) "Reflections on *Human Action* after 50 Years", *Cato Journal*, vol. 19, no. 2 (Fall), pp. 195–209.

Spencer, Herbert (1860) "The Social Organism", *Westminster Review*, vol. LXXIII, no. 143 (NS vol. XVII, no. 1) (January), pp. 90–121.

—— (1871) "Specialized Administration", *The Fortnightly Review*, vol. X (NS), no. 60 (December 1), pp. 627–54.

—— (1883) "The Americans: A Conversation and a Speech, with an Addition", *The Contemporary Review*, vol. XLIII, no. 1 (January), pp. 1–15.

—— (1885 [1897]) *The Principles of Sociology*. Vol. I. Third edn. New York: D. Appleton and Co.

—— (1886 [1912]) *The Principles of Sociology*. Vol. II. Second edn. New York: D. Appleton and Co.

—— (1897 [1978]) *The Principles of Ethics*. Two vols. Indianapolis: Liberty Classics.

—— (1898) "What is Social Evolution?", *The Nineteenth Century*, vol. XLIV, no. 259 (September), pp. 348–58.

—— (1904) *An Autobiography*. London: Williams and Norgate.

—— (1905) *Principles of Psychology*. New York: D. Appleton and Co.

—— (1954) *Social Statics: The Conditions Essential to Human Happiness Specified, and the First of Them Developed*. New York: Robert Schalkenbach Foundation.

Stapleton, Julia (1998) "James Fitzjames Stephen: Liberalism, Patriotism, and English Liberty", *Victorian Studies*, vol. 41, no. 2 (Winter), pp. 243–63.

Starr, Harris E. (1925) *William Graham Sumner*. New York: Henry Holt and Co.

Stephen, James Fitzjames (1859) "Mr. Mill on Political Liberty", *Saturday Review*, vol. 7, no. 172 (February 19), pp. 186–7; no. 173 (February 26), pp. 213–14.

—— (1861) "The Study of History: I", *Cornhill Magazine*, vol. III, no. 18 (June), pp. 666–80.

—— (1862) "Liberalism", *Cornhill Magazine*, vol. V, no. 25 (January), pp. 70–83.

—— (1863a) "Society", *Cornhill Magazine*, vol. VII, no. 37 (January), pp. 31–41.

—— (1863b) "Anti-respectability", *Cornhill Magazine*, vol. VIII, no. 45 (September), pp. 282–94.

—— (1864) "Sentimentalism", *Cornhill Magazine*, vol. X, no. 55 (July), pp. 65–75.

—— (1865) "Mr. Carlyle", *Fraser's Magazine*, vol. 72, no. 432 (December), pp. 778–810.

—— (1867) "Mandeville", *The Saturday Review*, vol. 23, no. 599 (20 April), pp. 500–2.

—— (1874 [1991]).*Liberty, Equality, Fraternity, and Three Brief Essays*. Edited by R. J. White. Chicago: University of Chicago Press.

—— (1884) "The Unknowable and the Unknown", *Nineteenth Century*, vol. XV, no. 88 (June), pp. 905–19.

Stephen, Leslie (1895) *The Life of Sir James Fitzjames Stephen, Bart., K.C.S.I., A Judge of the High Court of Justice*. Second edn. London: Smith, Elder and Co.

Sugden, Robert (1993) "Normative Judgments and Spontaneous Order: The Contractarian Element in Hayek's Thought", *Constitutional Political Economy*, vol. 4, no. 3 (Fall), pp. 393–424.

Sumner, William Graham (1878) "Socialism", *Scribner's Monthly*, vol. XVI, no. 6 (October), pp. 887–93.

—— (1883 [1952]) *What Social Classes Owe to Each Other*. Caldwell, Idaho: Caxton Printers.

—— (1887a) "The Shifting of Responsibility", *The Independent*, vol. XXXIX, no. 1999 (March 24), pp. 1–2.

—— (1887b) "Speculative Legislation", *The Independent*, vol. XXXIX, no. 2007 (May 19), p. 3.

—— (1887c) "The Banquet of Life", *The Independent*, vol. XXXIX, no. 2012 (June 23), p. 1.

—— (1887d) "The Abolition of Poverty", *The Independent*, vol. XXXIX, no. 2021 (August 25), pp. 1–2.

—— (1887e) "The State as an 'Ethical Person' ", *The Independent*, vol. XXXIX, no. 2027 (October 6), p.1.

—— (1887f) "The Boon of Nature", *The Independent*, vol. XXXIX, no. 2030 (October 27), pp. 4–5.

—— (1888) "The Family and Property", *The Independent*, vol. XL, no. 2063 (June 14), pp. 2–3.

—— (1889a) "Liberty and Responsibility", *The Independent*, vol. XLI, no. 2138 (November 21), pp. 3–4.

—— (1889b) "Liberty and Law", *The Independent*, vol. XLI, no. 2143 (December 26), p. 5.

—— (1906) *Folkways: A Study of the Sociological Importance of Usages, Manners, Customs, Mores, and Morals*. Boston: Ginn and Company.

—— (1913) *Earth-Hunger and Other Essays*. Edited by Albert Galloway Keller. New Haven: Yale University Press.

—— (1919) *The Forgotten Man and Other Essays*. Edited by Albert Galloway Keller. New Haven: Yale University Press.

—— (1992) *On Liberty, Society, and Politics: The Essential Essays of William Graham Sumner*. Edited by Robert C. Bannister. Indianapolis: Liberty Fund.

Sumner, William Graham and Albert Galloway Keller (1927) *The Science of Society*. Vol. I. New Haven: Yale University Press.

Taylor, Charles (1995) *Philosophical Arguments*. Cambridge, MA: Harvard University Press.

Tilman, Rick (2001) *Ideology and Utopia in the Social Philosophy of the Libertarian Economists*, Contributions in Economics and Economic History No. 223, Westport, CT: Greenwood Press.

Tönnies, Ferdinand (1935 [2001]) *Community and Civil Society*. English translation of the eighth edn. Edited by Jose Harris; translated by Jose Harris and Margaret Hollis. Cambridge: Cambridge University Press.

Turner, Jonathan H. (1985) *Herbert Spencer: A Renewed Appreciation*. Beverly Hills, CA: Sage Publications.

Unger, Roberto Mangabeira (1975) *Knowledge and Politics*. New York: Free Press.

Urbinati, Nadia (2002) *Mill on Democracy: From the Athenian Polis to Representative Government*. Chicago: University of Chicago Press.

Urmson, J. O. (1953) "The Interpretation of the Moral Philosophy of J. S. Mill", *Philosophical Quarterly*, vol. 3, no. 10 (January), pp. 33–9.

Vanberg, Viktor (1986) "Spontaneous Market Order and Social Rules: A Critical Examination of F. A. Hayek's Theory of Cultural Evolution", *Economics and Philosophy*, vol. 2, no. 1 (April), pp. 75–100.

Vaughn, Karen I. (1999) "Hayek's Implicit Economics: Rules and the Problem of Order", *The Review of Austrian Economics*, vol. 11, no. 1/2, pp. 129–44.

Vernon, Richard (1996) "John Stuart Mill and Pornography: Beyond the Harm Principle", *Ethics*, vol. 106, no. 3 (April), pp. 621–32.

Walzer, Michael (1983) *Spheres of Justice: A Defense of Pluralism and Equality*. New York: Basic Books.

—— (1990) "The Communitarian Critique of Liberalism", *Political Theory*, vol. 18, no. 1 (February), pp. 6–23.

Weber, Max (1947 [1964]) *The Theory of Social and Economic Organization*. Translated by A. M. Henderson and Talcott Parsons; edited by Talcott Parsons. New York: Free Press.

Whitaker, John K. (1996) *The Correspondence of Alfred Marshall, Economist*. Three vols. Cambridge: Cambridge University Press.

Wiltshire, David (1978) *The Social and Political Thought of Herbert Spencer*. New York: Oxford University Press.

Wonnell, Christopher T. (1994) "Liggio on Hayek: Systemic Knowledge, the Rule of Law, and Utility", *Southwestern University Law Review*, vol. 23, no. 3. pp. 531–7.

Yack, Bernard (1993) *The Problems of a Political Animal*. Berkeley, CA: University of California Press.

Index